GLOBALIZATION AND COMPETITION

Globalization and Competition explains why some middle-income countries, principally those in Asia, grow fast, while others are not as successful. The author criticizes both old-style developmentalism and the economics of the Washington Consensus. He argues, instead, for a "new developmentalism" or third approach that builds on a national development strategy. This approach differs from the neoliberal strategy that rich nations propose to emerging economies principally on macroeconomic grounds. Developing countries face a key obstacle to growth, namely, the tendency to overvaluate foreign exchange. Instead of neutralizing it, the policy that rich countries promote mistakenly seeks growth through foreign savings, which causes additional appreciation of the national currency and often results in financial crises, rather than genuine investment.

Luiz Carlos Bresser Pereira has taught economics and political theory at the Getulio Vargas Foundation, São Paulo, Brazil, since 1962. More recently, he has also taught at the École des Hautes Études en Sciences Sociales in Paris. Professor Bresser Pereira was minister of finance in the Jose Sarney administration in Brazil (1987) and, with the technical support of two major international banks, framed the proposal on how to solve the foreign debt crisis that formed the basis of the Brady Plan (1989). From 1995 to 1999, he served as Brazil's minister of public administration and reform of the state and minister of science and technology. In addition to numerous titles in Portuguese, Professor Bresser Pereira's works in English include *Development and Crisis in Brazil* (1984), *The Theory of Inertial Inflation* (1987), *Economic Reforms in New Democracies* (Cambridge University Press, 1993, with Jose Maria Maravall and Adam Przeworski), *Democracy and Public Management Reform* (2004), and *Developing Brazil* (2009).

Globalization and Competition

Why Some Emergent Countries Succeed while Others Fall Behind

LUIZ CARLOS BRESSER PEREIRA

Getulio Vargas Foundation, Brazil

CAMBRIDGE
UNIVERSITY PRESS

CAMBRIDGE UNIVERSITY PRESS
Cambridge, New York, Melbourne, Madrid, Cape Town, Singapore,
São Paulo, Delhi, Dubai, Tokyo

Cambridge University Press
32 Avenue of the Americas, New York, NY 10013-2473, USA

www.cambridge.org
Information on this title: www.cambridge.org/9780521144537

First published 2010

Printed in the United States of America

A catalog record for this publication is available from the British Library.

Library of Congress Cataloging in Publication data
Bresser Pereira, Luiz Carlos.
Globalization and competition : why some emergent countries succeed while others fall
behind / Luiz Carlos Bresser Pereira.
p. cm.
Includes bibliographical references and index.
ISBN 978-0-521-19635-2 (hardback) – ISBN 978-0-521-14453-7 (pbk.)
1. Economic development – Developing countries.   2. Developing countries – Economic
policy.   3. Finance – Developing countries.   4. Competition – Developing countries.
I. Title.
HC59.7.P447   2010
337.09172′4 – dc22   2009025690

ISBN 978-0-521-19635-2 Hardback
ISBN 978-0-521-14453-7 Paperback

Contents

Introduction

In global capitalism, there is a myth that nation-states have lost autonomy and relevance. In reality, given the competition that characterizes globalization, nation-states have become less autonomous, but, as a trade-off, their role has become more strategic. On the other hand, while the conservative Right transformed globalization into a neoliberal ideology confirming the economic and cultural hegemony of the United States, left-wing militants viewed it as a manifestation of imperialism and as a major obstacle to economic growth. But both sides have been proved wrong, as several middle-income countries – particularly the dynamic Asian ones – have achieved fast rates of growth. This fact confirms the economic doctrine that middle-income countries that have already overcome the poverty trap can catch up because they can count on cheap labor and are able to copy or buy relatively cheap technology. Indeed, since the 1980s, these countries have experienced such impressive growth that it has come to be generally acknowledged that the economic center of the world is moving from the United States to Asia. In the 1990s, after the collapse of the Soviet Union, the United States appeared as the only hegemonic power and the growth engine of the world, but in the 2000s, this has proved no longer to be the case, as

1

the impressive economic performance of the dynamic Asian countries has changed the world economic system. Yet a large number of emerging countries continue to record per capita economic growth rates inferior to those of the rich countries. Why does this happen? According to conventional neoclassical economics (whose hegemony is also in question for its repeated failure in explaining economic phenomena and orienting economic policies and for its responsibility for the 2007 global financial crisis), the cause is the lack of good institutions, particularly those that ensure property rights and contracts; according to conventional left-wing economics, it is because they lack industrial policies. In this book, I reject both explanations: neither the lack of institutional reforms nor the lack of industrial policy is behind such poor economic performance.

Instead, I propose three causes of such slow growth, one political and the other two economic. Middle-income countries fail to catch up (1) if, in the political sphere, they lack a nation strong enough to define a national development strategy and limit themselves to following rich countries' recommendations; (2) if, in the economic realm, their macroeconomic policies do not ensure a balanced budget, moderate interest rates, and a competitive exchange rate; and (3) if their income policies do not ensure that wages grow with productivity. This last problem is related to the fact that developing countries are defined by the existence of an unlimited supply of labor. Thus, wages tend to grow at a slower pace than productivity, which creates a chronic domestic demand problem, unless the ensuing concentration of income in the middle and upper classes is solved by the production of luxury goods and services. Latin American economists were already extensively discussing this question in the 1970s, when, in many countries, authoritarian rule was combined with increasing economic inequality; and with the transition to democracy, some countries like Brazil responded positively to the problem by increasing the minimum wage and social expenditures. For these reasons, I will not return to this issue in this book, even though the economic inequality problem is far from being satisfactorily dealt with in middle-income countries.[1] The first two problems are related to the distortions that the past thirty years of neoliberal ideological hegemony and financial globalization have imposed on the world economy. In this book, I first show how important a nation and a national development strategy are. Second, I show that the macroeconomic policies that are recommended to developing countries, particularly high interest rates and noncompetitive exchange rates, are inimical to growth. I argue that commercial globalization is an opportunity for developing countries insofar as it opens room for an export-led strategy, whereas financial opening is a curse. We are seeing now that the neoliberal deregulation of financial markets in rich countries, particularly in the United States, was disastrous for them as well. In the past, rich countries persuaded developing countries that they would be able to develop only with their financial support and that these countries should open their economies to international finance, but the rich countries kept their own domestic economies well regulated. In the past thirty years, however, the economic authorities of developed countries were persuaded that financial markets were efficient and that all markets self-regulate, and so they deregulated their economies. The major financial and economic crisis that was in full swing by 2008 is the outcome of this domestic financial liberalization coupled with financial globalization or liberalization. This book is not about the world financial crisis but rather about the reasons why many middle-income countries that have the necessary conditions for catching up did not do so, why their investment and growth rates were so modest, why their exchange rates tended to overappreciate, and why financial crisis was so frequent. The same financial globalization that

---

[1] In the 1970s, I devoted an early essay (Bresser Pereira [1970] 1984) and an entire book, *Estado e Subdesenvolvimento Industrializado* (Bresser Pereira 1977), to this subject, where I argued that the military regime sustained demand while inequality was increasing to the extent that the country's production was oriented to relatively sophisticated goods. This theme was present throughout the work of Celso Furtado (1963, 1965) and Maria da Conceição Tavares and José Serra (1972), and Edmar Bacha (1973) also wrote significantly on this subject.

recently boomeranged in the rich countries had been causing disruption in the developing countries' economies and causing slow growth rates since they liberalized their foreign accounts in the early 1990s.

I discuss these issues in light of a historical-structuralist approach that has its sources in Keynesian macroeconomics, in classical political economy, and in development economics as it was understood principally in the 1950s. While the classical economists (and Schumpeter) understood the logic of capitalist development, Keynes added to it the demand side. From the 1940s to the 1960s, development economists combined the two approaches, focusing on a problem that economics had not treated before: the development of poor or underdeveloped countries. After the crisis of the 1970s, Keynesian and development economics came under attack from the new and dominant neoliberal ideology and from neoclassical economics, yet the early 2000s witnessed a revival of development macroeconomics that still, however, lacks a systematic formulation. This book intends to make a contribution in this direction. It sees Marshallian microeconomics as a useful methodological instrument for analyzing markets, while rejecting neoclassical growth theory, neoclassical finance, and neoclassical macroeconomics, which is apparently more scientific because it adopts a hypothetical-deductive method that permits full use of mathematics but that is inconsistent with a social science that aims to understand economic systems and, so, requires an empirical or historical method.[2] Besides being incapable of explaining the real world, neoclassical finance and macroeconomics are ideological castles built in the air that are of no use to economists (who do not use them for economic policy), but are useful in justifying the deregulation of financial markets that allows rentiers to accumulate artificial financial

---

[2] I see Alfred Marshall as one of the four or five major economists, together with Adam Smith, Marx, Schumpeter, and Keynes. His microeconomics, however, is not part of what I see as the hard core of economics – a science that aims to explain the behavior of economic systems – but of a secondary economic science (economic decision theory), side by side with game theory. On this, see Bresser Pereira (2009b).

wealth, while leading the economy into financial bubbles and to recurrent crises. Neoclassical macroeconomist Gregory Mankiw (2006) well illustrated the pathetic irrelevance of neoclassical macroeconomics for macroeconomic policy making in the article "The Macroeconomist as Scientist and Engineer." I view this article as a confession of failure of this type of hypothetical-deductive macroeconomics. Mankiw, who was the chairman of the U.S. president's Council of Economic Advisors, begins his article by saying that during the two years he was in Washington, D.C., he was surprised that no one utilized the science as taught in the university. What policy makers and analysts do use is a collection of simple and pragmatic rules – a kind of engineering. Some pages on, however, he informs us that the economist who inspires policy makers in Washington, D.C., is John Maynard Keynes. He concludes by calling on "scientists" and "engineers" to get together.

Economists who have received neoclassical training in economics are certainly able to develop competent macroeconomic policies, but when they do so, it is a sign that they are not utilizing the economic theory that they have learned in their graduate courses. Instead, when they utilize methodological tools like econometrics, game theory, and certain parts of microeconomics, they combine them with Keynesian macroeconomics. Pragmatically, they abandon "science" and adhere to "engineering" – or, more precisely, they adopt the macroeconomic theory that is scientific.

In this book, I am not concerned with neoclassical economics or with the policies that economists adopt in developed countries but rather with the policy recommendations that rich countries, the North, offer their competitors – the middle-income or emerging countries. In other words, I am concerned with the Washington Consensus, or, as I have preferred to call it since the disappearance of the 1990s consensus in the 2000s, *conventional orthodoxy* – a body of knowledge developed by neoclassical economists. I am interested in criticizing the macroeconomic analyses, recommended policies, and political pressure originating in the North over developing countries. In many cases, the policy recommendations of conventional orthodoxy are substantially different from the actual policies conventional economists pursue in their own countries: they follow the "do what I say, not what I do" advice. This book is about development macroeconomics and a development strategy, but it also embodies a political economy approach. Although in the medium term, the interests of rich and middle-income countries coincide, in the short term, the fact that middle-income countries dispose of cheap labor often makes rich countries act collectively to neutralize middle-income countries' competitive capacity and to extract gains for their multinational firms. This behavior is seldom conscious or acknowledged, but it is the only explanation for the perverse content of conventional orthodoxy. Often the financial operations and investments involved are not in the interests either of people in developing countries, to whom, as we will see, they mean a mere substitution of foreign for domestic savings, or of people in rich countries, to whom they bring delocalization and reduced employment opportunities; however, they are in the interests of capitalist and professional elites in both types of country.

The central question addressed in this book is why, in global capitalism – a stage of capitalist development in which all markets are open and capitalist competition between business enterprises as well as between nation-states has become generalized – some developing countries are catching up while others are not. My answer is that those countries that are catching up have adopted a national development strategy that I call *new developmentalism*, whereas those that are falling behind have become subordinated to the North or to conventional orthodoxy. In opposition to old developmentalism, which, belonging to an earlier stage of economic development, presupposes a state-entrepreneur promoting forced savings, new developmentalism requires only a capable state and counts on markets and private entrepreneurial activity to achieve growth. The state is supposed to be the nation's main instrument of collective action, capable of organizing a nation around a national development strategy.

Introduction

New developmentalism has, as a basic long-term strategy, growth with domestic savings, not with foreign, and, in the short term, requires moderate interest rates and competitive or equilibrium exchange rates – precisely what sensible macroeconomic policies do in the rich countries, but the opposite of what conventional orthodoxy preaches.

For almost fifty years, I studied and taught economic development. The sources of my intellectual formation were development economics, Latin American structuralist theory, classical and Marxian political economy, and Keynesian macroeconomics. Today, I view myself as a Keynesian historical-structuralist economist who rejects mainstream neoclassical economics and any other orthodoxy whatsoever. I have been working on the ideas in this book since the early 2000s. Assuming that middle-income countries are supposed to present faster rates of growth than rich countries, I asked myself why, since the 1980s, this was happening only in some Asian countries, while the others fell behind. Gradually, I understood that the problem was neither the diminution of the size of the state, as the critiques from the Left claimed, nor the lack of further reforms, as claimed by the Right. The true causes were the lack of a national development strategy and a mistaken macroeconomic policy characterized principally by an overvalued exchange rate. Thus the problem was not the opposition between a hard, orthodox fiscal policy against inflation and a soft one; rather, the problem arose from the opposition between a growth policy privileging foreign savings and exchange rate populism, which appreciate the national currency, and an alternative policy based on domestic savings, fiscal or budgetary control, and the deliberate endeavor to neutralize the tendency to overvaluate the exchange rate. I knew that the exchange rate plays a strategic role in economic stabilization and growth, but the mechanisms that made it overvalued and inconsistent with economic development became clear to me only after 2001, when I began to systematically research the causes of the overvaluation. First, I criticized the policy of growth with foreign savings and explained why it does not usually cause growth but rather promotes, through the overvaluation of the currency, a high rate of substitution of foreign for domestic savings. Second, I realized that the Dutch disease is also a cause of overvaluation of the exchange rate, not only in oil-exporting countries but in practically all developing countries. After studying the problem with the help of students and assistants, I arrived at a central thesis or hypothesis: that the main obstacle to catching up faced by middle-income countries is the tendency to overvaluate the exchange rate – a tendency that economics still ignores and that conventional orthodoxy will probably dismiss. The latter admits that the exchange rate is volatile but believes that eventually it varies around the equilibrium price, while my contention is that if the tendency to overvaluate is not neutralized, market control will be expressed as a balance-of-payment crisis and a sharp depreciation of the national currency. There is a second structural tendency that is also an obstacle to growth – the tendency of wages to grow at less than the productivity rate because of the existence of unlimited supply of labor in developing countries – but the ensuing insufficiency of demand problem is often "solved" through the increase of luxury goods by the rich.

Conventional orthodoxy is the adversary that I criticize in this book. It is the Washington Consensus in the form in which it continues to be applied, even if its failure has eliminated the quasiconsensus existing since the late 1980s. It includes the sum of diagnoses, recommendations, and pressures that the North directs to developing countries. I call it "orthodoxy" because its adherents view it so. Yet whereas in the developed countries, this means fiscal austerity, moderate interest rates, and competitive exchange rates, Washington, D.C., and New York preach the exact opposite to developing countries, namely, high interest rates to fight inflation and overvalued exchange rates, also to fight inflation and to attract foreign capital. Despite its rhetoric of fiscal austerity, the conventional orthodoxy, in practical terms, adopts a soft fiscal policy so as to keep the internal debt high and thus remunerate the financial rentiers who hold local treasury bonds with high interest rates.

In fact, conventional orthodoxy suffers from the disease that it attributes to politicians in developing countries who lead the state to spend more money than it receives. It is populist not only from a fiscal standpoint but also and principally from an exchange rate standpoint insofar as it stimulates domestic consumption, rather than investment, by arguing in favor of policies that cause the local currency to appreciate. Conventional orthodoxy is a counterstrategy to growth that eventually neutralizes a country's competitive capacity. I do not discuss the political economy of this ideology, but it is the outcome of an informal political agreement between, on one hand, local financial rentiers and a domestic financial system that benefits from high interests and, on the other hand, multinational enterprises and competing countries that benefit from an overvalued local currency. The Bretton Woods international financial agencies act as intermediaries in the name of their controllers – the rich countries. The latter have reserve currencies, which limit their capacity to manage the exchange rate. It is principally for this reason that conventional orthodoxy insists that in the long term, it is impossible to manage the exchange rate, and rich countries rebuff the attempts of developing countries to neutralize the tendency of their exchange rates to overappreciate.

This book deals with middle-income or emerging countries that, today, together have almost five billion habitants and are divided between those countries that have succeeded in catching up and those that have not. The other two billion of the world's inhabitants are divided between the poor and the rich countries. I do not discuss the poor countries because their problems are different from those of the middle-income countries. They have low levels of education, noncohesive societies, weak states, and political elites that are often corrupt and have yet to undertake their capitalist revolutions. For the moment, they lack the capacity to compete with the rich countries that are interested in their mineral wealth. It is very important to discuss the policies that are necessary to enable these countries to overcome poverty, if not misery, and the ideas discussed in this book concerning national development strategies and exchange rates are applicable to them. But the diagnosis and the policies that are relevant to these countries are different from those applicable to middle-income countries.

In the seven chapters of this book, I develop two arguments that I believe to be simple. In Part I, I discuss the political economy of catching up. All middle-income countries are already capitalist societies that tend to grow at reasonable rates, but, while some are successful in catching up because they have adopted a national development strategy that I call new developmentalism, most of them display modest growth rates because they have subjected themselves to conventional orthodoxy. New developmentalism differs from old developmentalism because it attaches more importance to macroeconomic policy than to industrial policy, and it differs from conventional orthodoxy because it rejects the policy of growth with foreign savings and proposes a macroeconomic policy based on fiscal austerity, moderate interest rates, and competitiveness obtained through the neutralization of the tendency to overvaluate the exchange rate. In Part II, the theme is the development macro-economics of the exchange rate. I focus on the exchange rate because I believe that it is the strategic macroeconomic variable in economic development and also because I developed my research around it during the past nine years.

In Chapter 1, I discuss globalization and catching up and argue that, contrary to what neoliberal globalism asserts, nation-states have not lost their relevance but rather have become more strategic because the increased interdependence that characterizes globalization originates in the intense competition they face. This competition takes place not only among business enterprises, for profits and expansion, but also among nation-states, for higher rates of growth. The discussion presupposes that the competition between rich and middle-income countries is a game with positive-sum outcomes, but in the short term, some players gain more than others. In Chapter 2, the central idea is that a national development strategy is the key institution promoting growth. To invest, business entrepreneurs are not dependent on the security of property rights and contracts but rather are interested in good opportunities for profitable investment. The role of the informal agreements that constitute these national development strategies is precisely to create such opportunities. When a nation is able to formulate a national development strategy, it disposes of a set of laws, policies, understandings, orientations, and routines that ensured business enterprises sustained domestic and external demand. The rates of growth assured to countries that have completed their capitalist revolutions are modest. To achieve faster rates and gradually catch up with the growth levels of rich countries, developing countries should engage in national development strategies, with the state and its respective government or administration acting as an intermediary between the social classes and groups. Which strategy will eventually be effective? I discuss this question in Chapter 3, in which I compare the new developmentalism adopted by fast-growing Asian countries with the old national developmentalism that was successful in promoting economic growth in Latin America between the 1930s and 1980 but thereafter showed its limits. After the great crisis of the 1980s, conventional orthodoxy has been offering developing countries a stabilization and growth strategy. However, it is not surprising that it fails to bring about growth, insofar as it is a strategy proposed by competing countries and the International Monetary Fund (IMF), the World Bank, and the great international commercial banks. Observing high rates of growth of the dynamic Asian countries, I identify the new developmentalist strategy as an ideal type, in the Weberian sense. I concentrate on the middle-income countries because they have already completed their industrial revolutions and can count on a sizable class of entrepreneurs and a large middle class but remain underdeveloped because of their low level of income per capita and the dualist character of their societies, which implies the exclusion of large sectors of the population from the benefits of economic development. What are the characteristics of new developmentalism? If the neoliberal counterstrategy is ineffective, would this mean that I would nostalgically propose to return to old developmentalism – that is, to the protection of infant industries and strong state intervention in the economy? No, that is not the case. Manufacturing industry in middle-income countries is no longer an infant industry, and the stage of primitive accumulation (in which a central role of the state is to achieve forced savings) is well in the past. The challenge that middle-income countries face is the rejection of the macroeconomic policy supported by conventional orthodoxy and its replacement with a more competent one, proposed by new developmentalism. Fiscal policy should be austere because Keynesian public deficits are only temporarily legitimate; the interest rate should be moderate, as required by the law that established the U.S. Federal Reserve Bank, and the exchange rate should be competitive to ensure that competent local manufacturing industries have access to foreign markets. To neutralize the overvaluation of the currency and to ensure moderate interest rates (variables according to monetary policy), new developmentalism proposes a policy of growth with domestic savings and, if necessary, control of capital inflows. The chapter ends with an empirical study showing that countries that have a national strategy based on domestic savings and fiscal balance grow faster than countries that follow conventional orthodoxy.

The remaining four chapters, which form Part II, are dedicated to the exchange rate. Certainly there are other factors that help or hinder economic growth, but among them, the exchange rate is the most strategic. The other macroeconomic prices, such as the rate of interest or the rate of profit, and other variables, such as education, capital accumulation, technical progress, and institutions, are also important. But while there is a vast body of literature on the role that these variables play in economic development, the same is not true of the exchange rate. It is true that there are many studies of exchange rate regimes and of the volatility of the exchange rate, but these are not as relevant to developing countries as is the level of the exchange rate or, more precisely, its tendency to overappreciate. While this chronic overvaluation is not neutralized by economic policy, it leads to balance-of-payment crises and hinders economic development insofar as it reduces opportunities for export-oriented investment. I discuss this tendency in Chapter 4, which is introductory to the remaining three chapters. In Chapter 5, I examine the Dutch disease – a major market failure over which the market does not exercise any control. This major market failure, which we may also call the *natural resources curse*, derives from the existence in a country of an abundant and low-cost natural resource – principally oil, but several other resources as well – that may be economically exported at a substantially more appreciated or less competitive exchange rate than other goods this same country is able to produce using the best technology existing in the world. Such Ricardian rents benefit the country in the short term but eventually become a curse insofar as they render investments unviable in all tradable industries except those that cause it. I offer an interpretation of this problem that focuses on the overvaluation of the benefit exchange rate and extends its scope to the countries that count on cheap labor such as China. The condition for this is that wage differentials within the developing countries are substantially wider than those in developed ones. There are ways to neutralize the disease, but they are not simple. Given that it is consistent with current account equilibrium, if countries decide to neutralize it by depreciating their currencies, as China and Norway did, the rich countries will necessarily experience large current account deficits. In the model that I present in this book, the Dutch disease is characterized by the existence of two exchange rate equilibria: the *current equilibrium exchange rate*, which equilibrates the current account, and the *industrial equilibrium exchange rate*, which makes business enterprises using state-of-the-art technology competitive. Thus, the neutralization of the disease necessarily implies a current account surplus that will have as its counterpart a current account deficit in the developed countries, or, more broadly, in countries that derive no benefits from Ricardian rents. Although the neutralization of the disease in countries that are simultaneously advantaged and hampered by it is only partial, this outcome is already starting to appear. The large current account surpluses in developing countries and the creation of sovereign funds that have as their counterpart the deficit in the United States are manifestations of this partial neutralization. They are a logical consequence of the simple model developed here. In this book, I define the problem, rather than offering a solution to it. Given the win-win characteristic of global capitalist competition, rich countries will not be less rich insofar as developing countries are able to neutralize the tendency to overvaluation of the exchange rate. Yet to the extent that they prove to be able to perform this difficult task (as we will see, the domestic obstacles to this neutralization are huge), changes in the ownership of assets will be inevitable.

In Chapters 6 and 7, I discuss the policy of growth with foreign savings – the central strategy that conventional orthodoxy prescribes for developing countries. In Chapter 6, I show how foreign savings or current account deficits appreciate the domestic currency and lead to an often high rate of substitution of foreign for domestic savings. I criticize an idea that seems obviously true: capital-rich countries are supposed to transfer their capital to capital-poor ones. This may be true of poor countries and for business entrepreneurs, to whom credit is essential to finance innovation and investment. But for middle-income countries, it most certainly is not true, given the existence of the exchange rate. Usually, capital inflows cause the valorization of the local currency and consequent artificial increases in wages and domestic consumption, and so what we have is the substitution of foreign for domestic savings. As we will see, the policy of incurring chronic current account deficits makes sense only in special periods, when a country is already growing fast for other reasons. In that situation, foreign savings may cause an increase of investment, rather than consumption. Yet the policy of growth with

Introduction

foreign savings does not limit itself to increasing consumption at the expense of investment; it also causes financial fragility and financial crises – specifically balance-of-payment crises. This is the theme of the seventh and last chapter of the book, in which I focus on the financial crises of the 1990s.

The method that I utilize in this book is historical-deductive. I combine the long-term perspective on capitalist development that we find in classical political economy, particularly in Marx and in post–World War II development economics, with Keynesian macroeconomics. These authors used the same empirical method, which combines observation, particularly of new historical facts, with existing theory to arrive at new models – open models able to explain open and historical systems. There is no problem in combining a long-term analysis, such as the classical one, with a short-term Keynesian analysis because when we discuss economic development, long-term growth is the sum of short-term periods of growth. Besides, one line of thought completes the other: the Keynesian demand side completes the classical supply side. The historical-deductive method is empirical; thus, the models are supposed to be confirmed by econometric tests, whenever possible.

The ideas in this book were developed while I was writing some theoretical papers on development macroeconomics, and they are behind the macroeconomic model of the Brazilian economy that is outlined in *Developing Brazil* (Bresser Pereira 2009a). Chapters 1, 2, and 4 were written for this book. The other four have been published recently in academic journals (Bresser Pereira 2006, 2008; Bresser Pereira and Gala 2008; Bresser Pereira et al. 2008). To write this book I received the support of the Research Department of the School of Administration of São Paulo of the Getulio Vargas Foundation. Jan Kregel, Pierre Salama, Robert Boyer, and Yoshiaki Nakano were particularly helpful to me in writing this book. I am indebted to Adam Przeworski, Aldo Ferrer, Edwin Le Heron, Fernando Ferrari Filho, Gabriel Palma, Ha-Joon Chang, Helcio Tokeshi, Ignacy Sachs, Jan Kregel, José Luiz Oreiro, Julio

Introduction

Lopes, K. S. Jomo, Luiz Fernando de Paula, Marcio Holland, Osvaldo Sunkel, Paul Davidson, and Ricardo Ffrench-Davis and also to my students (and present colleagues) Nelson Marconi, Carmen Varela, and Alexandra Strommer de Godoi for their comments and suggestions. Cecilia Heise is responsible for the revision of the manuscript. My core debt is to my wife for life, Vera.

Part I

POLITICAL ECONOMY

1

Globalization and Catching Up

Despite conventional wisdom, globalization and nation-states are phenomena that do not contradict each other but are rather part of a same universe, which is the universe of contemporary capitalism. *Globalization* is a debatable term because the process that characterizes recent capitalist development has increased, rather than diminished, the international significance of nation-states, as stiffer competition between them for faster economic growth rates has made them even more strategic to their respective nations. In the early 1990s, soon after the collapse of Communism, globalization was presented as an indication of U.S. hegemony and of the affirmation of a single path to economic development – the neoliberal path of the Washington Consensus, or of conventional orthodoxy.[1] On the opposite side, economists and politicians who identify with the new hegemony have claimed that globalization would

---

[1] I have no sympathy for orthodoxy, which is a way of renouncing our faculty of thought, but I reject the adjective *heterodox*, which is often applied to economists who renounce influence or the chance to implement their ideas and policies, reserving for themselves the role of eternal minority opposition. A good economist is neither orthodox nor heterodox but rather pragmatic: he or she can frame good economic policy based on an open and modest theory that forces him or her to constantly consider and decide under conditions of uncertainty.

benefit everyone. Martin Wolf (2004: 4) summarized this view: "the fail-ure of our world is not that there is too much globalization but that there is too little." In a similar vein, the World Bank (2002) published a report in which it stressed globalization's success in promoting catching up and poverty reduction. To justify this conclusion, it divides nation-states into three groups – rich ones, more globalized developing ones, and less glob-alized developing ones – and shows that, in the 1990s, whereas the per capita growth rate of rich countries increased by nearly two percentage points per annum, and the growth rate of more globalized developing countries (corresponding to nearly three billion inhabitants) grew at rates of around 5 percent, in less globalized countries, the rates were negative, at around 1 percent. Next, the report regards both trade and financial globalization as positive, although it is obliged to acknowledge an increase in financial crises. This is where my key disagreement lies. Whereas I regard *trade globalization* as a competitive opportunity for middle-income countries – an opportunity of *catching up* – I maintain that *financial globalization* is usually disastrous for developing countries because it makes them unable to neutralize the tendency to overvaluate the exchange rate.

It is not surprising that so-called more globalized countries are suc-cessful because they are also more capitalistic countries – they are coun-tries that have already completed their capitalist revolutions. Unlike poor countries, these are middle-income countries that already have busi-ness and technical capabilities combined with cheap labor, which gives them an advantage in international competition. However, among these countries, we must distinguish the fast-growing from the slow-growing countries – we have to distinguish the countries that have their own national development strategies from those that do not. In this chapter, my main purpose is to discuss why trade globalization is an opportunity for middle-income countries from which many of them are profiting, while others are not. As we will see, while commercial globalization is an opportunity for middle-income countries, financial globalization is a threat. Trade liberalization is damaging only to those poor countries that are still trying to begin their process of industrialization and that have infant industries.

Trade globalization and financial globalization tend to move together, and there will always be economists ready to claim that it is impossible to separate one from the other, but experience shows that many countries, particularly Asian ones, were able to separate them. The condition that makes trade globalization an opportunity for a developing country, rather than a threat, is that it can neutralize the negative aspects of financial globalization, principally the tendency of the exchange rate toward overvaluation. This tendency, which I discuss in the last three chapters of this book, results primarily from two structural characteristics of developing countries: the Dutch disease, which affects practically all developing countries, and the attraction of foreign capital by the higher profit and interest rates usually prevailing in those countries. The Dutch disease is a particularly serious market failure because it appreciates the exchange rate without affecting the current account balance so that overvaluation can become permanent. For its part, the structural attraction of foreign capital also appreciates the national currency, but this would not be so bad if foreign capital increased the country's rate of investment. Yet, as we will see in Chapters 6 and 7, this is not the case; before the policy of growth with foreign savings brings about excessive foreign indebtedness and balance-of-payment crises, it promotes the substitution of foreign for domestic savings so that the country becomes indebted but does not grow. If the country is able to neutralize this tendency of the exchange rate toward overvaluation by retaining controls over financial flows, it will offer attractive opportunities for export-oriented investment and will grow fast; if it is not able to do so, it will lag behind.

Globalization is a comprehensive historical phenomenon and therefore a contradictory one. Some of the contradictions, such as the class struggles that characterized the first stages of capitalist development, lost their relative importance in the age of globalization; others, such as the contradiction between rich countries with expensive labor and middle-income countries with cheap labor, increased their significance. It is in light of this second contradiction and the new roles played by nation-states in globalization that I examine in this chapter the problem of catching up. As long as globalization implies a substantial increase in competition between countries or nation-states, we need to know how they compete, how they define their national development strategies, and how this competition affects and modifies the world economic system itself. To discuss this issue, the approach here will be economic, but it will also have to be political because any market system in which competitors compete regularly is also a system of cooperation that defines the rules of the competitive game.

THE PRESENT STAGE OF CAPITALISM

Globalization is, at the same time, an ongoing process of transformation – the process of accelerated economic, social, and political integration the world has been experiencing since the 1970s – and the name of the present stage of the capitalist economic system. It is the economic system in which all national markets become open and all nation-states start to behave according to the logic of capitalist accumulation and competition. The dynamic nature of this stage, which reflects the extraordinary speed of technological change, is disclosed in the very name chosen for it – a name whose suffix, -ization, implies the idea of change. Its technological basis is the reduction in the costs of transportation and, particularly, the information technology revolution, which made communications and the transfer of financial assets dramatically faster and cheaper. This technological revolution, by making it easier to create and integrate markets at a global level, promoted, on one hand, an increase in international economic competition and, on the other hand, a reorganization of production, sponsored by multinational corporations. As long as national economies opened up, their international competitiveness became a necessary condition for the continuation of their economic development.

In globalization, nation-states remain the decisive political-territorial unit. This is clear if we consider two definitions of globalization, one strong and the other weak. According to the first, globalization is the stage of capitalism in which economic competition between national states for faster growth rates becomes widespread. If the reader thinks this definition is strong, there is an alternative: globalization is economic competition at the world level between corporations, supported by their corresponding nation-states. In both cases, it is clear that the nation-state continues to play a strategic role in globalization. There is a third definition – globalization as competition at the world level between corporations without the support of their corresponding nation-states. In fact, there are corporations, especially consulting ones, that are genuinely multinational: Hirst and Thompson (1996) consider them as "genuinely transnational corporations."[2] But, in the absolute majority, so-called multinational corporations are national corporations because they are controlled by the capital and the knowledge of one or two countries. The readiest evidence for this lies in the activities of the ambassadors of rich countries in developing countries. Each ambassador well knows which are his or her corporations, that is, the corporations whose interests he or she is supposed to represent. The ambassador knows them, and he or she does not hesitate to protect their interests because this is one of the ambassador's two basic and legitimate missions (the other is to protect his or her country's commercial interests). These corporations are multinational because they have a presence in many countries, not because their ownership is divided among so many countries that they lose any

---

[2] To Hirst and Thompson (1996), multinational corporations are those that preserve a basis of national origin and are subject to regulation and control by the country of origin, whereas transnational corporations have entirely free capital, without specific national identification and with an international management potentially inclined to locate and relocate anywhere in the world in search of safer or greater returns.

national basis. Therefore, we can discuss which of the two definitions is the sounder – the strong one or the weak one – but what remains obvious in any of them is nations' highly strategic nature, from the economic point of view, at the present time: it is up to them to use their governments to formulate and implement a national competition strategy. Evidently, this does not mean that I am stating that nation-states compete internationally as corporations do. Competition between nations has a different economic logic. The process is conducted by politicians, not by entrepreneurs. The purpose is to achieve faster growth rates, rather than higher profit rates. The demand comes not from shareholders but from voters. On the other hand, whereas corporations are basically autonomous, nations are not because they face the serious problem of foreign ideological hegemony. Elites in developing countries are more easily identified with rich countries' elites than with their own people. Now, when this happens, the classical imperial process whereby local elites are associated with the imperial power recurs. Therefore, developing countries will actually be competitive with rich countries as long as they are able to reject this association and develop economic policies and institutional reforms compatible with the country's national interests.

A fourth definition along the same lines – with the difference, however, that its origin is not neoliberal or globalist, but Marxist – holds that the logic of capitalist accumulation has become global, that capitalists have no homeland, and that they invest where profit opportunities are greatest so that, once again, the nation-state has lost autonomy and importance. This theory, a classic tenet of international socialism, has an unacceptable essentialist aspect, but we must recognize the existence of a basic ambiguity in capitalists and enterprises. This ambiguity lies not in the fact that they look for profit wherever it may be found (this is part of the market's logic) but in the fact that, politically, capitalists actually sometimes feel themselves to be agents above nations but sometimes cling to nations for domestic protection or for support in their international actions. This ambiguity is usually greater in developing countries

24

than in rich countries, partly because in those countries the national interests with which entrepreneurs are associated are smaller than those in rich countries and partly because societies in developing countries tend to be culturally and ideologically dependent. However, if capitalists and corporations are ambiguous, the politicians who govern nation-states are not. For them – except in dependent developing countries – there is no doubt that their obligation is to protect national capital, work, and knowledge. They know that their election and reelection depend on their success in this endeavor. And therefore, their nationalist actions are evident in the international space. Capitalist nation-states have always acknowledged borders, but capital often ignores them; yet democracy is always national because politicians in democratic countries have no alternative but to represent their citizens: because there is no political globalization, there is no democratic globalization.

After the capitalist revolution turned the nation-states into political and territorial entities par excellence, capitalist competition became the fundamental economic law – competition that is not limited to enterprises, as presumed by conventional or neoclassical economics, but that directly involves nation-states. The world economic system was formed during the mercantilist era, dating from the development of the technology of maritime transportation and the great discoveries of new territories. Braudel (1979) and Wallerstein (1974) called this process of internationalization, which intensified from the seventeenth century on, the *economy-world* and *world system*, respectively. However, they were referring to partial systems that did not, in fact, embrace the whole world. Capitalism was then already becoming international from a mercantilist perspective that stressed the decisive economic role of nation-states. With the transition to industrial capitalism, the world's territorial organization in terms of nation-states speeded up, but it was only in the last quarter of the twentieth century that global capitalism materialized, as the world system began to encompass the whole surface of the earth. Never before had capitalism been so all embracing; never before had this type of independent political and territorial organization – the nation-state – been more dominant, and, as we will see, never before had the role of the nation-state been more strategic. Between the middle of the seventeenth century, when the treaties of Westphalia marked the formation of the European system of national states, and the twentieth century, competition between states became increasingly economic but was combined with military rivalry as long as, to define and expand the boundaries of the national market, it was necessary or profitable to resort to force. It was only as of the end of the nineteenth century that economic competition became predominant. Nowadays, in times of globalization, this competition dominates any other relation, as long as all major countries have settled borders and no longer threaten each other with war.[3]

With the Industrial Revolution and the steam engine, mercantile capitalism became industrial capitalism and gave rise, in the late nineteenth century, to what some have called the *first globalization* (Nogueira Batista 1998; Berger and Robert 2003). The Great Depression of the 1930s put a stop to the globalization process, as the failure of the liberal policies of that time was recognized and national economies became closed, but this did not prevent the process of political and social transformation from continuing and accelerating, as in World War II. Economic development had received a new impulse. During the twentieth century, the growth rates of capitalist countries practically doubled compared with those of the previous century. This accelerated growth in productivity or in per capita income was probably the consequence of four factors. First, Keynesian macroeconomic policies allowed markets to coordinate economies but, at the same time, limited their cyclic crises. Second, the better organization of workers made it possible to redistribute income

---

[3] As a symptom of this competition, in a supplement published by *Le Monde*, "Les Cahiers de la Competitivité," sponsored by French industry (August 29, 2007), the first story begins with the following sentence: "It is essential for France to preserve its world ranking and to ensure the competitiveness of its enterprises."

and to increase the domestic market. Third, technological development continued to accelerate, in a first phase characterized by mass production and the assembly line (the features that defined the Fordist regulation) and, later, by the information technology revolution that would characterize the globalization phase. Fourth, control of major enterprises was transferred to professional managers, and higher standards of administrative efficiency were established. In the professionals' capitalism, the very concept of capital has changed.

This latter cause of faster growth rates is related to the main social transformation that took place in the twentieth century: the expansion of bureaucracy and its transformation into a professional social class, alongside the bourgeoisie and the working class. As work began to be performed outside family units and mainly in bureaucratic organizations (such as large enterprises), a new professional or technobureaucratic middle class emerged between the capitalist class and the working class. *Professionals' capitalism*, or *knowledge capitalism* (instead of *entrepreneurs' capitalism*), was emerging – a form of capitalism characterized by faster rates of productivity increase, in which professionals or technobureaucrats took on the management and expansion of large enterprises, and the very concept of capital changed. In the nineteenth century, the period of classic economic theory, capital was defined as an advance of wages to the workers before the corresponding production was sold; capital was then essentially working capital. With the development of large capitalist manufacturing industry from the second half of the nineteenth century, capital was mainly understood as physical capital that could be measured by the stockholders' equity in each corporation. As of the second half of the twentieth century, however, in the framework of knowledge capitalism, capital is no longer fixed or circulating; rather, it is the present value of the corporation's cash flow, given a rate of return conventionally deemed as reasonable; to evaluate a company's capital, stock market analysts and investors discount its cash flow at the rate of return conventionally accepted in financial markets. This new concept corresponds to the greater power achieved by top professional executives and to the more strategic role they began to play, associated with the capitalist class and, at the same time, in a constant struggle with it for power and privilege. Through competent management, they can increase companies' cash flow, but they can also reduce it and the shareholders' capital if their management is incompetent.

As regards production, the twentieth century started with the major Fordist revolution, or the revolution of standardized production and the assembly line, and ended with the flexible and outsourced production that would predominate in globalization. Politically, the state ceased to be merely liberal, to become, in Europe, the *social state* or *welfare state*, democratic and guarantor of social rights.[4] Therefore the transition to professionals' capitalism, to Fordism, and finally to the social state would define the first three quarters of the twentieth century. However, in the 1970s, the end of the dollar convertibility, the first Organization of the Petroleum Exporting Countries oil shock, the widespread increase in commodity prices, and stagflation related to the cost inflation caused by pressures from trade unions put an end to thirty years of strong growth and falling inequality – the so-called thirty golden years.

The main cause of the ending of this golden age was the fall in the rates of profit growth and economic growth in the United States in the 1970s. The reaction that occurred in the 1980s defined a new ideology that would give it new strength – neoliberalism: instead of the state, the market should now coordinate the economy. Yet this change in the domain of political ideas coincided with the gradual materialization of a new stage of capitalism – the stage of globalization or global capitalism – in which

---

[4] Modern democracies are usually called "liberal democracies" in the United States. In my terminology, I call the state that arose in the early twentieth century, when universal suffrage was achieved in most of the rich countries, the *liberal democratic state*; after World War II, however, particularly in the more advanced European countries, the huge increase in social and scientific services provided by the state transformed it into the *social democratic state*.

all markets are open and capitalist competition encompasses the whole globe. The Fordist regulatory regime has gradually ceased to character-ize the advanced capitalist economies, whose technical progress is now headed by the information technology revolution; production methods have become more flexible and the outsourcing of activities is general-ized. In the frame of the new dominant ideology, the social state, with its Fordist and Keynesian regulatory component, is now fiercely attacked, as it would have contributed to increased wages, excessively benefited workers, and, in the 1970s, caused a profit squeeze and decreased growth rates. More generally, as pointed out by Correa de Moraes (2006: 29), it is the state itself, as the monopolist of legal rule, monopolist of the extraction of resources for collective consumption, and monopolist of legitimate coercion, that comes under attack on behalf of the market. A false dichotomy is therefore established between state and market, whereas in fact, a strong market is possible only when the state is also strong or capable.[5]

As for public policy, the new neoliberal times have been marked by four attempts, partly successful and partly failed: (1) by the failed attempt to formulate a neoclassical macroeconomic policy as an alter-native to the Keynesian one[6]; (2) by the successful attempt to privatize the government-owned corporations of developing countries; (3) by the partially successful attempt to add flexibility to labor relations (this was not completed by the abandonment of the social policies that had charac-terized the social state, but rather, by the increase in social expenditures, which came to be called *flexsecurity* in Europe); and (4) by the failed attempt to promote economic development through market-oriented

---

[5] This fact, curiously, has been acknowledged by Francis Fukuyama (2004), who attributes the failure of the Washington Consensus policies in developing countries to the fact that these policies have tried to weaken their national states.

[6] It was a failed attempt because the central banks adopted neoclassical monetary policies only rhetorically and continued to be essentially oriented by the Keynesian approach. Yet they adopted the neoliberal deregulation policies that were the direct cause of the 2007–8 major banking crisis.

reforms and so-called orthodox macroeconomic policies. This failure happened not so much because economic reforms do not work in the short term, but principally because the macroeconomic policies of conventional orthodoxy were the opposite of what is normally considered good macroeconomic policy in advanced countries; they were characterized not by moderate interest rates and competitive exchange rates but rather by high interest rates and noncompetitive or overvalued exchange rates.

Since then, we have witnessed, at the level of economic theory, the dominance of neoclassical theory based on rational expectations and, at the ideological level, the dominance of neoliberalism (a renewed and radicalized economic liberalism, endowed with a huge program of reforms), combined with its external expression, so-called globalism. According to the new neoliberal credo, on one hand, governments must implement market-oriented reforms aimed at economic deregulation, reductions in social security, and flexibilization of employment contracts to reduce wages in the rich countries themselves and, on the other hand, must pursue trade and financial liberalization to restrain the developmental nationalism of the middle-income countries that achieved industrialization and, as of the 1970s, competitively exported manufactured goods.

The new ideas have evidently encountered some resistance in developing countries. However, by the 1980s, those developing countries that had, in the 1970s, accepted without reservation the policy prescription of growth with foreign savings, particularly the Latin American and African countries, had already plunged into the great foreign debt crisis of the 1980s and lost power in the arena of international relations.[7] On

---

[7] In the 1970s, Latin American countries, associated with Asian ones, had organized themselves as so-called nonaligned countries under the banner of the "New Economic Policy" to urge rich countries to offer them commercial concessions. Affected by the foreign debt crisis, they went from the offensive to the defensive in their relations with rich countries.

the other hand, in the late 1980s, the Soviet Union, unable to continue to increase productivity after the growth phase based on heavy industry, collapsed. From the end of the 1980s on, developing countries, one by one, have surrendered to the Washington Consensus. The only exceptions are some Asian countries that remain faithful to their own strategy of capitalist development.

With the weakening of its competitors and opponents, the U.S. neoliberal hegemony reached its peak in the 1990s. As a consequence, globalization, which was already taking place because of the technological revolution that had reduced the costs of transportation and communications, gained strength with the liberalizing reforms that began to occur. We have, therefore, the transition from Fordist capitalism to the current global capitalism. Globalization, however, is a *real historical process*, not an ideological phenomenon. Even if we can talk of a neoliberal globalization or neoliberal capitalism, as neoliberalism emerged together with globalization, it is important to clearly distinguish one phenomenon from the other. If we understand globalization as the name of the present stage of capitalism, it follows that it should not be confused with an ideology. Global capitalism is the moment of capitalist development, just after the thirty golden years of capitalism (1945–75), in which individuals and enterprises relate with such a frequency and intensity that they begin to constitute a single, worldwide economic, social, and political system. It is the moment when capitalism really becomes a single system that encompasses the whole world. As a stage of capitalism, globalization encompasses every domain of human activity: economic, social, political, and cultural. Politically, globalization manifests itself at the United Nations and in all commercial and political treaties. Socially, one of its most interesting manifestations is the rise of a global civil society. It has many cultural manifestations.

Economic globalization can be seen from the angle of production, commerce, and finance. Trade globalization is the moment when all the national markets become reasonably open and practically all economic agents worldwide begin to be oriented by the logic of accumulation and capitalist competition. Financial globalization is the moment of capitalist development in which easy communication enables an astonishing increase in capital flows and causes the world's relative financial integration; it is also the moment when those developing countries that open their capital accounts (not all of them have done so) lose control over their exchange rates. Finally, productive globalization is the moment of capitalist development when the productive system becomes globally integrated through multinational corporations that reorganize their production in light of the relative costs they find all over the world. There is then a huge increase in intra-industrial and intrafirm exchanges. The international division of labor takes place no longer just between industries, but also within industries – the production of the same good is spread over several countries. This phenomenon has received several names such as *intra-industry trade*, *offshoring* (when we think of a multinational company producing components abroad; Blinder 2006), and *trade in tasks* (Grossmann and Rossi-Hansberg 2006) or *unbundling* (when we want to stress the division of labor; Baldwin 2006: 1). These two latter names clearly imply that the division of labor at the international level is not essentially a division of production between industries or between goods and services but rather between workers. Or as Baldwin (2006: 5), for whom globalization is a second historical unbundling, puts it, "this means that international competition – which used to be primarily between firms and industries in different nations – now occurs between individual workers performing similar tasks in different nations."

We can understand the poor economic performance of the majority of middle-income countries and of the rich countries since 1980 only if we consider the perverse consequences of, on one side, financial opening or financial globalization and, on the other, financerization or deregulation of financial markets coupled with the wild adoption of financial innovations aimed at increasing financial revenues. Financial opening coupled with the policy of growth with foreign savings is behind the noncompetitive exchange rate and slow growth rates of most middle-income countries; it is the strategy adopted by economic elites in rich countries to increase profits, while keeping these countries financially dependent and neutralizing their competitive capacity. This is essentially what the book deals with. In its turn, financerization, or the building of finance-based capitalism, although a phenomenon with global scope, was essentially a domestic strategy within the rich countries to increase returns on financial assets. To achieve this objective, bright and greedy financiers – professionals with MBAs or PhDs obtained at great universities – associated themselves with rentier capitalists in the task of raising the low interest rates that a relative abundance of capital had originated. With this objective, they engaged in classical financial speculation and developed financial innovations that completely distorted the aim of finance: to bring together the savings of many and to transform them into financial investment and long-term consumption. Instead, financerization meant an enormous increase in fictitious financial wealth that assured high revenues to rentier capitalists as well as generous performance commissions and bonuses to financiers. The resulting wealth was fictitious because it bore no relation to production – in the United States, since 1980, financial wealth increased around four times more than gross domestic product (GDP); figures in other countries are similar – and it also proved false because, once the 2008 banking crisis broke, this wealth melted down. Thus financial globalization, which originally appeared as a source of infinite wealth and as a tool to keep middle-income countries dependent, eventually turned on its creators and caused a financial and economic crisis comparable with the 1929 crisis. In this book, I discuss not this domestic side of financial globalization – financerization and the 2008 financial crisis – but rather, its international side: the one related to financial opening of developing countries' economies, their loss of control over their respective exchange rates, an artificial increase in domestic consumption, and the increase in financial instability.

To sum up, in contrast to commercial globalization as something that works well if reasonably regulated, neoliberal and financerized globalization was a distortion of capitalism, a reactionary regression in relation to the thirty golden years (which also are the years of Bretton Woods and of the welfare or social state). In the time of democracy – a time in which we should predict that market economies would become more efficient or productive, more stable, and less unequal – we saw the rise of neoliberal and financerized capitalism, in which growth rates fell, financial instability greatly increased, and economic inequality also significantly increased. The 2008 financial crisis demoralized both the unregulated markets and the wild financial innovations that characterized neoliberalism and financial globalization and opened the way for a better-regulated global capitalism.

GLOBALISM

Because of the increased interdependence between nation-states in global capitalism, it was said that nation-states were no longer sovereign; moreover, they would have lost relevance. Globalization brought with it new ideologies: *neoliberalism*, the ideology of self-regulating markets, and *globalism*, the ideology of globalization. Whereas neoliberalism is the contemporary form of aggressive, nineteenth-century laissez-faire, globalism praises globalization, proclaims the irrelevance of the nation-state in this economic and social setting, and views globalization as an inevitable process whereby markets increasingly dominate in the coordination of economic systems. Whereas neoliberalism is an ideology for internal use, aimed at legitimizing the reduction of expenditures with the assurance of social rights, globalism is mainly useful in an external context and is focused on developing countries. Ankie Hoogvelt (2001: 154–5) defines globalism from another angle, which is complementary to the one I am offering: "globalism is the reification of the globalization process as a meta-historical force that develops outside human agency, limiting and conditioning the field of action of individuals and communities, whether they are nation-states or local groups. Globalism is the ideology that adds to neoliberal beliefs the belief in the *unavoidability* of the transnationalization of economic and of financial flows." I would just add that this unavoidability, which the author put in italics, means not only that the economy internationalizes, but that it does so according to a single model: the model prescribed by neoliberalism.

By revealing to developing societies the growing lack of autonomy and significance of their nation-states, this ideology is useful for limiting nationalist manifestations in those societies and for leading their dependent elites to subordinate themselves to rich countries' elites. According to globalism, the world would be, or would tend to be, a "borderless society" (Ohmae 1990), or else borders would lose relevance as long as many subnational problems became more pressing than national ones (Sassen 2005).[8] This assumption may assume a deterministic nature that appears, for instance, in Octavio Ianni's (1995: 40) assertion that because of technological and economic changes as well as the logic of capital accumulation, "the sovereignty of the nation-state is not just being limited, but shaken at its base. When the principle of capital accumulation is pushed to its last consequences, it translates as an intensive and extensive development of productive forces and relations of production, at a global level."

The central idea of globalism is that under globalization, nation-states became more interdependent, lose autonomy to implement policies, and therefore lose their significance. Yet it is easy to show the opposite starting from the same assumptions. Indeed, globalization is characterized by a greater interdependence between nation-states, and greater interdependence means some loss of autonomy. But what is the

---

[8] This author's position is contradictory because she thinks both that "globalization is partly a system located inside the national states" and that "highly specialized and therefore obscure factors denationalize specific components of the State's work" (Sassen 2005: 524).

reason for this greater interdependence? It is the increase, not in cooperation, but in competition between countries – an increase in competition that has made states and their governments much more economically strategic than they were before globalization, when each country had to compete with a limited number of other countries, often neighboring ones.

Besides being a fact, interdependence is, as of the 1970s, rhetoric or ideology. As Keohane and Nye (2001: 6) remark, "for those who wish the United Sates to retain world leadership, interdependence has become part of the new rhetoric, to be used against both economic nationalism at home and assertive challenges abroad." It is not surprising, therefore, that Henry Kissinger declared as early as 1975 that "now we are entering a new era. Old international patterns are crumbling; old slogans are uninstructive; old solutions are unavailable. The world has become interdependent in economics, in communication, in human aspirations."[9] In the 1990s, when U.S. ideological hegemony reached its peak, the leitmotiv of President Bill Clinton's speeches was globalization and interdependence. Both would lead all countries to reduce their conflicts and to cooperate – naturally, under the command of the United States. Actually, with the end of the Cold War, the old idea of balance-of-power diplomacy, whereby major countries were permanently threatening each other with war, was abandoned, but as a trade-off, economic competition greatly increased.

It was also in the 1990s that the theory of *global governance* appeared, whose more systematic presentation was made by David Held and Anthony McGrew (2002). According to this theory, which became popular within international organizations, including the United Nations, nation-states would cease to have a key role because now a large number

---

[9] "A New National Partnership," speech by the secretary of state of the United States, Henry Kissinger, in Los Angeles, January 24, 1974. Quoted in Keohane and Nye (2001: 3).

of other international organizations, whether official or nongovernmental, would participate in a hypothetical world regime, no longer called "government," but rather, "governance."[10] Once again, we are faced with a hegemonic rhetoric that makes no sense. Although the global political system developed in the frame of globalization, we are still far from the moment when nation-states can retire. Ulrich Beck (2000: 10–11) is correct when he says that globalization or globalism "means that we have been living for a long time in a world society." Yet he fails to acknowledge that we have a global society without a global state. Thus, his conclusion makes little sense: "globalization denotes the *process* through which sovereign national states are criss-crossed and undermined by transnational actors with varying prospects of power, orientations, identities and networks." This is to overestimate the global civil society that is really emerging and to underestimate the nation-states that have never been so strategic in global economic competition as they are today.

The emergence of such ideas, in a moment of the history of mankind in which, after all, the surface of the earth is completely covered with nation-states, has one paradoxical aspect. Until World War II, the world map was dominated mainly by empires – no longer the classic empires, but the capitalist empires, particularly of Britain and France. Later, we saw the emergence of a growing number of nation-states, as the old colonies became independent. For some time, the constitution of the Soviet Empire implied the retrogression in this process, but with its collapse, the world capitalist society fully assumed its intrinsic character of an economic system politically and geographically organized on the lines of nation-states. This is why José Luís Fiori (2002: 36) correctly asks, "How to explain this paradox that announces the death of the

---

[10] Note that I am not using *government* as a synonym of *state*, as is usual in American English; rather, I use *government* to refer to either the elite of top elected and nonelected civil servants who run the state organization or to the process of governing the country. Governance would be the governing process in which other groups and individuals – civil society – participate.

states' sovereignty as a result of globalization, exactly at the time when they are multiplying and becoming a global phenomenon?"

A second assumption of globalism is that there is only one path to economic development, and its model is U.S. capitalism. Therefore, the loss of autonomy of nation-states should not be deplored, but welcomed, because this will make easier for all countries to follow the same path toward development – the one presumed to be the more successful: the U.S. path. There is, however, no reason to consider the U.S. model of capitalism superior to western European capitalism. On the contrary, I understand that the social capitalism built in Europe during the thirty golden years, although hurt by the neoliberal hegemony, remains a political and economic system more democratic, more equal, more stable, and, as it will be finally made clear after the 2008 crisis, more capable of promoting growth than the U.S. one. Likewise, there is no reason to assume that globalization forces all countries to follow a same economic and political model. As Layna Mosley (2005: 356) points out, "domestic institutions play an important role in mediating pressures from the global economy." Just as there are many models or varieties of capitalism, so there are different national strategies of economic development. The countries that have achieved the best results use very different strategies from those recommended by rich countries through their agencies. On the other hand, the assumption of the solidarity of rich countries toward developing countries is belied every day in newspaper reports of discussions concerning the World Trade Organization. Even if there is some solidarity, particularly regarding poorer countries, what really characterizes the relationship of rich countries with other countries is still the attempt to gain all kinds of advantages over weak, or even corrupt, governments. Yet, with regard to middle-income countries, we must make a distinction between countries with autonomous national elites and countries with dependent elites. With both, the main relation is that of competition, but with the latter, there is also a relation of exploitation. While they negotiate the opening of their domestic markets to exports from other countries demanding reciprocity, they open them to investment by multinational corporations without any compensation. The justification for this uneven practice is the argument that it is natural that capital-rich countries transfer their capital to capital-poor countries. Complementing this argument is the saying that "economic growth is nothing more than a competition among developing countries to attract foreign direct investment."[11]

As globalism is based on real facts, and particularly because it is an ideology of the hegemonic center, it also attracts left-wing critics, who, instead of denying globalization, deplore the alleged loss of the autonomy and significance of nation-states.[12] To these two opposing groups, a third can be added, consisting of progressive European intellectuals like Jürgen Habermas, who confuse the consequences of globalization with the loss of national autonomy resulting from the harmonization process of the European Union and do not realize that the European Union is not evidence of the weakening of the idea of national states but rather is an attempt to form a European multinational state stronger than its individual member nation-states.[13]

Today, there is a large body of literature criticizing globalism. Robert Wade (1996), for instance, made a careful analysis of the problem and concluded, as indicated in the title of his chapter, that "reports of the death of the national economy are greatly exaggerated." Robert Boyer

---

[11] I discuss this problem more broadly, criticizing growth with foreign savings, in the last chapter of this book.

[12] The basic left-wing book on globalization and on the loss of autonomy of nation-states is by François Chesnais (1994). It is impressive how, in this book, Chesnais criticized financial globalization and predicted the coming major financial crises. Gilberto Dupas (2006: 150), for his part, points out that "the globalization process has progressively constrained the power of the states." We have seen that Octavio Ianni thought likewise in his pioneer works on globalization.

[13] See Habermas (2000). In the 1998 and 2000 essays, the concern with Europe is mixed up with globalization; in the 1999 essay, attention is turned more toward extending democratic policy to a system in which the nation-state inevitably loses autonomy. The idea that, despite their growing interdependence, nation-states should firmly defend their interests, particularly economic ones, is erroneously discarded by Habermas.

(2001: 12), summing up the conclusions of a broad study of the models of capitalism or modes of regulation, remarked that "regarding this issue there is almost complete unanimity: each chapter develops an original argument regarding the lack of convergence of institutional reforms, even if they respond to the same imperatives."

The fact that, through their financial systems and multilateral agencies, rich countries force developing countries to adopt neoliberal reforms by imposing "conditionalities" just hastens an inevitable process. For example, at the World Trade Organization, during the Uruguay Round, which ended in the 1990s, these countries were able to substantially reduce the scope for economic policy on the part of developing countries by making illegal a number of practices that they themselves had largely used in the past (Wade 2003; Chang 2006).

THE STRATEGIC ROLE OF THE NATION-STATE

Thus, the fact that countries are interdependent and cooperate does not mean they have "lost sovereign power." *Sovereignty*, as Jean Bodin defined it, is a concept of political philosophy that has always had partial or precarious historical existence. When political philosophers attributed absolute sovereignty to nation-states, those states were probably less sovereign than today because they were always threatened by wars and invasions – threats that today are almost nonexistent for the major countries. The nation-states that did not become involved in agreements to create more extensive regional sovereignty (as European countries did) remain sovereign because they are still the final source of law and order for their inhabitants, and they are more economically strategic today than at any other time. Yet those that made such agreements, such as the countries of the European Union, and, particularly, those of the euro area, transferred part of their sovereignty to a multinational state in formation, but they transferred it freely to increase their power within the frame of globalization, not to submit to it. As a result, we will understand the logic of international political and economic relations only if we think of nation-states – particularly the most powerful ones – as autonomous units promoting their national interests in the global arena in any way they can.

By making these statements, am I not being so-called mercantilist and therefore making a mistake that became manifest after the publication of the *Wealth of Nations* in 1776? The misconception that existed in mercantilism was metallism: it was the confusion between the wealth of nations, on one hand, and the trade surpluses they achieved and the amount of gold they accumulated, on the other. But mercantilists were correct when they saw in the newly emerging nation-states not only the fundamental political, but also economic, units. Adam Smith's main criticism of mercantilists was concentrated on metallism, showing that the true wealth of a nation-state lies in its production of goods and services, not in the trade surpluses and the amount of gold it accumulates. Smith also criticized the protectionist nature of mercantilist policies. He continued, however, to think of economics as political economy, in which the fundamental units of study were nation-states. He was interested not in the wealth of individuals or of the world, but in the wealth of nations. The classical economists who followed him thought likewise. Ricardo, for instance, showed clearly that international trade is not a zero-sum game, as mercantilists thought, but a positive-sum game, in which all nation-states involved could win. It was only in the 1870s, when conservative economists responded to Marx's interpretation of classical political economy with a new and essentially flawed school of thought – neoclassical economics – that the nation-state lost its key role in economics. By using the hypothetical-deductive method, instead of a historical or empirical method, neoclassical economics emptied economic theory of its real content and turned it into a method of market analysis. Although neoclassical economics has become dominant in university graduate courses, government leaders never seriously considered such highly abstract laissez-faire theory when framing their policies, given its impractical nature. They ceased to think in mercantilist terms, to have trade balances and the accumulation of international reserves as goals, but, correctly, from the point of view of their nations, became what neoclassical economists disparagingly call *neomercantilists* – they remained concerned about increasing employment and national production or wealth. Keynesian macroeconomics in the 1930s and development economics in the 1940s brought back to economic theory this national developmental approach central to classical political economy, as both schools view economic development as a national process.

Globalization has taken place on the economic, social, and cultural levels but has scarcely advanced on the political level; we cannot talk of political globalization. Although during the twentieth century, a global political system has emerged, headed by the United Nations, we are still far from the formation of a world state. Despite being interdependent, nation-states are the lead players in globalization: they are the sources of citizenship and law, and they define peace and war. The fact that the transition to and consolidation of democracy in rich and middle-income countries took place in this century only strengthened the autonomy of the nation-states, as their citizens/voters demanded from their government leaders the pursuit of the major political goals of modernity: security, freedom, economic development, social justice, and the protection of nature. This is why the political level lacks the ambiguity that exists on the economic level: whereas entrepreneurs and executives of major enterprises waver between nationalism and globalism, politicians, to be reelected, have no alternative but to identify themselves with their own nations. Government leaders take into account the globalization process in which they are involved, and the interdependences deriving from this do not preclude them from adopting national policies. Indeed, although the substitution of the term *internationalization* for *globalization* would imply that nations have lost significance, they remain crucial.

Global capitalism is a world economic system whose basic components are enterprises as well as the sovereign nation-states. Marx made the great analysis of capitalism on the economic and social levels but failed in his analysis of the political or state domain. There is no theory of the nation-state in Marx, even though the nation-state is the political and territorial unit characteristic of capitalist societies. Whereas in pre-capitalist societies, the classical empires were the political and territorial units, under capitalism, it is the nation-state that takes on this role.[14] Nation-states are sovereign political and territorial entities, consisting of three elements: a nation, a territory, and a state. This latter, therefore, cannot be confused with the nation or with the nation-state (or with the government that heads the state). Whereas the nation is a type of society, and the nation-state is a political and territorial unit, the state is an institution: it is the constitutional system and the organization that underpins it; it is the law and the state apparatus.[15] Under capitalism, nations use their states as instruments of collective action to achieve their political goals, among which is always the maintenance of their own sovereignty and economic development. As shown by Ernest Gellner (1983), the empires' aristocratic elites, when promoting territorial expansion, had no concept of productivity increase or economic development, and therefore they left untouched their colonies' social organization and culture and confined themselves to collecting taxes from subjugated populations. In contrast, in the nation-states, nations are the result of a national social agreement turned to common political purposes. The new economic

---

[14] I use the term *classical empires* to refer to precapitalist empires. During the long capitalist revolution, there were also empires such as the British one; these, however, should not be confused with the classical empires – the last one being the Austro-Hungarian Empire. The industrial capitalist empires of the nineteenth century, such as the British and the French, and even the mercantile empires of the seventeenth and eighteenth centuries, such as the Spanish and the Portuguese, were mixed forms, sharing characteristics of the ancient empires and modern nation-states.

[15] I know that these distinctions are not always clear, and this is partly why these three words are used with different meanings. In the literature on international relations, *states* in the plural is also commonly used as a synonym for nation-states. In the United States, *nations* is commonly used also as a synonym for nation-states, rather than being reserved for national societies. Authors rarely make the necessary clear distinction between *state* and *nation-state*.

and political elites do not confine themselves to concentrating military and police power to ensure their security; their other, principal goal is the economic development that legitimizes them. To do that, contrary to what happened with classical empires, the nation-states extend public education to the whole population living in the national territory, and thus, at the same time, they ensure productivity increase or economic development and turn their subjects into citizens by successively acknowledging their civil, political, and social rights. As long as markets opened and the logic of profit, capital accumulation, and technical progress prevailed everywhere, new nation-states were formed.

NEOLIBERAL DECLINE

In the 2000s, neoliberalism and globalism have lost the dominance they enjoyed in the two previous decades, while the hegemony of the United States, which was the basis of that dominance, has declined sharply. Several factors have contributed to this: the failure of the neoliberal reforms to promote growth, the political disaster that is the Iraq War, the 2007–8 financial crisis in the United States, the elections of left-wing and nationalist politicians in Latin America, and last but not least, the shift of the world's economic axis from the United States to Asia. Thus, while globalism expected that the U.S. model would prevail worldwide, the opposite is the case. As Aglietta and Berrebi (2007: 8) remark, "globalization should be seen as a system of multilateral interdependences, in which the emerging powers have a determining influence on developed economies." This is one of the consequences of the catching up process, whereby a group of countries compete successfully with rich countries, grow faster than those countries, and take on a decisive role among the world's nations. Although this phenomenon had favored the growth of the United States and Europe (if China had grown, since the early 1980s, by 2 percent per annum, instead of 10 percent, the United

States and Europe would have grown less during that period), there is a feeling of defeat with regard to international competition, which leads to a negative view of globalization. Globalization is increasingly seen by rich societies as a threat, rather than an advantage, and as a consequence, globalism has lost its luster. Research conducted in the United States in 2008 revealed that more than 50 percent of the population already view globalization negatively.[16] Paul Krugman (2008: 4; see also Krugman 1995), who in the 1990s was certain that globalization did not cause wages in developed countries to fall, has since changed his mind:

> The developing countries that account for most of the expansion in trade since the early 1990s are substantially lower-wage, relative to advanced countries, than the developing countries that were the main focus of concern in the original literature [on the consequences of globalization for wages]. China, in particular, is estimated by the Bureau of Labor Statistics to have hourly compensation in manufacturing that is equal to only 3 percent of the U.S. level. Again, this shift to lower-wage sources of imports seems to suggest that the distributional effects of trade may well be considerably larger now than they were in the early 1990s.

In other words, commercial globalization, which I see as an opportunity for low-wage, middle-income countries, is far from being so favorable to rich countries. It causes delocalization of manufacturing industries and depresses the wages of the poor. In contrast, my argument is that the rich in developed countries gain from financial globalization, which is disastrous for developing countries insofar as they become unable to neutralize the tendency of the exchange rate toward overvaluation and hence become excessively indebted. The 2008 financial crisis showed that, eventually, it is also disastrous for rich countries.

---

[16] According to the president of the U.S. Council of Foreign Relations, Richard Haass (2008), "globalization dilutes the influence of big powers, including the US."

Political Economy

GLOBALIZATION AND CATCHING UP

In globalization, the international division of labor between rich and middle-income countries follows a simple rule: tasks with higher value added per capita, which are not standardized or codified and require more skilled labor, composed primarily of managers and communicators, would be performed in rich countries that have plenty of this kind of labor, whereas standardized or codified tasks would be transferred to low-wage workers in developing countries. This process enables developing countries to catch up, profiting from their advantages of cheap labor and their capacity for importing technology at a relatively low cost, and at the same time guarantees that rich countries continue to grow at satisfactory rates, even if facing problems of delocalization and deindustrialization. As long as the new jobs in manufacturing industry and services have a higher technological content, demanding more skilled labor compatible with a higher value added per capita and therefore with higher wages, rich countries should continue to grow satisfactorily in the frame of globalization. Their real cost would be the greater concentration of income in the short run because initially the wages of their less skilled workers would suffer a relative decline and would increase only if those workers went through a qualification process inherent to development centered on industries with more technological content.

The assumption of economic theory that developing countries should catch up appears to be confirmed. An increasingly significant group of developing countries are fast-growing economies, profiting from the advantage of their lower labor costs and exportation to rich countries; these developing countries continue to industrialize because they are still transferring labor from agriculture and underemployment to manufacturing industry. However, not all middle-income countries have been successful in this transfer, and in the catch up, because not all such nations are strong enough to face the ideological hegemony of the North. Whereas the dynamic Asian countries have succeeded,

46

Latin American middle-income countries have failed, with the exception of Chile and, more recently, Argentina: they grow at slower rates than the rich countries and do not catch up. In these low-growth economies, societies lacking cohesion and with alienated ruling elites do not know how to use their states strategically and to grow. This will depend on each country's national cohesion and on the autonomy of its ruling elites with respect to rich countries.

Globalization is being accompanied by income concentration. Yet the increase in inequality is a consequence not mainly of more open markets but of the information technology revolution, which has increased the demand for skilled labor and decreased the demand for unskilled labor, and also of neoliberal ideology, which aims at precisely such an outcome. Trade opening and immigration cause some income concentration in rich countries because they force local workers to compete with cheaper labor, but rich countries have the means to defend themselves against it. Besides erecting higher barriers against immigration (because there is no political globalization, there is no migratory globalization), they adopt countervailing social measures. As observed by John Stephens (2005), the possible reductions in wages caused by competition from middle-income countries tend to be compensated by measures increasing social protection. The Scandinavian institution of flexsecurity has this purpose.[17]

The assumption that globalization increases inequality within each country is confirmed by the facts, whereas the assertion that it is an obstacle to developing countries has fallen into discredit.[18] Despite the

---

[17] For an excellent short description of flexsecurity or of the so-called Copenhagen Consensus, see Kuttner (2008).

[18] The participants of the World Social Forum, for instance, no longer define their movement as antiglobalization and now fight for "another globalization," a more equitable one. Marxist analysts, such as Ben Fine (2004: 212), have ceased to view globalization negatively and consider it "a reaction, or even an absolute rejection of neo-liberalism," as long as it is not a mere ideology but capitalism materially in movement.

imperialist strategy implicit in the globalist attempt to neutralize national strategies, a significant number of middle-income countries, such as China, India, South Korea, Taiwan, Thailand, Malaysia, and Indonesia, and more recently, Russia, Argentina, and Vietnam, are growing at substantially higher rates than the rich countries – they are catching up and therefore approaching the income levels of the rich countries. Yet in other middle-income countries, particularly in Latin America, but also in the Middle East and sub-Saharan Africa, growth rates are much more modest. In other words, we have fast-growing and slow-growing developing countries. Commercial globalization implies a major opportunity for developing countries, which is being used by the dynamic Asian countries, including two population giants, China and India, so that globalization – in global, not national, terms – is becoming a process of redistribution of income and wealth on behalf of the fast-growing developing countries. As Grunberg and Laïd (2007: 137) remark, "over the years, globalization will appear as it really is: a historical process of redistribution of wealth and power on behalf of world regions that were deprived of them during at last two centuries." This comment absolutely does not announce the funeral of the West because international trade is a positive-sum game, but it indicates that the banner of globalization carried by the United States in the 1990s is far from being as favorable to rich countries as presumed. Globalization also acts in their favor because the accelerated growth of a growing number of middle-income countries and the ever-growing trade in which they are involved are factors that benefit rich countries as well. Contrary to what an increasing number of people in rich countries believe, globalization does not reduce but rather increases those countries' growth rates and, although posing new challenges, particularly for the social state that developed in northwestern Europe, does not destroy them (Glatzer and Rueschmeyer 2005). What occurs is just a process of flexsecurity, whereby the workers' stability in enterprises is reduced but, as a trade-off, the state's social expenditure is increased. The relations of power between rich countries and dynamic middle-income countries change on behalf of these latter, but standards of living continue to rise in both groups of countries.

COMMERCIAL AND FINANCIAL GLOBALIZATION

The participation of developing countries as a whole in world exports rose from 20 percent in 1970 to 43 percent in 2005, and their participation in the global product in purchasing power parity terms, which corresponded to 80 percent at the end of the eighteenth century, thanks mostly to China and India, fell to 20 percent in 1950, as a consequence of the imperialism to which those two countries were subjected; however, since the early 1980s, it has risen again, and it already, by 2005, represented 45 percent of world GDP.[19] Globalization is therefore reorganizing production worldwide. Rich countries as well as a good number of developing countries are growing at faster rates than in the past, but among them, the dynamic middle-income Asian countries, Russia, and Argentina are growing faster and catching up. Asia, which for centuries was the world's richest region, has regained its importance in the world economy.

The accelerated economic development that we are witnessing in middle-income countries is not happening by accident. Those countries have nationalist business and bureaucratic elites that adopt national development strategies based on domestic savings and on competent macroeconomic policies. A national development strategy is an informal agreement among the social classes under the leadership or the intermediation of government, aiming at economic development. It presumes the existence of a developmental state – that is, a state that makes economic development one of its central concerns, as has always been the case with the U.S. state (despite the fact that its orthodox economists

---

[19] The source of these data is Woodall (2006), based on Organisation for Economic Co-operation and Development (OECD) data collected by Angus Maddison.

49

insist on rejecting developmentalism). In Latin America, between the 1950s and 1970s, when growth rates were high, the corresponding states were called "developmentalist." More recently, after the pioneering contribution of Chalmers Johnson (1982) regarding Japan, the term *developmental state* has been reserved in international political economy mainly for dynamic Asian countries (Evans 1995; Woo-Cummings 1999). However, a state does not have to be called "developmental" for it to have a national development strategy. Ireland, for instance, has grown at extraordinary rates since the late 1980s as a result of a national strategy (Godoi 2007). Regarding national development strategies, for now we must consider that they constitute an institution, or more precisely, a set of laws, policies, and agreements aimed at creating lucrative investment opportunities for entrepreneurs.

Although the rich countries realized the competition they were experiencing from the developing countries only as of the 1970s, when the so-called newly industrializing countries appeared, there have always been conflicting, rather than cooperative, relations between them. At first, it was not the financial opening, but the commercial one, that the rich countries used ideologically to limit the competitive ability of the new countries. After the first Industrial Revolution took place in Britain, this country tried to obstruct the catching up of other European countries. Friedrich List ([1846] 1999) coined the phrase "kicking away the ladder" to illustrate this behavior, and Ha-Joon Chang (2002a) gave it empirical content. After the beginning of the nineteenth century, the countries that industrialized early tried to neutralize the competitive ability of the countries that came after them, arguing and pressing for open international markets. This strategy worked for a certain time, but in the end, each country realized that it needed to protect its infant industry and tried to create high tariffs to achieve this. The United States and Germany industrialized in the nineteenth century based on this understanding. In Latin America, from the 1930s on, the region's most important countries also industrialized by protecting their infant industries, and the same occurred in Asia soon after World War II. Therefore, although the strategy of neutralizing competitors based on the law of comparative advantage of international trade was effective for some time in persuading competitors not to industrialize, it eventually became exhausted, as middle-income countries achieved industrialization in defiance of neoliberal arguments based on the law of comparative advantage. Trade globalization lost appeal as an ideological weapon. Today, protective measures emanate increasingly from rich countries, not from middle-income countries, which know how to take advantage of the opportunity represented by the trade opening.

Yet, while commercial globalization is an opportunity from which some developing countries are able to profit, financial globalization is a threat insofar as it leads countries to lose control over their exchange rates and to become excessively indebted in foreign currencies. Financial opening is favorable to rich countries[20] because an overvalued exchange rate in developing countries favors rich countries' commercial interests and also increases the amount of hard currency multinationals transfer to headquarters with a given revenue in the local currency. It is also favorable because there is no more effective way of making countries (and people, as in the limiting case of present slavery episodes)[21] dependent. This is why, since the early 1990s, when the neoliberal hegemony seemed invincible, pressures grew on developing countries to open their capital accounts and try to grow with the use of foreign savings. Although many are the diagnoses, recommendations, and pressures made by rich countries through the World Bank, the International Monetary Fund, and other agents of the international financial system, the core of conventional orthodoxy is currently devoted to keeping developing countries'

---

[20] Note that the 2008 financial crisis was not the consequence of financial opening but of domestic financial deregulation.

[21] In developing countries, slavery usually takes place in rural and underdeveloped areas, and in all countries, it happens with immigrant labor. In both cases, indebtedness is the instrument to reduce people to a condition of slavery.

exchange rates relatively appreciated. This orthodoxy is not yet commit-
ted to denying that the tendency toward exchange rate overvaluation I
have recently identified exists, but merely insists that managing this rate
is unfeasible. Conventional orthodoxy knows that only by means of an
overvalued exchange rate can rich countries compensate for the advantage that middle-income countries derive from their low-cost labor.
Therefore, as I discuss in Part II of the book, it denies the existence or
the relevance of the Dutch disease for developing countries; insists on
recommending the policy of growth with foreign savings; and, unable
to distinguish a depreciated from a competitive exchange rate, claims
that any intervention in the exchange rate is unfair as it is a way of
growing at one's neighbors' expense ("beggar thy neighbor").[22] Besides,
it insistently argues that the use of so-called competitive devaluations
weakens technological progress, and so productivity, as it artificially protects business enterprises from foreign competition, even though what
I am proposing is no more than the neutralization of the tendency of
the exchange rate toward overvaluation. The best efforts of conventional
orthodoxy are directed to protecting the policy of growth with foreign
savings, ignoring the fact that a current account deficit implies a high
rate of substitution of foreign for domestic savings (Chapter 6). Actually,
the policy of growth with foreign savings is positive for a country only
in a very particular situation, namely, when the national economy is
already growing fast and the prospects for profits are very good, because
at that moment, the wage increases caused by exchange rate appreciation are oriented to consumption rather than to investment. Outside
this particular situation, the consequences of the exchange rate appreciation, besides a decrease in exports and an increase in imports, will be,
successively, an increase in real wages; an increase in domestic consumption; the substitution of foreign for domestic savings; growing financial

[22] In Chapter 4, I define the equilibrium or competitive exchange rate as the one corresponding to *industrial equilibrium* – the one in which the exchange rate makes viable
economically tradable industries utilizing state-of-the-art technology.

fragility, accentuating dependence; and eventually, if the country does not wake up in time, a balance-of-payment crisis (Bresser Pereira and Gala 2008).

To successfully compete under globalization, the necessary national development strategy of the successful Asian countries was always based on severe fiscal adjustment and a competitive exchange rate. Unlike in Latin America, the land reform that strongly reduced the differences of income between households made it possible for governments not to try to offset the concentration of income with social expenditure. This prevented fiscal populism. Yet, as far as the exchange rate was concerned, the dynamic Asian countries imposed strict limits on foreign indebtedness and limited capital inflows whenever necessary. They did not need to limit capital outflows because, except for the 1990s, when four Asian countries were attracted by the policy of growth with foreign savings and, not surprisingly, endured the 1997 crisis, they have always kept their foreign accounts balanced, and when they went into debt, they did so only moderately, and always when the country was already experiencing fast growth.

2

The Key Institution

Since the 1960s, institutions have been a central concern of political scientists and, since the 1980s, also a major research program for economists. Before that, social scientists used to adopt a structural or socio-economic approach, in which institutions had a role but the economic structure conditioned them, whereas neoclassical economists simply ignored institutions. Thus, when mainstream economists focused on institutions, it was progress; it was a way of broadening the scope of economics, which had been narrowed by neoclassical economics. Yet the form that this inclusion of institutions in development economics took ended up being excessive and reductionist: excessive insofar as institutions suddenly gained autonomy from social structures and reductionist because the new institutionalist economists claimed that if the rules of law or property rights and contracts were assured, economic development would automatically ensue in the market. In this chapter, my central concern is not to criticize this claim, the weakness of which is self-evident; rather, I offer an alternative set of institutions that, on one hand, enjoy relative autonomy in relation to economic structures and, on the other, play a key role in promoting economic growth: a *national development strategy*.

The Key Institution

The central weakness of the new institutionalist approach to economic development stems from the strong correlation between each society's levels of economic development of its institutions, or more generally, between the three social instances (the economic, the institutional, and the cultural) existing in all societies. There is, to be sure, some degree of freedom between these instances insofar as at certain moments, the economic structure advances more than the institutional and the cultural instances, whereas at other moments, the opposite occurs. The reasonable hope that all reformers share is that the second alternative is true – sometimes it is, but only rarely. Usually, good institutional reforms go hand in hand with, on one hand, technological and economical change and, on the other, cultural and ideological change. This fact, which Marx and Engels discovered more than a century and a half ago, has been confirmed in many ways, but few imagined that econometric studies would confirm it. Yet this happened after institutions became fashionable objects of study among conventional economists, and they decided to relate the institution to economic growth. What most econometric tests have demonstrated is that there is a strong correlation between good institutions and the *level* of economic growth but practically no correlation between respect for property rights or contracts, or the rule of law, or even democracy, and the *rate* of economic growth. In other words, the three societal instances – economic, institutional, and cultural – are strongly correlated in terms of outcome (the richer countries tend also to be more democratic, socially more equitable, and more protective of the environment), but in the growth process, we cannot find sensible correlations between institutional variables and the yearly percentage increase in per capita income or improvement in standards of living. The tight correlation between the structural and the institutional instances is confirmed, whereas the hope that institutional reforms will generate growth is not. Institutional reforms remain essential to development, but they do not explain why some countries begin to grow faster than before and, gradually, catch up.

What we need to find is the institutional historical fact that explains the beginning of the catching up, or more broadly, of periods of reasonably high and sustained growth. Although what I will discuss applies to middle-income countries, it also applies partially to poor countries. Usually, the growth process begins when a cluster of reforms and policies to which a nation is able to informally agree opens new opportunities for profitable investment, thus creating the conditions for Schumpeterian entrepreneurs to invest and innovate. This new historical fact is an institution – a national development strategy – that, on the demand side, (1) creates a demand for investments oriented to the domestic market, neutralizing the tendency for profits to increase faster than wages (due to the unlimited supply of labor prevailing in such countries) and so contributing to sustained domestic demand, and (2) keeps the exchange rate competitive so as to ensure that industries using state-of-the-art technology remain profitable, despite the tendency of the exchange rate toward overvaluation. Once a country is able to agree on the cluster of formal and informal institutions that is a national development or competition strategy, it will be able to adopt the macroeconomic policies that will really make a short-term difference: besides the competitive exchange rate that promotes export-oriented investment and an income policy that keeps wages and salaries increasing with profits so as to stimulate consumption and investment, this strategy will also be austere in fiscal terms so as to keep the state financially healthy and will keep the interest rate at a moderate level, while using it to manage monetary policy.

Economic development tends to be self-sustained inasmuch as, in an environment of rapid technological change, firms have no choice but to reinvest their profits. It is, however, perennially subject to crises, slow growth rates, and eventual long-term quasistagnation, as was the case in Latin America in the 1980s and 1990s. It speeds up at certain times, indicating the presence of a national development strategy; at other times, it becomes quasistagnant, either because the previous strategy has become exhausted and the country is unable to replace it or because the country is subordinated to its competitors. The challenge each nation faces in overcoming these difficult transition phases involves national autonomy and societal cohesiveness – two factors that tend to depend on many circumstances. These factors will be stronger in Asian countries than in Latin American ones because their people never thought to be European: they improve after a revolution, making the country free from formal or informal international subordination, as was the case in Iran; they are subdued when external domination is overwhelming, as happens in the Middle East and Africa for geopolitical reasons, specifically, their natural resources; and they are restrained when soft ideological power exerted by dominant countries persuades local elites to follow their recommended policy reforms.

In modern democracies, the state is the nation's instrument of collective action, and the government is the body of elected officials and high-ranking bureaucrats who rule it in the name of the citizens.[1] The strategic nature of economic development arises from the need and opportunity of a nation to organize efforts to raise living standards and from the strong correlation between economic growth and the achievement of other major political objectives. Even though development may, in the short run, take place at the expense of social justice and environmental protection, in the medium term, the positive correlation will show up because social justice and defenders of the environment will be empowered by economic growth. Yet the key factor making a national growth strategy necessary is the highly competitive nature of capitalism.

---

[1] In English, the term *government* is often used synonymously with *state*, whereas *administration* denotes what, in Europe and Latin America, is called *government* (*governo*, *gobierno*, *gouvernement*). I use *state*, not *government*, to mean the organization that defines and enforces the law; administration or government is formed by the group of politicians and senior officials who direct the state; *nation-state* is here a synonym for *country* or *national state*. *States*, in the plural, is often used as a synonym for *nation-states* or *countries*, but I avoid that. Note also that I distinguish *nation* and *state* from *nation-state*: a nation or a national society plus a state and a territory form a nation-state.

Today, within the framework of globalization, where commercial and technological rivalry among nations is stronger than ever, the need for a national development or competition strategy has become evident. Although nation-states do not have the same cohesiveness as organizations, they, too, need a kind of strategic plan to succeed in international competition. In governing, a large share of politicians' efforts and struggles is centered on how best to promote a country's economic growth. On the economic relations front, with regard to trade and technological and financial matters, nation-states and their private business enterprises experience tough competition that requires constant initiative on the part of their governments. Nation-states also cooperate because in all cases in which there is frequent competition, cooperation is necessary to define the rules of the game and to avoid conflicts damaging to both sides, but, in general, competition prevails over cooperation.

In the past two centuries of capitalist development, experience shows that when a middle-income country that has already completed its capitalist revolution is enjoying full growth, this is a sign that its nation is strong – that politicians, business entrepreneurs, bureaucrats, and workers are operating within the framework of a loose but concerted national strategy. A nation's strength is expressed in its commitment to the political objectives of contemporary societies – security, freedom, economic development, social justice, and protection of the environment – and in its ability to bring together and formulate strategies to achieve these objectives. The more developed or the more capitalist a country is, the more economic development tends to be facilitated by free markets that foster the efficient allocation of factors of production. But in developing countries, economic development is the outcome of a nation's deliberate endeavor to use the state as its principal institutional instrument of collective action. It is the result of an informal agreement involving entrepreneurs, workers, and the middle classes, with the intermediation of government. Together with governments, business associations and unions often play a major role in defining it and also in putting it into

action. Such a national development or competition strategy materializes into laws, policies, common understandings, and shared beliefs that
orient innovation and stimulate investment; it is not formal or written,
but it can easily be intuited by the observer. At the present time, for
middle-income countries, domestic savings and a competent macroeconomic policy are the two key factors in this national strategy that will
make the country competitively successful, that is, that will enable it to
catch up.

The politically oriented society that is behind a state and its government may be viewed as a civil society or a nation. When society is viewed
as civil society, civil liberties are the focal point; when it is viewed as a
nation, security and economic growth are the central concerns. A nation
that is able to agree on a national development strategy is strong and
lively. In contrast, as Fábio Konder Comparato (2005: A3) underlines,
"when a nation no longer defines a historical horizon to be pursued with
courage and hope, it enters the unhappy state of awareness that Hegel
referred to: the inability to take a harmonic stance before life."

DEFINITION

What is a national strategy? This is not an easily answered question as
national strategies vary widely across time and space, yet a historical definition attempting to capture its main characteristics may be offered. A
national development strategy is an international competition strategy;
it is concerted economic action oriented toward economic growth that
has the nation as its collective actor and the state as its basic instrument
of collective action. It is an informal or implied political coalition in
which social classes, under the leadership of the government, suspend
their domestic conflicts and cooperate when the problem they face is
international economic competition. It is an institution or a cluster of
institutions that guide the main political and economic actors in their
decision-making processes – politicians on how to define new public

policies or reform existing ones, businesspeople on when and where to invest. Thus, a national development strategy always involves the inducement to innovation and capital accumulation. It is a nationalist institution insofar as it gives clear priority to the interests of national labor, national knowledge, and national capital, but the higher the stage of development, the more moderate and democratic this nationalism will be, open to international cooperation and rejecting ethnic criteria.[2]

Because people in the modern world are organized on three levels – families, organizations, and nation-states – that compete and cooperate among themselves, a national development strategy is the form in which each nation chooses to perform this double competition and coopera-tion role. Cohesive and autonomous nations will have stronger national development strategies than divided and dependent ones. The cohesive-ness of a nation tends to increase with economic growth, but the process is far from being monotonic: gradual deterioration followed by crisis is common, as we have seen in Latin America since the 1980s. Insofar as nations gain and lose cohesiveness, their national development strate-gies will be clear or blurred and their economic achievements corres-pondingly variable.

A national development strategy is made up of a set of institutions defining the rules of the game of economic growth. Some are laws that should be relatively general and permanent, expressing basic values and objectives; others are institutional reforms that respond to basic changes in the social and economic structures; and still others are policies that may be more specific and temporary, defining means. Several forms

---

[2] Nationalism is here understood as the ideology that legitimizes the formation and consolidation of the nation-state. Citizens will be nationalists if they have no doubt that their governments are supposed to protect national capital, labor, and knowledge. According to this definition, all developed societies are nationalistic – so much so that they can dispense with the adjective or use it pejoratively, generally together with *populist*, to refer to political movements from the Right or Left that oppose hegemonic global views.

of planning, starting with public and infrastructure investments, are an essential part of it. If they are matched with strategic planning by business enterprises, this is a sign that a national development strategy really is in place. Yet national development strategies or national projects must not be confused with economic planning. In most successful national development strategies, there has been some sort of planning, particularly in the early stages of growth, when investment in the economic infrastructure and heavy industry took priority. Later on, market coordination becomes essential, and any general planning will be of the indicative variety only.

Since the capitalist revolution began, but principally under globalization, a national development strategy has been a competition strategy. It must always consider the reactions of so-called adversaries, which will be either other national competitors or new facts creating obstacles to growth that demand policy change. A national development strategy is the result of a collective and informal decision-making process. It is, therefore, a means to manage the national economy, to pursue options capable of steering it competitively toward development. Just as firms plan their activities strategically, so nation-states outline national development strategies in a necessarily less systematic, but nevertheless effective, way. Herbert Simon and Peter Simon ([1962] 1979: 176) identified strategy with program and regarded the latter as a means whereby economic actors with incomplete information and limited rationality appraise alternatives and make choices, instead of permanently optimizing, as assumed by neoclassical economics. On the basis of the analysis of a chess match, they write that a program or strategy is a series of decisions carried out in a well-defined manner that enables vast economy in terms of memory and the assessment of alternatives. On defining a strategy, the player must take three principles into consideration: (1) the attacker must consider strong games only (like checks on the opposite king); (2) all alternatives available to the opponent must be explored; and (3) if any of the games that the attacker is considering, regardless of how strong they may be, allow the opponent to make moves in response, the attack move is abandoned for lack of promise.

It is no different with national strategies. Strategists must begin by diagnosing the situation and then must search for alternatives, always bearing in mind the fact that they cannot pursue every alternative but, within the framework of a program, only those that appear more promising or satisfactory. Strategists are under no illusion as to optimization but know that they have limited time to make a decision, to choose under uncertainty. To implement the eventually defined strategy or program, those in charge of it will use all means available: they will draft laws, adopt economic policies, and define public investment plans and the national budget and all sorts of other institutions; they will try to make the most of the market's resources but will not hesitate to intervene, as needed.

When social scientists discuss models of capitalism as mutually distinct as the Anglo-American and corporative models, the Scandinavian and Japanese, they are also discussing the respective national growth strategies that have proved effective in promoting economic development in rich countries.[3] As models or varieties of capitalism, national growth strategies are also ideal types. The difference is that models are oriented toward describing and looking for the interrelations among all the social, economic, and political variables, whereas strategies concentrate on the variables that cause (or preclude) growth: a national strategy implies accelerated growth, whereas a model of capitalism may be consistent with relatively low per capita growth rates. National growth strategies are specific to each country, but, as in the case of models of capitalism, we can devise and analyze national growth strategies that encompass several countries. Describing the East Asian

---

[3] There is already a large and competent literature on models of capitalism (see, among others, Schmitter 1974; Esping-Andersen 1990; Albert 1991; Goodin et al. 1999; Hall and Soskice 2001; Boyer and Souyri 2001; Huber 2002; Stephens 2002).

model of capitalism, Ha-Joon Chang (2002b: 229) lists six characteristics that are typical traits of the respective national growth strategies:

(1) the pro-investment rather than anti-inflationary macroeconomic policy; (2) the control of luxury consumption, which serves both economic and political functions; (3) the strict control of foreign direct investment, which is contrary to the popular impression that these economies (except perhaps Japan) have an "open" FDI policy; (4) the integrated pursuit of infant industry protection and export promotion; (5) the use of exports as a tool to exploit scale economy and, thus, to accelerate the maturation of infant industries; (6) and the productivity-oriented (as opposed to allocation-oriented) view of competition.

To this list I would only add the neutralization of the tendency of the exchange rate toward overvaluation to define what I call the new developmentalist strategy that I discuss in Chapter 3.

SOME HISTORY

In the case of Latin America, to search for national development strategies makes sense only after 1930, when some countries that had been formally independent since the early nineteenth century became effectively independent and industrialized. In the case of Asia and Africa, such a search must be made after World War II, when countries in these continents became formally and, in most cases, substantively independent (such as the dynamic Asian countries). For the Latin American countries, the Great Depression of the 1930s created an opportunity to begin or boost industrialization. The national revolution, which began formally more than a century before with political independence, got under way. In Brazil, in Mexico, and, to a lesser degree, in other Latin American countries, a national-developmentalist strategy based in import substitution and state intervention attempted to emulate and adapt the experience of late-development central countries such as Germany and Japan.

Aiming to neutralize the Dutch disease or, more broadly, the tendency of the exchange rate toward overvaluation (of which economists had no knowledge at the time, but which policy makers intuited), countries used multiple exchange rates that effected a transfer of income from exported agricultural and mining products to industrial firms. Countries also resorted to several forms of planning and industrial policy to stimulate investment in higher per capita value-added industries. Between 1930 and 1980, national developmentalism was successful in Latin America.

At first, these national development strategies used local resources to finance development. This was the correct approach because it avoided the appreciation of the local currency and the loss of competitiveness of local industries that is inevitable when capital inflows are bigger than the demand for hard currency. However, from the early 1970s, in light of the assumption that rich countries are supposed to transfer capital to capital-poor countries, they increasingly resorted to foreign loans and to direct investment, while maintaining protectionist strategies and a pessimism about exports of manufactured goods, which no longer made sense. These two mistakes led to a major crisis in the early 1980s, which Latin American countries have yet to overcome fully. From around 1990, as a result their own national fragility and their response to the increasing ideological pressure from the North – the neoliberal wave – Latin American countries fell back into the condition of quasicolonies, and their elites accepted an imported strategy – conventional orthodoxy – which neutralizes, rather than promotes, economic development.

In contrast, at this time, some Asian countries that remained subject to European imperialism until World War II gained autonomy.[4] Some of them, like Korea and Taiwan, underwent agrarian reform in the 1950s. At first, they adopted an import-substitution strategy, but, whether because

---

[4] Japan was never a colony, and this was one of the reasons why it was the first Asian country to be part of the center. China, too, was not a formal colony, but it fell under foreign rule after the loss of the Opium War. India was a colony and, for that reason, lost even more than China in the nineteenth century.

their natural resources were limited or because their elites, being indigenous instead of transplanted from Europe, were better able to assert their national interests, they changed to an export-led strategy as early as the 1960s, while retaining industrial policies. Japan's successful economic growth served as a model for them. This was the beginning of the so-called flying geese strategy, whereby countries acquired conditions needed for development in successive waves: Japan was first, in the 1950s; Korea, Taiwan, Hong Kong, and Singapore followed in the 1970s; in the 1980s came Malaysia, Thailand, and Indonesia; and in the 1990s, China, India, and Vietnam came last. In all of these countries, the more strategic macroeconomic price – the exchange rate – was deliberately kept competitive, and industrial policies were markedly active, while tariff protection was gradually reduced. By practicing competent macroeconomic policies that kept state finances sound, limited finance from foreign savings, and managed exchange rates, they avoided the foreign debt crisis of the 1980s (which paralyzed development in Latin America) and kept their economies competitive and growing.[5]

The dynamic Asian countries, with their manufactured-goods, export-led strategy, had crucial advantages over Latin American countries. The first Asian tigers were small and soon changed from import substitution to export-led growth; many underwent agrarian reforms that ensured a more equal income distribution; they always adopted strict fiscal policies; they avoided the great foreign debt crisis of the 1980s by limiting foreign indebtedness (growth with foreign savings); they imposed limits on foreign investment; and any version of the Dutch disease from which they suffered was much weaker than in Latin America. All this permitted them to keep their exchange rates competitive. In the 1980s, while Latin Americans were immersed in debt crisis and economic populism (a perverse and unforeseen outcome of the transition

---

[5] As we see in Chapter 5, although the policy of growth with foreign savings usually has a negative effect on economic growth, in periods of high growth, it may be positive.

to democracy, or a reaction against the military regimes' policies that characterized this decade in several Latin American countries), Asian countries were making their transition from the first to the second stage of economic growth, or from old national developmentalism to new developmentalism.

What explains this difference of behavior between the Latin American and fast-growing Asian countries? Why did the Latin American elites surrender to the North, when the Asian ones did not? One explanation for the greater national autonomy of the Asian countries may be that they were subjected to industrial imperialism in the nineteenth century, but, except for the Philippines, their elites remained native, whereas the elites in Latin American countries, albeit of mixed race, considered themselves Europeans, and probably for this reason, had always had a greater problem in identifying themselves as national elites. Thus, it is probably not by chance that, among the Asian countries, the Philippines has dismal growth rates.

SUPPLY SIDE AND DEMAND SIDE

National development strategies vary from moment to moment and from country to country. Two countries that, since the 1980s, have adopted national development strategies – China and Ireland – could not be more different. Yet national development strategies have certain common traits that are related to the concept of economic development and its causes. On the supply side, economic development results from the increase in productivity caused by capital accumulation with the incorporation of technological knowledge, from investments in infrastructure that have positive externalities, from entrepreneurial innovations, and from the transfer of manpower to the production of goods and services involving higher per capita value added. Still, on the supply side, economic growth depends on technological progress and innovation; on education, food, and health care; or more broadly, on human capital.

On the demand side, economic growth depends on the elements that compose effective demand: investment, consumption, state expenditures, and exports minus imports. When demand is sustained, entrepreneurs will face investment opportunities to use the existing resources created on the supply side. To determine whether a country has a national strategy, we need to look not only to its main outcome – gross domestic product (GDP) growth per capita – but also at whether the main characteristics of the supply and demand sides of economic development are present.

On the supply side, all development strategies require or presuppose a financial system to finance investment or capital accumulation. In the early phases of development, when countries are beginning their capitalist revolutions, finance is obtained through so-called forced savings organized by the state, through profits realized in some primary goods industries using natural resources in which the country is rich, and through foreign investment. The essential task is to profit from the positive externalities caused by state and foreign investment (the big push model; see Rosenstein-Rodan 1943) and to transfer manpower from traditional activities to capitalist ones (see Lewis 1954). The existence of a primary goods industry using local natural resources from which the country is able to collect Ricardian rents is a standard form of initiating capitalist development that will be effective in neutralizing the Dutch disease to the extent that the state can tax such rents, using the revenues to finance its own investments and increase social expenditures. As industrialization proceeds, or the industrial revolution is completed, profits will tend to become the main source of investment finance. On the other hand, private and state financial systems develop and become capable of providing investment finance. The main agents of the accumulation process are business entrepreneurs, but in the first stages of development, the state plays a strategic role in promoting forced savings through the creation of social security funds, through taxes, or through investment banks.

A second trait of national development strategies is informal planning and industrial policy. Liberals reject both, but all countries have used them, particularly in the early stages of growth. National development strategies involve channeling idle funds or funds derived from forced savings toward public investment or toward business firms for investment by means of incentives or subsidies. In almost every country in the world, the state played an important role in the creation of the basic infrastructure of the economy and in increasing the rate of capital accumulation from around 5 percent to more than 20 percent of GDP. Yet, as the economy's complexity and diversity increase, forced savings cease to be required, while industrial policy loses relative significance as markets assume a larger role in resource allocation. As shown by Gerschenkron (1962), in the early stages of growth of backward central countries, the state plays a decisive role in bringing about capital accumulation and growth. Yet, after some time, as national economies become more complex, markets assume the coordinating role. In the transition from one to the other mode of development, there will usually be a crisis, after which the nation will have to devise a new national development strategy that accords a greater role to markets and entrepreneurs. In any circumstance, the state will conserve its capacity to achieve public savings to finance the strategic public investments that are always necessary. In this second stage, national growth strategies will develop a national financial system able to finance investment and technological progress. They will also continue to be involved in industrial policy, even though conventional orthodoxy condemns this. It could not be otherwise because globalization has made nation-states more interdependent, but, despite what we are usually told, no less relevant; on the contrary, globalization has made nation-states more strategic because it is characterized by acute competition among nation-states through their business enterprises.

A third common trait of national development strategies are policies connected with public education, health care, science, and technology. All theories of economic development emphasize human capital and technical progress, where the role of state agencies is strategic, but business enterprises are supposed to bear an increasing responsibility. Innovation lies, naturally, in the hands of business entrepreneurs – whether classical individual entrepreneurs or executive entrepreneurs.

A fourth canonical trait of national development strategies on the supply side is state investment in infrastructure, principally in energy, transportation, and communications. The state-owned enterprises, many of which were privatized in the 1990s, are the best examples of this characteristic. They are also on the demand side, together with capital accumulation in other industries, but all investments, and particularly those in infrastructure, play a major role in increasing productive capacity.

Fifth, a national development strategy is usually involved in making the state organization or public administration effective and efficient so that it can function as a tool of development. The public service reforms that took place in developed countries in the nineteenth century are the classic reforms in this area. In Britain, France, and the United States, however, they happened after industrialization. Many Latin American countries between the 1930s and the 1970s, and several Asian countries after 1950, adopted "developmentalist public administration reforms," aiming to make their bureaucracies flexible and modern. Finally, since the 1980s, many developed countries, and since the 1990s, some middle-income countries, responding to the growth of the social state or welfare state, have become involved in managerial or public management reforms to make public services more efficient.[6]

These five common traits are on the supply side of economic growth. Yet many developing countries have unused specialized labor, including highly educated people, that migrates to rich countries for lack of

---

[6] I have worked extensively on this subject since 1995, when I was minister of federal administration and reform of the state, and developed a model of public management reform (Bresser Pereira 2004a).

internal demand or have capable entrepreneurs who are unable to innovate and invest for lack of demand – in other words, for lack of investment opportunities. That is why, in every national development strategy,
a central characteristic is its capacity to ensure strong aggregate demand.
How? Usually, Keynesian economists underline the need for fiscal and
monetary policy to increase investment and consumption. This is sound,
but the limits of such policies are well known: fiscal deficits must be temporary because fiscal balance is a condition for state capability; monetary
policy is also a short-term anticyclical policy, not a development policy; and careless policies in these two areas may cause inflation rather
than growth. A competent macroeconomic policy that ensures, in the
long run, moderate interest rates and a competitive exchange rate is a
condition for growth, but in this domestic arena, the policy maker is
permanently constrained by tight checks. He or she must, above all,
keep the public deficit and public debt under control to ensure that
the state retains its capacity to be an effective instrument of collective
action.

There is, however, a form of effective demand that is less constrained
economically. I refer to exports. Strong increases in exports are a major
developmental factor on the demand side. If a country has, on the supply side, efficient productive capacity, the key issue is the exchange rate:
an export-led growth strategy requires a competitive exchange rate. For
some time, at the beginning of the process, a country may resort to
import substitution, but economies of scale establish definite limits to
this option, while there are no limits to an export strategy, except domestic ones: a country's productive and technological capacity. That is why
all countries that grow strongly are able to keep the exchange rate competitive. To achieve that, the main problem that national development
strategies must solve is how to neutralize the tendency of the exchange
rate toward overvaluation. The problem is related to the Dutch disease,
the policy of growth with foreign savings, and to exchange rate populism.
I discuss this problem in Part II of this book.

A country is supposed to manage its exchange rate to keep it competitive and to cope with the Dutch disease and wild capital inflows. For a long time, developing countries did so indirectly through complex systems of tariff protection and export subsidies. In consequence, the resulting effective exchange rate was less than the nominal exchange rate.[7] Today, when such practices are no longer compatible with the complexities of the industrial economies of developing countries, the exchange rate is managed more directly and in a more market-friendly way through the imposition of export taxes on the commodities causing the Dutch disease, through the purchase of foreign currencies and the buildup of international reserves, and, when these measures are not enough, through the adoption of controls on capital inflows. This was what Latin America did up until the 1980s, and it is what the Asian fast-growing countries continue to do today.

THE KEY INSTITUTION

It is easier to understand the role of national development strategies in development if we view them as the *key institution* in economic growth. In societies where the modern nation emerged as the central political actor and the state is the main instrument of collective action, a national development strategy is the institution, or collection of associated institutions, for achieving economic growth. It is a cluster of laws, policies, agreements, understandings, and shared beliefs – that is, of formal and informal institutions – that create investment opportunities and orient competitive economic actions undertaken, on one hand, by business entrepreneurs, workers, and the professional middle class and, on the other hand, by politicians and state bureaucrats.

---

[7] Note that the nominal exchange rate here is not the opposite of the real exchange rate (inflation controlled) but rather of the effective exchange rate (implicit after protection and export subsidies are taken into account).

After Douglass North (1990) published his book on institutions, aiming to make neoliberal economics broadly consistent with institutional analysis, and won a Nobel Prize, institutions again became fashionable in economics. Classical, Marxist, German historicists, and above all, the U.S. institutionalists had always attributed a central role to institutions, whereas neoclassical economics practically ignored them for around a century. When, in the early 1990s, institutions were eventually brought back into mainstream economics, many hailed this as good news. Yet this revival of institutions did not widen the horizons of economic analysis or make it more realistic because it adopted a reductionist approach: growth would take place in a country whenever one institution was present, namely, the guarantee of property rights and contracts. In this way, the new institutionalists were just repeating the old laissez-faire or the new neoliberal argument that the crucial condition of economic growth is that society ensures that markets function well.

This view is not empirical – it does not correspond to historical reality; rather, it is ideological, for several reasons. First, the protection of property rights and contracts or, more broadly, the rule of law is a consequence, rather than a condition, of economic development. The liberal states that emerged in Britain, France, and the United States in the early nineteenth century and ensured the rule of law did not precede but rather coincided with and followed the respective industrial revolutions. Second, in capitalist development, the protection of property rights and contracts is a relevant, but not a sufficient or even the most important, condition. Entrepreneurs are neither *bureaucrats* nor idle *rentiers* who prize security over all things; rather, they are risk-taking agents aiming for profits and self-achievement; they are interested in security, but they are much more interested in monopolist profits derived from innovation and in the expansion of their enterprises. Growth-oriented institutions sometimes may not guarantee property rights and contracts but may offer excellent investment opportunities. In China, national and foreign firms have invested and are investing so much, and the country is growing

72

so extraordinarily fast, not because Chinese institutions guarantee property rights (only recently have they begun to do so) but because there is a national development strategy in place that, combined with fast rates of growth, offers entrepreneurs extraordinary opportunities to realize profits and expand their enterprises.

Rather than the protection of property rights and contracts, my claim is that a national development strategy is the key institution for fast and sustained growth. Although a country cannot, from one day to the next, protect property rights and contracts or the rule of law, because this achievement depends on a long and difficult economic and political process, its people have shown that at certain moments they are able to develop a national growth strategy. This will happen principally when the people realize that it is either backward in relation to its competitors or that it is being dominated by foreign powers. The former consideration was the classical motivation for Germany to become a unified state in the second part of the nineteenth century; the latter has many examples, but probably the most telling is that of China, which was a major empire up until the eighteenth century and came under foreign domination in the nineteenth and the first part of the twentieth centuries, but, from 1949, adopted national development strategies – first adopting a statist strategy (which the Chinese called "socialist," though it was really a radical version of other statist early industrializations like that of Japan or, to a lesser extent, Brazil) and later an overtly capitalist one.

Marx regarded economic development as a process in which institutions change at a slower pace than economic and technological infrastructure so that they eventually face a revolutionary updating process. Thus, he viewed institutions as an obstacle rather than an incentive to development. During the twentieth century, however, as nations learned how to devise and implement national development strategies using their states, the state became more capable, and so institutions, beginning with national development strategies, became more effective and positive social tools. Marx, living in the time of the liberal state but not yet of the democratic state (which would only arise in the twentieth century), saw the state not as an instrument of democratic collective action but solely as an instrument of political domination. Even at that time, however, the state was already nations' main instrument for promoting economic growth. In the era of globalization, despite neoliberal attempts to diminish the size of the state organization and its capacity for intervention, its active responsibility for advancing economic growth was eventually enhanced as competition among nation-states intensified.

Historically, the forms of state intervention and national growth strategies depended on the stage of economic growth of each individual country and on the model of capitalism that each adopted. In all circumstances, the state was an effective instrument insofar as the government was able to initiate a national agreement. Such an agreement did not eliminate domestic class conflicts but showed that such conflicts were not strong enough to prevent the nation from working together when the problem was to compete internationally. Besides being an organization that guarantees the law, the state is the legal system itself; thus, it is both an organizational and a normative institution – the constitutional matrix of other formal institutions. When this complex organizational system becomes dynamic, when the officials that staff it (politicians and bureaucrats) are embedded in a society oriented to hard work, innovation, and investment, the corresponding normative institutional system will also be dynamic and forward-looking – and we will realize that we are in the presence of a national development strategy. The guarantee of property rights and contracts is only one, and not necessarily the most important, of the institutional aspects of this strategy.

If it is true that national development strategies do not presuppose overarching planning experiences, it is also true that those responsible for the strategy will not assume that self-regulated markets are capable of allocating resources. According to the new institutionalist assumption, the market is the default means of coordinating production, while organizations and institutions are a second-best means of such coordination, which becomes necessary when transaction costs are too high. This kind of reasoning is alien to the actual assumptions behind successful national development strategies. Neoclassical economists assume that to draw up a strategy, the policy maker proceeds from a general equilibrium situation and then successively abandons unrealistic assumptions, finally to arrive at the reality of the country's economic and political system. Instead, the pragmatic policy maker proceeds from the existing mixed reality, and from an open macroeconomic model that must be constantly adapted and updated, to examine the impact of the strategic macroeconomic variables: exchange rate, interest rate, public deficit, public savings, current account, and so on. Equally alien to the pragmatic policy maker drafting a national development strategy is the statist assumption that the state should be able to plan or manage the entire economy. National development strategies are always pragmatic institutions that arise from social practice and therefore cannot be driven by ideological dogmatism, whether interventionist or neoliberal. The market is an extraordinary institution for resource allocation, but as Polanyi (1957) remarked, it is just one of the institutions that exist in a given society, and it is intrinsically limited in its capacity to coordinate the economic system. State intervention is similarly constrained. Thus national development strategies imply viewing the state and the market not as competitors but as complementary institutions, which a national growth strategy is supposed to make the best use of.

To sum up, national development strategies differ, depending on the stage of growth and the model of capitalism. At the early development stages, the two main development strategies countries adopt are forced savings and protection of infant industries; at later stages, they resort to dynamic macroeconomic policies that (1) maintain the fiscal budget in long-term balance; (2) keep the exchange rate competitive, neutralizing the tendency of the exchange rate toward overvaluation; (3) ensure a clear differential between a satisfactory expected profit rate and a low interest rate; (4) allow for wages and salaries to increase with productivity; and (5) keep prices stable and employment reasonably full.

In the short term, national development strategies promote capital accumulation and technical progress by achieving a dynamic macroeconomic stability that includes full employment. Additionally, they involve industrial policies stimulating or protecting high per capita value-added industries. However, unlike in the era of the old national developmentalism, under new developmentalism, industrial policies and tariff protection are less important than competent, market-friendly macroeconomic policies, which necessarily involve a competitive exchange rate. In the 1950s, when the manufacturing sector was an infant industry, the assumption was that developing countries would not be able to compete in this area. Yet manufacturing industry soon ceased to be infant, and since the 1970s, the countries that adopted an export-led strategy have become major exporters of manufactured goods. Yet the exchange rate remained an essential problem. While developing countries' policy makers were not aware that the Dutch disease and the policy of growth with foreign savings were the main causes of the tendency of the exchange rate toward overvaluation, they adopted confused policies that, in some cases, were effective and caused growth. Now, they have begun to be more consistent in their policies, aiming to guarantee a competitive exchange rate.

National development strategies involve the participation of the different social classes in the nation. Thus, they imply negotiations between the classes, in which government is supposed to play an intermediary role. At the same time, a strategy must be able to provide more profits to business entrepreneurs and higher wages and salaries to the workers and the professional middle class – something that can be achieved only with economic growth or productivity increases. One of the central reasons why capitalism remains the only option for social-economic organizations is that productivity increases may be shared by workers and the professional middle class, without reducing the profit rate (Bresser Pereira 1986). If labor negotiations cannot count on growth, they degenerate either into aggressive behavior among the classes or into a loss of societal cohesiveness, or anomy. The more democratic and economically advanced a country is, the more attention to equality of opportunities and political freedom will be required from the strategy. In a developed country, where social and democratic values are better entrenched, social justice and democratic constraints will be stronger than in developing countries, but in no country can they be ignored. National development strategies involve political agreements, and politics always implies argument and compromise to create new institutions – to develop new and better rules of the game.

3

New Developmentalism

After the failure of conventional orthodoxy to promote macroeconomic stability and development, Latin America – the region that adopted its policies most strictly – has become home to a clear movement for rejecting its "macroeconomics of stagnation." Africa also adopted such policies, but there, the rejection has not been so clear. In this chapter, after examining the crisis of old, or national, developmentalism, I compare the rising new developmentalism with the old as well as with the set of diagnoses and policies that rich nations have prescribed and pushed on to developing countries, that is, conventional orthodoxy.

OLD DEVELOPMENTALISM AND ITS CRISIS

Between the 1930s and the 1970s, Brazil and other Latin American countries grew at an extraordinary pace. They took advantage of the weakening of the capitalist center to formulate national development strategies that, in essence, implied forced promotion of savings through the state and protection of national infant industries mixed with the neutralization of the Dutch disease on the import side, even though policy makers knew nothing about the disease.[1] The designation "national developmentalism" emphasized, first, that the basic objective of the policy was to promote economic development, and second, that for this to happen, the nation – that is, businesspeople, state bureaucracy, middle classes, and workers, joined together in international competition, which was needed to define the means to reach this objective within the framework of the capitalist system, with the state as the principal instrument of collective action. The notable economists, who, at that time, studied development and made economic policy proposals, along with the politicians, government officials, and businesspeople who were most directly involved in this process, were called "developmentalist economists" because they chose development as the ultimate goal of their economic analysis and political action. This group of international economists, which included some Latin American ones, created a branch of economics – *development economics* – that was affiliated with three complementary schools of thought: the classical school of Smith and Marx, Keynesian macroeconomics, and Latin American structuralist theory.[2] Development economics was a theory or group of theories, while *developmentalism* was the corresponding national development strategy. Development economics, whose heyday, as with Keynesian macroeconomics, was in the 1950s and the 1960s, combined pure market-based economic theories with theories of political economy that cast the state and its institutions in a leading role as auxiliary coordinators of the economy. Developmentalism faced opposition from neoclassical economists, who already, at that time, were called "orthodox" and also "monetarists"

---

[1] As we see in Chapter 5, to neutralize the Dutch disease on both the import and the export sides, it is necessary to impose a tax on exports of the goods that cause the overvaluation of the exchange rate by shifting up their supply curve. An import tax neutralizes the Dutch disease only partially. It does not necessarily represent protectionism if it limits itself to neutralizing the disease.

[2] The founding group of development economists or pioneers of development economics includes Paul Rosenstein-Rodan, Arthur Lewis, Hans Singer, Ragnar Nurkse, Michal Kalecki, Gunnar Myrdal, Raúl Prebisch, Celso Furtado, and Albert Hirschman.

because of the emphasis they placed on the control of money supply as a means of controlling inflation.

Because Brazil and Mexico were peripheral or dependent countries, whose industrial revolution was taking place 150 years after that of Britain and more than 100 years after that of the United States, their remarkable development between the 1930s and 1970s was possible only inasmuch as these countries were able to use the state as an instrument to define and implement a national development strategy. The role of the state was not about replacing the market with the state; rather, it was about strengthening the market to enable it to create the necessary conditions for business enterprises to invest and innovate. All countries, beginning with Britain itself, required a national development strategy to bring about their industrial revolutions and to continue to develop. The use of a national development strategy was particularly evident among late-development countries, such as Germany and Japan, which were never characterized by dependence. Peripheral countries, on the other hand, like Brazil and other Latin American countries that had lived through the colonial experience, remained ideologically dependent on the center after their formal independence. Both late-development central countries and former colonies needed to formulate national development strategies, but the task was easier for the former. For peripheral countries, there was the additional hurdle of facing their own dependence, that is, the submission of the local elites to those in central countries, who were interested in nothing other than their own development. Developmentalism was nationalist because to become industrial, these countries needed to form their national states. The nationalism present in developmentalism was the ideology for forming a national state; it was the affirmation that to develop, countries needed to define their own policies and institutions.[3] Late central countries also used developmentalist

---

[3] Nationalism can also be defined, as, e.g., by Gellner, as the ideology that attempts to endow every nation with a state. Although this is a good definition, it is applicable to

strategies, although they were not called by that name, except in the case of Japan, which Chalmers Johnson (1982), in his classic study of MITI (Ministry of International Trade and Industry), called a "developmental state." Because they were nationalistic, they always followed their own criteria, rather than their competitors' criteria, in formulating policies, and they used their states deliberately to promote development.

In the 1940s, 1950s, and 1960s, developmentalists and Keynesians prevailed in Latin America; they were the mainstream. Governments used their theories first and foremost in economic policy making. From the 1970s, however, in the context of the great neoliberal and conservative wave that began to form, neoclassical economists, most of whom adopted a neoliberal ideology, challenged Keynesian theory, development economics, and Latin American structuralism. Since the 1980s, in the context of the great foreign debt crisis that added to the rich nations' political power, these economists managed to redefine their prescriptions for developing countries in neoliberal terms. The neoliberal ideology targeting these countries became hegemonic, expressing itself through what became known as the Washington Consensus, which I prefer to call *conventional orthodoxy*, not only because this is a more general expression but because if some such consensus existed in the 1990s, in the 2000s it has broken down.

During the 1980s, the national development strategy – national developmentalism – faced a major crisis and was replaced with a foreign strategy: conventional orthodoxy. Several factors help explain this. First, during the 1960s, the national alliance that served as the political foundation for developmentalism fell apart as a direct consequence of the military coup supported by Brazilian industrialists and the

central Europe rather than Latin America. At the moment of political independence, the Latin American nations were not yet fully formed and yet were endowed with states. The nations, however, were incomplete, and their regimes were semicolonial; with independence, the main change was that the dominant power shifted from Spain or Portugal to Britain and other major central European countries.

81

U.S. government. The national-developmentalist approach assumed the existence of a nation and thus of a national agreement involving industrialists, workers, and the state bureaucracy – a reasonable assumption insofar as, after a lengthy period of dependence following the independence movements of the early nineteenth century, these countries, since 1930, had taken advantage of the crisis in the North to begin their national revolutions and form autonomous national states. On the basis of this fact, developmentalism proposed that each country's new industrial businesspeople were, or should become, a "national bourgeoisie," as had been the case in developed countries, and associate themselves with government officials and urban workers to bring about a national and industrial revolution. Therefore, in every country, the sense of nation, of national society, was reinforced, and the possibility dawned that this society might implement a national development strategy, using the state as its instrument for collective action. It was at once a proposal and an assessment of the reality confirmed by the accelerated industrialization process that Latin America was then experiencing. The Cuban revolution of 1959, however, by radicalizing the left wing, and the economic crisis of the early 1960s led to the dissolution of the national developmental alliance and set the stage for the establishment of military regimes in Brazil, Argentina, Uruguay, and Chile, with support from each country's businesspeople and from the United States. As a consequence, the national alliance that was so essential to the constitution of a nation broke up, and Latin America's moderate Left embraced the theses of the theory of associated dependence, which rejected the possibility of a national bourgeoisie. In doing so, it rejected the very ideas of nation and of national development strategy on which national developmentalism was based.

Second, because old developmentalism was based on import substitution, it contained the seeds of its own demise. Protection of national industry, the focus on the market, and the reduction of an economy's openness coefficient, even in a relatively large economy such as Brazil's, are greatly constrained by economies of scale. For certain industries, protection becomes absurd. As a result, when the import-substitution model was maintained through the 1970s, it was leading Latin American economies into a deep distortion. On the other hand, as Celso Furtado remarked as early as 1965, after the initial import-substitution phase of consumer goods industries, continued industrialization implied a substantial increase of the capital to labor ratio, with two consequences: income concentration and reduced capital productivity, or reduced product to capital ratio (Furtado 1965). The response to income concentration was to be an expanded production of luxury consumer goods, characterizing what I have termed the *industrial underdevelopment model*, which, besides being perverse, contains the seeds of the dissolution of the national pro-development alliance.

Third, the great debt crisis of the 1980s, which was not directly related to the import-substitution model but already an outcome of the growth-with-foreign-savings strategy, further weakened the national alliance that was behind national developmentalism. The debt crisis paved the way for the rise of high inertial inflation, which would be the scourge of the Brazilian economy for fourteen years. The military government had indexed prices since 1964, but it was only in the early 1980s that inflation topped 100 percent a year as a result of exchange rate depreciations caused by the foreign debt crisis: from this moment up to 1994, inflation would be measured in monthly terms (5, 10, 20 percent a month), configuring high inertial inflation (Bresser Pereira and Nakano 1987). After that, developmentalism was supported only by a populist left wing, which, while in office in the second half of the 1980s, proved unable to manage the Brazilian economy. This became apparent in the Cruzado Plan – the 1986 attempt to control inertial inflation – which ended in a major, disastrous populist episode (Sachs 1989).

The fourth reason for the replacement of developmentalism with conventional orthodoxy lies in the strength of this ideological wave, which was coming from the North. In the early 1980s, in response to the foreign debt crisis, a new and stronger conventional orthodoxy established itself bit by bit. The Baker Plan of 1985, named after U.S. secretary of the treasury James Baker, completed the definition of the new ideas by adding market-oriented institutional reforms to orthodox macroeconomic adjustment. Developmentalism then became the target of a systematic attack. Taking advantage of the economic crisis that derived from the fact that this kind of development model was in part overcome because primitive accumulation and the industrial revolution had been completed, and also from the distortions it had suffered in the hands of populist politicians and the middle classes, conventional orthodoxy imparted to developmentalism a negative connotation, identifying it with populism or irresponsible economic policies. In its stead, it proposed a panacea of orthodox and neoliberal institutional reforms. It further proposed that developing countries abandon the antiquated concept of nation that national developmentalism had adopted and accept the globalist thesis, according to which, in the age of globalization, nation-states had lost autonomy and relevance: worldwide free markets (including financial ones) would be charged with promoting the economic development of all.

More than twenty years later, what we see is the failure of conventional orthodoxy to promote Latin America's economic development. While developmentalism prevailed, between 1950 and 1980, per capita income in Brazil grew by almost 4 percent a year; since then, it has grown by around 1 percent a year, that is, four times less. The performance of other Latin American countries has been no different, with the exception of Chile. In the same period, however, dynamic Asian countries, including China since the 1980s and India since the 1990s, have maintained or achieved extraordinary growth rates.

Why such different growth rates? At the more immediate level of economic policy, the fundamental problem relates to loss of control over the most strategic macroeconomic price in an open economy: the foreign exchange rate. Latin American countries lost control over it through open financial accounts and saw their foreign exchange rates appreciate, as, from the early 1990s, they accepted the proposal, emanating from Washington, D.C., and New York, of growth with foreign savings. Yet, at the same time, Asian countries mostly ran current account surpluses and retained control over their foreign exchange rates. At the reform level, Latin American countries indiscriminately accepted all liberalizing reforms, irresponsibly privatizing monopoly utilities and opening their capital accounts, while Asian countries were more prudent. However, it gradually became clear to me that the main difference was to be found in a new, fundamental fact: Latin American countries interrupted their national revolutions and watched as their nations became disorganized and lost cohesiveness and autonomy; as a consequence, they were left without a national development strategy. The national strategy that Latin American countries, in general, and Brazil, in particular, adopted between 1930 and 1980 was known as *developmentalism*. In this period, and mainly from 1930 to 1960, many Latin American countries were firmly nationalist, finally providing their formally independent states with a basic solidarity when it came to competing internationally. Yet the weakening brought about by the great economic crisis of the 1980s, combined with the hegemonic force of the ideological neoliberal wave coming from the United States since the 1970s, caused the interruption of the process of national and state formation in Latin America. Local elites stopped thinking for themselves and accepted advice and pressure from the North, while the countries, devoid of a national development strategy, saw their development stall. Conventional orthodoxy, which came to replace national developmentalism, had not been developed locally; it did not reflect national concerns and interests but rather the visions and objectives of rich nations. In addition, as is typical of neoliberal ideology, it was a negative proposal that assumed the markets' ability to coordinate everything automatically, proposing that the state stop playing the economic role it always had in developed countries: that of supplementing the market's coordination to promote economic development and equity.

I have been critical of conventional orthodoxy and of the macroeconomics of stagnation that it implies since it became dominant in Latin America. I was probably the first Latin American economist to criticize the Washington Consensus, in my keynote lecture during the annual congress of the Brazilian National Association of Post-Graduate Economics Courses (Bresser Pereira 1991a). My criticism, however, gained a new dimension from the first quarter of 1999, after I had been for four and a half years a member of the Cardoso administration, whose economic policies, after the successful and innovative Real Plan of 1994, became fully orthodox. Between 1999 and 2001, my close associate Yoshiaki Nakano and I began a more systematic critique of conventional orthodoxy, based on our common structuralist and Keynesian views of economics (see Bresser Pereira [1999] 2002a; Bresser Pereira and Nakano 2002a, 2002b). Our criticism showed that the conventional proposal, albeit inclusive of certain necessary policies and reforms, did not, in fact, promote a country's development but rather kept it semistagnant, incapable of competing with wealthier countries and easily falling prey to a form of economic populism: foreign exchange populism. The alternative economic strategy present in these works was innovative in that it acknowledged a series of new historical facts that implied a need to review the national development strategy. How to name this alternative? We decided that "new developmentalism" would be a good name. What does new developmentalism involve? I define it as a third discourse – as an alternative strategy to both old developmentalism and conventional orthodoxy, and as a critique of the diagnoses, policies, and reforms conceived mainly in Washington, D.C., for use in developing countries.

NATION AND NATIONALISM

New developmentalism, like the national developmentalism of the 1950s, at once assumes the presence and implies the formation of a true nation, capable of formulating an informal, open, national development strategy, as is proper for democratic societies whose economies are coordinated by the market. A nation is a society of individuals or households that, sharing a common political fate, manages to organize itself as a state with sovereignty over a certain territory. A nation, therefore, like the modern state, makes sense only within the nation-state framework that arises with capitalism. For a nation to be able to share a common fate, it must have common objectives, chief among which, in historical terms, is development. Other objectives, such as freedom and social justice, are also fundamental to nations but, like the state and capitalism, arise with economic development as part of their reasoning, of their intrinsic manner of being. Nations, nation-states, capitalism, and economic development are simultaneously and intrinsically correlated historical phenomena. In its most developed form – today's globalization – capitalism's economic constituents are not only firms operating at the international level, but also, if not mainly, nation-states or national states. It is not just firms that compete worldwide in the markets, as conventional economic theory proposes; nation-states, too, are fundamental competitors. The main criterion of success for the political rulers of every modern nation-state is comparative economic growth. Rulers are successful in the eyes of their people and internationally if they achieve greater growth rates than countries regarded as direct competitors. Globalization is the stage of capitalism in which, for the first time, nation-states span the entire globe and compete economically through their firms.

A nation involves a basic solidarity among classes when it comes to competing internationally. Businesspeople, workers, state bureaucrats, middle-class professionals, and intellectuals may come into conflict, but they know that they share a common fate and that this fate relies on their successful competitive involvement in the world of nation-states. It involves, therefore, a national agreement. A national agreement is the basic social contract that gives rise to a nation and keeps it strong or cohesive; it is the compact among social classes of a modern society that enables this society to become a true nation, that is, a society gifted with a state capable of formulating a national development strategy. The great national agreement or compact that established itself in Brazil after 1930 joined the infant national industrial bourgeoisie to the new bureaucracy or the new state technicians; added to these were the urban workers and the more domestic, market-oriented sectors of the old oligarchy, such as the ranchers, from which Getúlio Vargas came. Their adversaries were imperialism, represented mainly by British and U.S. interests, and the affiliated exporting rural oligarchy. The most strategic accord in a modern nation-state is that between industrial businesspeople and the estate bureaucracy, which includes significant politicians but also workers and the middle classes. And there will always be domestic adversaries, somehow identified with imperialism or today's colonyless neoimperialism as well as with local collaborationist or globalist groups. In the case of Brazil today, they are the rentiers who rely on high interest rates and the financial industry that collects commissions from the rentiers.

A nation is always nationalist inasmuch as nationalism is the ideology of the formation of a national state and its permanent reaffirmation or consolidation. Another way to define nationalism is to say, after Ernest Gellner (1983), that it is the ideology that pursues a correspondence between the nation and the state – that stands for the existence of a state for each nation.[4] This, too, is a good definition, but one typical of a thinker from central Europe; it is a definition that becomes exhausted as soon as a nation-state is formed – when nation and state begin coinciding over a given territory, formally establishing a "sovereign state." It fails, therefore, to take into account Ernest Renan's ([1882] 1992: 55)

---

[4] Ernest Gellner, a Czech philosopher who took refuge from Communism in Britain, was probably the most astute analyst of nationalism in the second half of the twentieth century.

celebrated statement: "a nation is a daily referendum."[5] It fails to explain how a nation-state may formally exist in the absence of a true nation, as in the case of Latin American countries, which in the early nineteenth century saw themselves endowed with a state because of not only the patriotic efforts of nationalist groups but also the good services of England, whose aim was to oust Spain and Portugal from the region. In this way, these countries saw themselves endowed with a state in the absence of true nations, as they ceased to be colonies and became dependent on England, France, and, later, the United States. For a true nation to exist, the several social classes must, despite the conflicts that set them apart, be in solidarity when it comes to competing internationally, and they must use national criteria to make policy decisions, particularly those that involve economic policy and institutional reform. In other words, the rulers must think with their own heads, instead of dedicating themselves to confidence building, and the entire society must be capable of formulating a national development strategy.

New developmentalism will become a reality when Brazilian society again becomes a true nation. This is what happened in Brazil between 1930 and 1980, particularly from 1930 to 1960. Under the rule of Brazil's twentieth-century statesman Getúlio Vargas, the country took national decisions into its own hands and formulated a successful national development strategy. In those thirty years (or fifty, if we include the military period, which remained nationalist, despite its political alliance with the United States against Communism), Brazil changed from an agricultural to an industrial country, from a mercantilist social formation to a fully capitalist one, from a semicolonial status to a national status. Developmentalism was the name given to the national development strategy and to its driving ideology. Therefore, the process of defining the new

---

[5] In the immediately preceding part, Renan wrote, "A nation is a great solidarity made up of the sentiment of the sacrifices made and those people are still willing to make. It assumes a past; its present summation is a tangible fact: the consent, the clearly expressed desire to go on with common life."

developmentalism equally involves resuming the idea of nation in Brazil and other Latin American countries. It implies, therefore, a nationalist perspective in the sense that economic policies and institutions must be formulated and implemented with the national interest as their main criterion and with each country's citizens as actors. Such a nationalism aims not to endow a nation with a state, but rather, to turn the existing state into an effective instrument for collective action by the nation, an instrument that enables modern nations, in the early twenty-first century, to consistently pursue their political objectives of economic development, social justice, and freedom within an international framework of competition, but also peace and collaboration among nations. It implies, therefore, that such nationalism is liberal, social, and republican, that is, that it incorporates the values of modern industrial societies.

THIRD DISCOURSE

New developmentalism is a third discourse between the old developmentalist discourse and conventional orthodoxy; it is a set of ideas, institutions, and economic policies through which medium-income countries attempt, in the early twenty-first century, to catch up with developed countries. Like the old developmentalism, it is not an economic theory, but a strategy; it is a national development strategy, based mainly on Keynesian macroeconomics, whereby such countries may gradually catch up with rich nations. It is the set of ideas that enables developing nations to reject rich nations' proposals and pressures for reform and economic policies, like a fully open capital account and growth with foreign savings, inasmuch as such proposals are neoimperialist attempts to neutralize development – the practice of kicking away the ladder. It is the means by which businesspeople, government officials, workers, and intellectuals can stand as a true nation to promote economic development. I do not include poor countries in the new developmentalism, not because they do not require a national development strategy, but because they still need to accomplish their primitive accumulation and industrial revolutions, and the challenges they face and the strategies they require are different.

In terms of discourse or ideology, we have, on one hand, the dominant, imperial, and globalist discourse that flows from Washington, D.C., and is embraced in Latin America by the neoliberal, cosmopolitan right wing, comprising mainly the rentier class and the financial industry.[6] This is conventional orthodoxy: an ideology exported to developing countries; an antinational strategy that, despite its "generous" offer to promote prosperity among medium-income countries, in fact serves rich nations' interests in neutralizing these countries' ability to compete. Four basic beliefs define it: first, the country's major problem is the lack of microeconomic reform capable of enabling the market to operate freely; second, even after the end of runaway inflation in 1994, controlling inflation remains the main purpose of economic policy; third, to achieve such control, interest rates must be high because of the sovereign risk; and fourth, because economic development is a great race among countries to obtain foreign savings, the implicit current account deficits and foreign exchange appreciation brought about by capital inflows are no cause for concern. The disastrous effects of this discourse in terms of balance-of-payment crises and low growth for the Latin American countries that have adopted it since the late 1980s are well known today (Frenkel 2003).

The opposite discourse is that of the bureaucratic-populist left wing. From this perspective, developing countries' ills are due to globalization and financial capital, which burdened the countries with high foreign and public indebtedness. The proposed solution was to renegotiate the countries' foreign and public debt at a great discount. The second ill

---

[6] By *rentier class*, we no longer mean the class of large landowners but rather that of inactive capitalists whose livelihood depends mainly on interest income. The *financial industry*, in turn, involves, besides rentiers, businesspeople and managers who collect commissions from rentiers.

was insufficient demand, which could be resolved with increased public spending, entailing chronic public deficits. And the greatest ill – unequal income distribution – could be resolved by increasing the minimum income, the salaries of civil servants, and the coverage of the Brazilian welfare system. This option was adopted, for example, in Peru under Alan García. In Brazil, it was never fully put into practice.[7]

The first discourse served the interests of the North and reflected its deep ideological hegemony over Latin American countries. Locally, it sprang chiefly from the Brazilian rentier class, which depends essentially on interest for a living, and from economists affiliated with the financial industry; a confused, disoriented upper middle class also shared it. The second came from the lower middle class and labor unions, reflecting the old bureaucratic left wing's perspective. Neither discourse had a chance of achieving a reasonable consensus in Brazilian society because of their irrationality and biased nature. Neither ideology reflected national interests. Might there be a third discourse capable of achieving such a reasonable consensus? Certainly this third discourse is possible and is being formulated, little by little. It is the *discourse of new developmentalism*. But is not new developmentalism also an ideology, as are conventional orthodoxy and the bureaucratic-populist discourse? Yes and no. Yes, because every national strategy implies an ideology, a set of political, action-oriented ideas and values; and no, because, unlike conventional orthodoxy, which is no more than an outside proposal, new developmentalism will make sense only if it rises from internal consensus and therefore stands as a true national development strategy. A full consensus is impossible, but a consensus that brings together businesspeople from the production sector, workers, government officials, and middle-class professionals – a national agreement, therefore – is now forming, taking advantage of the failure of conventional orthodoxy.

---

[7] The Workers Party adopted such a discourse in Brazil, but once in power in 2003, it adopted policies recommended by conventional orthodoxy.

This emerging consensus regards globalization as neither a blessing nor a curse but rather as a system of intense competition among national states through their firms. It realizes that in such a competition, the state must be strengthened fiscally, administratively, and politically and at the same time must provide national firms with the conditions to become internationally competitive. Like Argentina's reaction to its 2001 crisis, it acknowledges that development in Brazil is prevented, in the short term, by exceedingly high short-term interest rates determined by the Central Bank of Brazil, which push long-term rates upward. It assumes that for development to occur, investment rates must necessarily rise and the state must contribute by means of positive public savings that are the outcome of curbing current government expenditures and not of increased taxes. Finally, and more generally, new developmentalism assumes that development, in addition to being held back by the absence of democratic nationalism (an absence that favors conventional ortho-doxy), is also hampered by income concentration, which, besides being unfair, is a cultural medium for all forms of populism and thus for the bureaucratic-populist discourse.

What is a national development strategy? More than a simple ideol-ogy developed abroad, like conventional orthodoxy, it is a set of economic development–oriented institutions and policies. It is less than a national development plan because it is not formal; it lacks a document that accu-rately describes objectives to be attained and policies to be implemented to attain such objectives because the inherent accord among the social classes has neither text nor signatures. And it is more than a national development plan because it informally embraces the whole of society, or a large share thereof; it shows all a path to tread and certain very general guidelines to be observed; and although it does not assume a conflict-free society, it does require a reasonable union of all when it comes to competing internationally. It is more flexible than a project, and it always considers the actions of opponents or competitors. It rec-ognizes that the factor that drives individual behavior is not just personal interest, but competition with other nations. A national development strategy reflects all this. Its leadership falls to the government and the more active elements of civil society. Its fundamental instrument is the state itself: its norms, policies, and organization. Its outcome, when a major accord establishes itself, when strategy becomes truly national, when society begins sharing, loosely but effectively, methods and goals, is accelerated development – a period during which the country enjoys high per capita income and high rates of growth of living standards.

A national development strategy implies a set of fundamental variables for economic development. These variables are both real and institutional. The nation's increased savings and investment capacities; the means by which it incorporates technical advances into production; human capital development; increased national social cohesiveness, resulting in social capital or in a stronger, more democratic civil society; a macroeconomic policy capable of ensuring the financial health of the state organization and of the nation-state or country, leading to conservative domestic and foreign indebtedness ratios – these are all constituent elements of a national development strategy. In this process, institutions, instead of mere one-size-fits-all abstractions, are seen and construed concretely, historically. A national development strategy will gain meaning and strength when its institutions – whether short-term ones, which I call policies or public policies, or relatively permanent ones (institutions proper) – respond to societal needs, and when they are compatible with the economy's production-factor endowment or, to put it more broadly, with the elements that make up society at its structural level.

OLD AND NEW DEVELOPMENTALISM

The developmentalism of the 1950s and the new developmentalism differ in terms of two variables that emerged in the second half of the twentieth century: on one hand, new historical facts that changed world capitalism,

Chart 3.1: *Old and new developmentalism compared*

Old developmentalism	New developmentalism
1. Some complacency about public deficits and inflation.	1. No complacency about fiscal imbalance and inflation.
2. The state plays a leading role in terms of forced savings and investment in firms.	2. The state has a subsidiary but important role in forced savings and investment in firms.
3. Industrialization is based on import substitution and trade is export-pessimistic.	3. Growth is export-led and trade is export-realistic.

which moved from its golden age to the globalization phase, and on the other hand, medium-income countries, such as Brazil, that changed their own development stages and are no longer marked by infant industries. A summary comparison of the two strategies appears in Chart 3.1.

The main change at the international level was from the capitalism of the golden age (1945–75), when the welfare state was put together and Keynesianism ruled, while development economics prevailed as a theory and a practice of economic development, to the neoliberal capitalism of globalization, where growth rates are slower and competition among nation-states is far fiercer. In the golden age, medium-income countries still posed no threat to rich nations. Since the 1970s, however, when these countries have come to include the newly industrializing countries and, since the 1990s, China, they have become much more competitive: the threat their cheap labor poses to rich nations is clearer than ever. In the golden age, rich nations, and the United States, in particular, in need of Cold War allies, were far more generous; today, only the poorest African countries can expect some generosity – but even these must be wary because the treatment the rich nations and the World Bank afford them and the help, or alleged help, they receive are often perverse.

The main difference at the national level is that industry was in its infancy at that time; it is now mature. The import-substitution model was effective, between the 1930s and 1960s, in establishing the industrial bases of Latin American countries. Since the 1960s, however, those countries should have begun lowering protectionist barriers and orienting themselves toward an export-led model, under which they might show themselves as competitive exporters of manufactured goods. But they did not, probably due to an export pessimism that faded only in the 1970s. It was only in the early 1990s that trade was liberalized, in the middle of a major economic crisis, often hurriedly and haphazardly. This twenty-year lag in changing the strategy was one of the greatest distortions endured by developmentalism.

New developmentalism is not protectionist: it simply emphasizes the need for a competitive exchange rate. It assumes that medium-income countries have already overcome the infant industry stage but still face the Dutch disease. Unlike old developmentalism, which embraced the export pessimism of development economics, new developmentalism counts on developing countries' ability to export medium value-added manufactured goods or high value-added primary products. Experience since the 1970s has clearly shown that this pessimism was a mistake. In the late 1960s, Latin American countries should have begun shifting decisively from the import-substitution model to the export-led model, as did Korea and Taiwan. In Latin America, Chile was the first to effect such a change, and as a result, its development is often cited as an example of a successful neoliberal strategy. In fact, neoliberalism was fully practiced in Chile only between 1973 and 1981, coming to an end with a major balance-of-payment crisis in 1982 (Diaz-Alejandro 1981; Ffrench-Davis 2003). The export-led model is not specifically neoliberal because, strictly speaking, the neoclassical economic theory that underlies this ideology has no room for development strategies other than the indiscriminate opening of markets. Dynamic Asian countries, having adopted import substitution in the 1950s, switched to a manufactured-goods exporting strategy in the 1960s and, since the 1980s, can be regarded as new developmentalist countries. The export-led model has two main advantages over the import-substitution model. First, the market available to industries is not limited to the domestic market. This is important for small countries but equally relevant to countries with a relatively large domestic market. Second, if a country adopts the export-led model, the economic authorities have access to an efficiency criterion to guide the industrial policy they frame to benefit the nation's firms: only firms that are efficient enough to export will benefit from the industrial policy. Under the import-substitution model, inefficient firms may enjoy the benefits of protection; under the export-led model, the likelihood of this happening is substantially smaller.

The fact that the strategy that new developmentalism stands for is not protectionist does not mean that countries should be willing to open their markets indiscriminately. They should negotiate pragmatically at the level of the World Trade Organization and regional accords to secure mutual openness. They should always ascertain whether the Dutch disease is being neutralized by export or sales taxes because if it is not, tariffs are a second-best policy. And finally, export-led growth does not mean that the country should give up industrial policies. The scope for these has been reduced by the highly unfavorable agreements made in the World Trade Organization's Uruguay Round, but there is still some scope for them, if considered strategically, in consideration of future comparative advantages that may arise as some supported firms achieve success.

New developmentalism rejects misleading notions of growth based chiefly on public deficits that became popular in Latin America in the 1980s, in the aftermath of democratization. This was one of the most severe populist distortions that developmentalism endured in the hands of its latter-day advocates. The notable Latin American economists who formulated the developmentalist strategy, such as Furtado, Prebisch, and Rangel, were Keynesians, and they regarded aggregate demand management as an important tool for promoting development. But they never defended the economic populism of chronic deficits. Those who came in their wake did, however. When Celso Furtado, faced with the severe crisis of the early 1960s, proposed his Plano Trienal in 1963, these second-class followers accused him of an "orthodox bounce back." In fact, what Furtado already acknowledged, and what new developmentalism firmly defends, is fiscal balance. New developmentalism defends it not because fiscal balance is orthodox, but because the state, being strategic to economic growth, must be strong in financial terms, and its debt must be moderate and long in maturity. The worst thing that can happen to a state as an organization (the state also underpins the legal system) is to lose the trust of creditors, whether domestic or foreign. Foreign creditors are particularly dangerous, for at any time, they can decide to suspend the rolling over of debts and lead the country into a balance-of-payment crisis, but domestic creditors may also be perverse, as they can coalesce with the financial system to capture monetary policy and impose high basic interest rates on the country, as has been the case in Brazil.

The final difference between the developmentalism of the 1950s and new developmentalism lies in the state's role in promoting forced savings and investing in economic infrastructure. Both forms of developmentalism cast the state in a leading role in ensuring the proper operation of the market and providing the general conditions for capital accumulation such as education, health, transportation, communications, and power infrastructure. In addition, however, under the developmentalism of the 1950s, the state also played a crucial role in promoting forced savings, thereby contributing to countries' primitive accumulation process; furthermore, the state made direct investments in infrastructure and heavy industry, where the investments required exceeded the private sector's savings. This has changed since the 1980s. With new developmentalism, the state still can and must promote forced savings and invest in certain strategic industries, but the national private sector now has the resources and managerial ability to provide a sizable portion of the investment needed. The new developmentalism rejects the neoliberal thesis that the state no longer has resources because whether the state has resources depends on how its finances are managed. But new developmentalism understands that, in all sectors where reasonable competition exists, the state must not be an investor; instead, it must concentrate on defending and ensuring competition. Even after these investments have been excluded, there are many left for the state to provide, financed by public savings rather than debt.

In sum, and again, because medium-income countries are at a different stage, new developmentalism regards the market as a more efficient institution, one more capable of coordinating the economic system, than did old developmentalism, although this perspective is far from the irrational faith in the market evinced by conventional orthodoxy.

NEW DEVELOPMENTALISM AND CONVENTIONAL ORTHODOXY

We now turn to the differences between new developmentalism and conventional orthodoxy. Conventional economic orthodoxy or conventional economic knowledge is made up of the set of theories, diagnoses, and policy proposals that rich nations offer to developing countries. It is based on neoclassical economics but is not to be confused with it, because it is not theoretical but rather openly ideological and oriented toward proposing institutional reforms and economic policies. Although neoclassical economics is based in universities, particularly in the United States, conventional orthodoxy springs mainly from Washington, D.C., home to the U.S. Treasury Department and to the two agencies that are supposedly international but are, in fact, subordinate to the U.S. Treasury: the International Monetary Fund (IMF) and the World Bank. The former is charged with macroeconomic policy and the latter with development. Secondarily, conventional orthodoxy originated in New York, the seat or point of convergence of major international banks and multinationals. Therefore, we may say that conventional orthodoxy is the set of diagnoses and policies intended for developing countries and originating in Washington, D.C., and New York. Conventional ortho-doxy changes over time. Since the 1980s, it has become identified with the Washington Consensus, which cannot be understood simply as the ten reforms or adjustments that John Williamson (1990) listed in the chapter that gave birth to the expression. (His list included reforms and adjustments that are, indeed, necessary.) The Washington Consensus is, in fact, the effective shape that the neoliberal and globalist ideology has taken in the economic policies recommended to developing countries.

Conventional orthodoxy is the means by which the United States, at the level of economic policies and institutions, expresses its ideolog-ical hegemony over the rest of the world and mainly over dependent, developing countries that lack nations strong enough to challenge this hegemony, as has traditionally been the case in Latin American coun-tries. This hegemony purports to be benevolent, whereas in fact it is the arm and mouth of neoimperialism – that is, the imperialism without (formal) colonies that established itself under the aegis of the United States and other rich nations after the classic colonial system ceased to exist in the aftermath of World War II.

Inasmuch as conventional orthodoxy is the practical expression of neoliberal ideology, it is the ideology of the market against the state; while new developmentalism wants both a strong state and a strong market and sees no contradiction between them, conventional ortho-doxy wishes to strengthen the market by weakening the state, as if the two institutions were participants in a zero-sum game. Since the sec-ond half of the twentieth century, therefore, conventional orthodoxy has been a version of the laissez-faire ideology that prevailed in the previous century. Disregarding the fact that the state has grown in terms of the tax burden and of the degree of market regulation as a result of the increased dimensions and complexity of modern societies, and disregarding the fact that a strong and relatively large state is a requirement for a strong and competitive market, conventional orthodoxy is the practical reac-tion against the growth of the state's apparatus. In some cases, the state has also grown out of mere clientelism, to create jobs and employ the bureaucracy, but essentially the state increased first to invest in the infrastructure and second to increase social services. Yet conventional orthodoxy is not interested in distinguishing legitimate state growth from the illegitimate variety. It is the ideology of the minimal state, of the self-regulated market, of the night watchman state, of the state that is concerned only with domestic and foreign security, leaving economic coordination, infrastructure investment, and even social services like health care and education to the devices of the market. It is the ideology of individualism that assumes that all are equally capable of defending their interests. It is, therefore, a right-wing ideology, an ideology of the powerful, the rich, the better educated – the high bourgeoisie and the high technobureaucracy. Its goal is to drive down direct and indirect real wages by leaving labor unprotected and thus making business enterprises more competitive in an international market of developing countries and cheap labor.

The central difference between conventional orthodoxy and new developmentalism lies in the fact that conventional orthodoxy is market fundamentalist, believing that the market is an institution that coordinates everything optimally if it is free of interference, whereas new developmentalism is pragmatic. New developmentalism views the market as an extraordinarily efficient institution in coordinating economic systems but is aware of its limitations. Factor allocation is the task that it best performs, but even here, it faces problems. It fails to stimulate sufficient investment and innovation. It fails to ensure an exchange rate that is consistent with the transfer of manpower to higher value-added per capita industries. And, in the distribution of income, it is a clearly unsatisfactory mechanism because markets privilege the stronger and the more capable. While conventional orthodoxy acknowledges market failures but asserts that state failures are worse, new developmentalism rejects such pessimism about the possibilities of collective action and demands a strong state – not as a trade-off for a weak market but rather to complement a strong market. If men are able to build institutions to regulate human actions, including the market itself, there is no reason why they should not be able to strengthen the state organization or apparatus – making its administration more legitimate, its finances more solid, and its management more efficient– or to strengthen the state constitutional or legal system, making its institutions increasingly well adapted to social needs. Politics and democracy exist precisely for that purpose, and the more advanced democracies made major progress in this area in the twentieth century.

Insofar as one of the foundations of new developmentalism is classical political economy, which is essentially a theory of the wealth of nations (Smith) or of capital accumulation (Marx), social structures and institutions are fundamental to its reasoning. Besides, as it adopts a historical approach to economic development, the teachings of the German Historical School and of the U.S. institutionalists are an essential part of its vision.[8] Thus, institutions are fundamental, and reforming them is a constant task insofar as, in the complex and dynamic societies in which we live, economic activities must be constantly reregulated. In contrast, conventional orthodoxy, based on neoclassical economics, has only recently acknowledged the role of institutions, in the context of so-called new institutionalism. In contrast to historical institutionalism, which, in relation to economic development, sees obstacles to economic growth in precapitalist institutions and in the distortions of capitalist ones and seeks actively to develop a set of institutions forming a national growth strategy, new institutionalism offers a simplistic answer to the problem: it is sufficient that institutions guarantee property rights and contracts or, more broadly, the efficient working of markets, which will automatically promote growth. According to the neoliberal jargon

---

[8] The Historical School is the school of Gustav Schmoller, Otto Rank, Max Weber, and, in a different line, Friedrich List; the American Institutionalist School is the school of Thorstein Veblen, Wesley Mitchell, and John R. Commons.

adopted by, for instance, *The Economist,* a good government will be a reformist one, involved in market-oriented reforms. According to new developmentalism, a government will be effective in economic terms if it is able to promote economic growth and a more even distribution of income by the adoption of economic policies and institutional reforms that are oriented, wherever possible, to the market but often correcting it; in other words, an effective government increases state capability and the efficiency of markets within the framework of a national development strategy. According to conventional orthodoxy, institutions should limit themselves almost exclusively to constitutional or quasiconstitutional norms; according to new developmentalism, economic policies, and particularly monetary policies, must undergo permanent reform – permanent and gradual adjustment within the framework of a broader growth strategy. Industrial policies are also required, but whereas old developmentalism gave a major role to them, new developmentalism adopts a moderate industrial policy: government should act strategically only when the business enterprise that needs support shows that it is capable of competing internationally; an industrial policy that becomes confused with protectionism is not acceptable. For new developmentalism, a moderate interest rate and a competitive exchange rate are more important than industrial policy.

New developmentalism and conventional orthodoxy share many institutional reforms, but their objectives are often different. Take, for instance, public management reform. New developmentalism supports it because it wants a more capable and more efficient state apparatus; conventional orthodoxy supports it because it sees in such reform an opportunity to reduce the tax burden. To new developmentalism, such a consequence may be desirable but relates to a different issue. The tax burden is a political issue that depends on how democratic societies assign roles to the state and on how efficient public services are. Another example is that both approaches favor more flexible labor markets, but new developmentalism looks at the experiences of northern

Europe and does not mistake flexibility for lack of protection, whereas conventional orthodoxy wants to make labor standards more flexible to weaken the labor force and reduce wages. With other reforms, the difference is one of degree. New developmentalism favors, for instance, an open and competitive economy because it sees commercial globalization as an opportunity for middle-income countries, but it rejects unilateral opening and requires reciprocity from trade partners. And there are cases in which there is definitive disagreement, such as with regard to opening the capital account. Whereas conventional orthodoxy strongly favors it, new developmentalism rejects it because the middle-income country loses control over the exchange rate. New developmentalism views commercial globalization as an opportunity but sees financial globalization as a risk that developing countries should not take.

In comparing new developmentalism and conventional orthodoxy, we can distinguish growth strategies from macroeconomic policies, although the two are closely correlated. Because growth is impossible without stability, we may begin by comparing macroeconomic policies. As we can see in Chart 3.2, both positions value macroeconomic stability, but whereas conventional orthodoxy reduces macroeconomic stability to price stability and control of public debt, new developmentalism requires, in addition, a moderate interest rate and a competitive exchange rate that guarantee the intertemporal equilibrium of public accounts (of the state) and of foreign accounts (of the nation-state), respectively. Conventional orthodoxy's approach may be summed up as follows: to guarantee macroeconomic stability, a country should achieve a primary surplus that keeps the public debt to gross domestic product (GDP) ratio at a level acceptable to creditors. The central bank is supposed to have a single mandate, namely, to control inflation, because it has at its disposal a single instrument, namely, the short-term or basic interest rate. This rate is essentially endogenous, corresponding to the equilibrium or non-inflation-accelerating rate of interest, and given the fiscal unbalance, it should be high. The exchange rate

Chart 3.2: *Macroeconomic policies compared*

Conventional orthodoxy	New developmentalism
1. The primary surplus is the central fiscal standard.	1. The budget deficit and public savings are the central fiscal standards.
2. The central bank has a single mandate: inflation.	2. The central bank has a triple mandate: inflation, exchange rate, and employment.
3. The central bank uses a single instrument: the exchange rate.	3. The central bank may buy reserves or impose controls on capital inflow to control the exchange rate.
4. The short-term interest rate is endogenous and should be high.	4. The short-term interest rate is exogenous and may be moderate.
5. The exchange rate is floating, endogenous, and tends to equilibrium.	5. The exchange rate is floating but is managed to avoid the tendency of the exchange rate toward overvaluation.

is also endogenous, that is, it is market defined, and its equilibrium will be automatically ensured by the market once a floating exchange rate is adopted. New developmentalism adopts a substantially different, Keynesian approach combined with the pragmatic practices prevailing in the dynamic Asian countries: fiscal adjustment should not have as its parameter the primary surplus, but rather, the budget deficit and positive public savings that finance the required public investments. The central bank, in association with the finance ministry, should not be limited to a single mandate but should have a triple one: to control inflation, to keep the exchange rate competitive (neutralizing the tendency toward overvaluation of the exchange rate, which we discuss in the next chapter), and to achieve reasonably full employment. To perform these tasks, the central bank functions not with a single instrument (which is, contradictorily, viewed by conventional orthodoxy as endogenous), but with several instruments, in addition to the interest rate: it may buy reserves and establish capital inflow controls to avoid the tendency of the exchange rate to relative appreciation, which is common in medium-income countries. The interest rate is an instrument to control inflation, but it may be considerably less than conventional orthodoxy envisages; the exchange rate should be kept floating, but managed – there is no such a thing as a completely free exchange rate. To sum up the comparison, whereas orthodox macroeconomic policy is based on high interest rates (to achieve so-called financial deepening and to fight inflation) and on an overvalued currency (again to control inflation), new developmentalist macroeconomic policy views inflation as under reasonable control and demands modest interest rates, a competitive exchange rate, and hard fiscal adjustment to reduce the public debt (if it is high) or to keep it low (if it is already low).[9]

We may now compare the growth strategies that I present in Chart 3.3. Conventional orthodoxy supports institutional reforms that reduce the size of the state and strengthen the market. It ascribes a minimum role to the state in investment and industrial policy, and it does not see any role for the nation (an absent concept). It proposes the opening of the capital account and a policy of growth with foreign savings.

In contrast, new developmentalism wants institutional reforms that strengthen the state as well as the market – only a capable state organization and state normative institutions endowed with legitimacy can serve as an instrument of collective action by the nation. New developmentalism sees the nation as a national society with a sense of common destiny and solidarity when competing internationally, as the fundamental actor defining a national growth strategy. It views the national

---

[9] According to Roemer (1994: 1), the economic strategies of Asian countries "contained four common elements: (1) exchange rates were managed to provide constant and rewarding incentives to exporters; (2) budget deficits were kept small in relation to GNP; (3) exporters had access to inputs and could sell outputs at world market prices despite protection for home-oriented industries; and (4) labor and credit markets were flexible enough to allocate resources to rapidly growing industries."

Chart 3.3: *Growth strategies compared*

Conventional orthodoxy	New developmentalism
1. Reforms reduce the state and strengthen the market.	1. Reforms strengthen the state and the market.
2. There is no economic role for the nation.	2. The nation defines a national growth or international competition strategy.
3. Government institutions are supposed to merely protect property rights and contracts.	3. The national growth strategy is the key development institution.
4. The state plays a minimal role in investing and in industrial policy.	4. The state plays a moderate role in investing and in industrial policy.
5. Growth is financed by foreign savings.	5. Growth is financed by domestic savings.
6. Capital accounts are open, and the exchange rate is not managed.	6. Capital inflows are controlled, when necessary, to manage the exchange rate.

development strategy as the fundamental institution for this growth, creating incentives for entrepreneurs to innovate and invest. It gives priority to export industries and to industries characterized by high per capita value added, that is, industries with high technological or knowledge content. It believes that growing domestic savings is not only possible, but necessary, for all developed countries did so in the past. The Dutch disease, the policy of growth with foreign savings recommended by conventional orthodoxy, is a major cause of exchange rate appreciation – appreciation that must always be prevented because a competitive exchange rate, relatively depreciated, is the central condition for growth.

Before the 1990s, conventional orthodoxy was concerned with foreign exchange rates and, during balance-of-payment crises, always demanded foreign exchange depreciations in addition to fiscal adjustments. Since the 1990s, however, the IMF has practically forgotten current account deficits (they represented foreign savings, after all) and exchange rate depreciations. The twin-deficit hypothesis exempted it from worrying about current account deficits: all it had to do was concern itself with the primary surplus. For a while, it chose to talk about foreign exchange anchors and dollarization; after that strategy failed in Mexico, Brazil, and, above all, Argentina, the IMF turned to fully floating exchange rates to solve all external problems.

The new developmentalism is strongly critical of this perspective and wants control not only over the state's public accounts (public deficit) but also over the nation's total accounts (current account). It not only wants the state's debt to be low but also wants the state to show positive public savings. It also wants a nation-state to have foreign accounts that ensure its national security and autonomy. It wants not only interest rate management but also foreign exchange rate management, even if within the framework of a floating rate regime – which it does not call "dirty," as conventional orthodoxy is wont to do, but rather "managed."

Each of the preceding points is deserving of a lengthy analysis, but that is beyond the scope of this chapter. In both comparative charts, my objective is to show that, contrary to the hegemonic ideology that assumes that conventional orthodoxy is a straitjacket for all countries (Friedman 1999), there is a viable and responsible alternative. The experience of the East Asian countries that never accepted conventional orthodoxy was already clear on the existence of this alternative; it became even clearer with the more recent experience of Russia and Argentina. In the 1990s, these two countries adopted conventional orthodoxy models and then fell into deep crisis; after rejecting this economic model in the 2000s, the two countries are now performing in high-growth mode. Thus new developmentalism is not a theoretical proposal but expresses successful national experiences. And conventional orthodoxy is neither a growth strategy nor a derivation of sound development macroeconomics; it is stagnation macroeconomics.

The policies derived from sound development macroeconomics must necessarily be oriented toward responsible fiscal practices, a moderate average interest rate, and a competitive exchange rate; this is the policy tripod of new developmentalism. When macroeconomists in rich countries discuss monetary and fiscal policies in their own countries, they do diverge, but they agree on these three points. Conventional orthodoxy as applied in developing countries, however, shows a quite different practice. Although it is always asking for fiscal discipline, it is soft on this matter; Brazil, for instance, has achieved each year since 1999 the fiscal target defined by conventional orthodoxy,[10] but fiscal problems have not been overcome. Conventional orthodoxy shows no discomfort in asserting that Brazil's real equilibrium interest rate is 9 percent a year, and in defending the central bank's interest rate policy, that has resulted in an average rate of 12 percent in real terms in recent years – a short-term interest rate that, in the special case of Brazil, directly increases the public debt.[11] And conventional orthodoxy insists, against the evidence, that it is impossible to manage the long-term exchange rate; this may be true for the United States, whose dollar is the international reserve currency, but it is not true for other countries.

Of these three policies, the crucial one is the requirement of a competitive exchange rate. By *competitive* or *real equilibrium* exchange rate, I understand the exchange rate that not only equilibrates intertemporally the current account but ensures the competitive viability of tradable industries using state-of-the-art technologies. As we see in Chapter 4, developing countries face a tendency of their currencies to relative overvaluation, which new developmentalism neutralizes.

[10] Between 1999 and 2002, the primary surplus target defined by IMF was 3.5% of GDP; the target was subsequently increased to 4.25%.
[11] In Brazil, there is no difference between the short-term and the long-term interest rates because it is the short-term interest rate set by the Central Bank that determines the interest paid on Brazilian domestic treasury bonds. This is an absurd financial practice – an inheritance of the times of high inertial inflation that is carefully conserved by the representatives of conventional orthodoxy.

EMPIRICAL COMPARISON

To develop a growth strategy, we need to find the key economic policies or short-term institutional variables required by growth. We should not seek long-term institutions because they are strongly correlated with the level of economic and cultural development; rather, we should seek short-term policies that may be changed relatively more easily and rapidly. Problems that can be solved with short-term macroeconomic policies can be addressed relatively effectively, and outcomes may be significant in the short term, whereas long-term policies – usually legal, if not constitutional – are difficult to frame and take time to yield results. What, then, are these policies? One way to arrive at them is by simple observation and comparison, as I have tried to do in this chapter; another way is to look for a hierarchy of causes or for the causal chain behind the variable that directly affects growth, namely, the investment rate. Yet, if we are able to identify the strategic policies in this causal chain, this will be a complementary method to define the strategic variables within new developmentalism. This is a difficult task because in economic and social relations, causes frequently overlap and operate in different directions: cause and effect are mutually reinforcing. Although these causes will vary from country to country, my claim is that the problem is essentially a macroeconomic problem: on the demand side, high interest rates and noncompetitive exchange rates reduce the opportunities for profitable investment and leave unemployed a huge proportion of the human and material resources that the country disposes of. High interest rates discourage enterprise and productive investment, while the overappreciated exchange rate reduces expected profits on export-oriented investment. On the other hand, the domestic market suffers from the existence of an unlimited supply of labor that keeps wages growing more slowly than productivity. Together, these two out-of-balance macroeconomic prices and this distortion in the labor market lower the country's investment and savings capacity, besides causing greater inequality.[12] For the investment rate to grow, effective demand needs to be increased, and for that to happen, the exchange rate should not be chronically overvalued and wages should not grow more slowly than productivity. As we see in this chapter, the exchange rate tends to be overvalued in developing countries, and thus only an economic policy that neutralizes this tendency will ensure the competitive exchange rate that is required for sustained economic growth.

Although other policy variables are also relevant – particularly an austere fiscal policy and monetary policy that keeps the average basic interest rate at a moderate level – these are obviously desirable policies that do not need much discussion. If the state is supposed to be strong or capable – a true instrument of collective action for each nation – it must keep its accounts balanced. Only at times of recession, and temporarily, did Keynes recommend an expansive fiscal policy. On the other hand, a moderate short-term interest rate is essential to economic development because the opportunity to invest depends on the difference between the expected rate of profit and the interest rate.

Thus, using either one or the other method of defining the key growth policies that have short-term outcomes, we arrive at a simple list. Although catching up depends on other variables, it depends essentially on a country's rate of accumulation, and this rate, in turn, depends

[12] Ferreira et al. (2006) have undertaken a significant econometric study to determine why Brazil's investment rate did not rise after 1994. They find two main culprits: the high interest rate and the high tax burden. Their test does not include the exchange rate: had it done so, they would probably have found that this rate, too, was significant. Miguel Bruno (2006), in turn, has also used econometric studies to show that the average gross profit rate and the rate of accumulation dropped systematically in Brazil between the mid-1970s and the early 1990s. Since then, however, the two rates have become uncoupled, with the rate of accumulation dropping and the profit rate rising. The increase in the profit rate, which partially offsets the interest rate hike, is related to the reduction in the share of wages in national income.

Table 3.1: *Growth of average income per capita in the dynamic Asian countries and major Latin American countries: 1990–2005*

Asia		Latin America	
Dynamic countries	Annual growth (%)	Major countries	Annual growth (%)
China	11.2	Argentina	4.3
Korea	7.4	Bolivia	3.4
India	6.2	Brazil	2.9
Indonesia	5.5	Chile	6.5
Malaysia	6.1	Colombia	3.5
Thailand	6.4	Guatemala	2.8
Taiwan	7.0	Mexico	3.9
Vietnam	8.1	Peru	4.2
Average rate	7.2	Average rate	3.9

Note: Major countries have more than ten million inhabitants. Table excludes countries specializing in oil exports.
Source: International Monetary Fund (IMF), *World Economic Outlook.*

(1) on the existence of a competitive exchange rate, (2) on a moderate interest rate paid on the public debt, and (3) on a small public deficit, so that the state, along with the private sector, is able to save and invest. In the remainder of this chapter, I use these variables to present a simple comparison between the Asian countries that adopted national development strategies and the Latin American countries that, as of the late 1980s (Bolivia and Mexico) or the early 1990s (Argentina and Brazil), adopted conventional orthodoxy.

I limit my comparison to the countries listed in Table 3.1. A more comprehensive ranking of the developing countries would consider, in addition to the dynamic Asian countries and the Latin American ones, the other middle-income countries that grow unsatisfactorily and the poor or low-income countries. However, I limit my comparison to the two groups in Table 3.1 because there is a clear contrast between the independence of the Asian counties and the dependence of the Latin American countries. My simple hypothesis is that the better performance of the dynamic Asian countries is due to the fact their national development strategies were based on a competitive exchange rate, on greater fiscal balance, and, consequently, on a greater rate of investment than the same variables in Latin American countries. I limit my comparison to the eight dynamic Asian nation-states and to the major Latin American countries[13] listed in Table 3.1 along with their corresponding growth rates. I make the comparison from 1990 because in the previous year, the solution to the foreign debt crisis was drawn up by the Brady Plan; also, it was around that year that Latin American countries, weakened by the great foreign debt crisis of the 1980s, surrendered to conventional orthodoxy, whereas the dynamic Asian countries continued with their own national development strategies.[14] Table 3.1 shows the huge difference in growth rates of the two groups of countries. If we compare the simple average per capita growth rates of the two groups (7.2% for the dynamic Asian countries vs. 3.9% for the Latin American countries) with the average growth rate of rich OECD countries in the period,[15] namely, 4.3 percent, we observe that Asian countries are catching up, whereas Latin American countries are not. During the period of the comparison, only Chile attained good growth rates. If we considered the last five years (2003–7), Argentina would also show high rates.

A national development strategy for middle-income countries does not mean strong state intervention in the economy. Certainly the state

---

[13] The criterion for the inclusion of Latin American countries in the comparison was the combined incidence of an annual per capita income of more than US$3,000 (according to the purchasing power parity measure) and a population of more than ten million inhabitants. Countries specializing in oil or natural gas exports were excluded.

[14] In the 1990s, some fast-growing Asian countries, specifically Korea, Indonesia, Malaysia, and Thailand, also partially submitted to conventional orthodoxy by accepting the theory of growth with current account deficits. The outcome was the 1997 financial crisis and the prompt return of those countries to growth with domestic savings.

[15] Korea, Slovakia, Hungary, Mexico, Poland, Portugal, the Czech Republic, and Turkey were not included in the calculation of this average.

will have a greater role than just ensuring the rule of law or liberties, property and contracts, and price stability, as recommended by conventional orthodoxy. But it will not need to become involved in aggressive industrial policy, as suggested by the old developmentalism,[16] nor act again as a direct production state by renationalizing privatized corporations, because it already relies on a market structure, with entrepreneurs, professionals, and workers, and on a stock of capital and a private sector able to invest and to save and not in need of the interventionist policies that were pursued in the era of national developmentalism. Neither will the state need to be protectionist, unless protection contributes to neutralizing the Dutch disease,[17] because manufacturing industry is no longer an infant industry; on the contrary, it is or should be the agent of an export-oriented economy.

The decisive policy revealing the presence of a national development strategy in a middle-income country is neither strong state intervention in the economy, which is necessary only in the early stages of economic growth, nor adequate institutions, because their quality tends to be highly correlated with the country's development level; rather, it is a competent macroeconomic policy that also suffers from this constraint, but competent policy makers are more often able to get around it. This policy relies on three pillars: a severe fiscal adjustment, a moderate interest rate (which may vary according to the monetary policy being implemented), and a competitive exchange rate. The severe fiscal adjustment keeps the state financially healthy and prevents it from becoming excessively indebted. The moderate interest rate contributes to fiscal adjustment (if the state still has high public debt) and encourages private investment. The competitive exchange rate, which may be inferred from the existence of a current account surplus or small deficit, opens

---

[16] It will always need to have some industrial policy, as rich countries do.

[17] Import tariffs are a way of partially neutralizing the Dutch disease because they depreciate the currency only for the domestic market, not for exports (Bresser Pereira 2008).

New Developmentalism

lucrative investment opportunities oriented to exports; it also shows that actual wages and consumption are not being artificially increased by an overvalued exchange rate, that the nation-state's financial health is sound, and that the country is not at risk of recurring balance-of-payment crises. The assumption is that the state, besides being in a position to manage its finances and the basic or short-term interest rate (there is little dispute on that), is also able, in the frame of a floating exchange rate regime, to manage its exchange rate and thus neutralize the tendency to exchange rate overvaluation existing in developing countries as a result of the Dutch disease and to the attraction that those countries exert on rich countries' capital. Therefore new developmentalism – the name of the strategy that is used today by the most successful middle-income countries – may be identified in a country if we can observe in it three economic indicators that are reasonably easy to detect: a low or zero public deficit, which indicates fiscal balance; a surplus or a small deficit on the current account, which indicates a competitive exchange rate; and a high ratio of investment to GDP – the main consequence of the other two variables and the fundamental condition for catching up. Although the three variables are important, the current account surplus or small deficit is, in my view, the most important because it reveals that the exchange rate is being correctly managed and that the tendency to exchange rate overvaluation is being neutralized. This is a fundamental issue because the exchange rate is the most strategic macroeconomic price to the extent that it influences practically all macroeconomic aggregates. If we ask ourselves what the secret is of the extraordinary growth of the dynamic Asian countries, the answer will probably be the policy of growth with domestic savings based on a competitive exchange rate. This does not mean that these countries have rejected foreign investment but simply that they do not incur current account deficits, except for brief periods. Foreign investment in China, for instance, is not meant to finance the current account deficit, as happened in Latin America, but to provide access to technology and foreign markets.

115

Political Economy

Table 3.2: *Rates of investment, public deficits, and current account balances in two groups of countries (average annual percentage of gross domestic product, 1990–2005)*

	Rate of investment	Public deficit	Current account balance
Dynamic Asian countries	28.11	1.42	0.76
Major Latin American countries	18.32	1.98	−2.72

Source: IMF, World Bank, Economic Commission for Latin America and the Caribbean, Asian Development Bank, and United Nations Conference on Trade and Development.

On the basis of the preceding remarks, I hypothesize that there should be a positive correlation between, on one hand, economic growth and, on the other hand, a low public deficit, a current account surplus, and a high rate of investment – and therefore that, when we compare countries and their economic performance, those three variables are a good indicator of the presence in a country of a national development strategy. The data in Table 3.2 confirm this hypothesis in the comparison between the dynamic Asian countries and Latin American countries in terms of their public deficits, their current account deficits, and their average rates of investment for the period 1990–2005. The predictions that the dynamic Asian countries would have lower public deficits; current account surpluses, rather than deficits; and greater rates of investment than Latin American countries are fully confirmed: in Asian countries, there are smaller public deficits, current account surpluses, and much greater rates of investment. The coefficients of correlation between those three factors and growth rates are significant and positive; the correlations of growth with the rate of investment (0.83) and with the current account balance (0.6) are more significant than the correlation of growth with the public fiscal balance (0.18).[18]

[18] We calculated the correlation between the average values (of said variables) in the various countries during the period under consideration (1990–2005). Instead of the public

116

To reinforce this argument, we performed an econometric test in which we defined GDP per capita as the dependent variable (in PPP – purchasing power parity – adjusted U.S. dollars) and, as explanatory variables, the current account balance, the public sector fiscal outcome (so positive indicates a surplus), and the rate of investment (all three calculated in relation to GDP). The data were organized in a panel of sixteen countries (those included in Table 3.1) covering the period from 1990 to 2005. A regression was initially conducted in a panel with fixed effects, whose tests pointed to the occurrence of autocorrelation between the series. Therefore, we decided to carry out a regression from a first-difference equation of those variables and from the use of robust standard errors.[19] The equation used in the test and the econometric results can be found in the appendix to this chapter.

The coefficients and the (robust) standard errors indicate that the three variables are significant in explaining the behavior of GDP per capita. With regard to the public deficit and the current account deficit, the coefficient is 10 percent, as compared with the rate of investment, which is 5 percent. The three coefficients are positive, confirming the role of those variables in an economy's faster or slower growth rate of GDP per capita.[20]

These three variables are associated with a strong state, free of debt, that works as an instrument of collective action for the nation and therefore as an instrument of the national development strategy. They are also connected to a policy of growth with domestic savings, which, combined with the policy aimed at neutralizing the tendency of the exchange rate

deficit, we used the public sector fiscal outcome, and therefore, in this case, the positive correlation occurs between the public sector surplus and the GDP per capita.

[19] Actually, heteroskedasticity – robust standard errors. Regression includes generalized least squares estimators.

[20] It is also worth mentioning that because the variables relating to the current account balance and to the rate of investment lag by one period: their impact on GDP per capita occurs in the next period, whereas the impact of the public deficit occurs in the current period.

toward overvaluation, ensures, on the demand side, profitable invest-ment opportunities. Usually, papers and studies on economic develop-ment privilege the supply side, focusing their attention on the devel-opment of human capital, technology, and economic infrastructure. Without denying the significance of this issue, I assume in my analysis that developing countries have abundant human and capital resources that are idle or poorly used as a result of the chronically overvalued exchange rate. The success of the dynamic Asian countries is partly due to their permanent control over their exchange rates, preventing them from appreciating, and therefore they ensure the existence of good investment opportunities for entrepreneurs and the full employment of factors.[21]

In conclusion, trade globalization represents an opportunity for middle-income countries to the extent that they have competitive advan-tages derived from their cheap labor and from the possibility of imitat-ing or buying technology at relatively low cost. However, to profit from this opportunity, the nation-state must be autonomous and able to formulate a national strategy of competition or development. The the-ory that globalization, by making nation-states more interdependent, has reduced their relevance is false because the greater interdependence derives not from greater cooperation, but rather, from greater interna-tional competition. It is true, however, that financial globalization is damaging to middle-income countries as long as it leads them to lose control of their exchange rates, which cease to be competitive because of the existence in those countries of a tendency toward exchange rate overvaluation.

---

[21] In the 1990s, some Asian countries (Korea, Thailand, Malaysia, and Indonesia), influ-enced by the force of the argument encouraging developing countries to grow with foreign savings, abandoned their classical exchange rate controls, opened their external financial accounts, and agreed to grow with foreign savings. The outcome was the 1997 crisis. Yet they learned the lesson, came back on track, depreciated their currencies, and since then have experienced large current account surpluses.

Given the strategic nature of the exchange rate and its tendency to overvaluation in developing countries, the distinction between economic trade globalization and financial globalization becomes essential. Whereas trade globalization provides an opportunity for middle-income countries, financial globalization, by opening of the capital account, leads them to lose control of their exchange rates. The overvaluation of this rate limits lucrative investment opportunities in tradable industries that are not those giving rise to the Dutch disease, resulting in growth rates that are less than the country's potential supply capacity. What we see, then, in middle-income countries is the emigration of a substantial part of their human resources – the most educated part – to rich countries as a result of a lack of job opportunities in their own country.

Although we are in the age of globalization, this does not mean that countries cannot manage their exchange rates by imposing taxes on the sales of commodities that give rise to the Dutch disease and by controlling capital inflows when the mere acquisition and sterilization of reserves is not enough to neutralize the tendency to exchange rate overvaluation. The neoliberal and neoclassical theories that the exchange rate cannot be managed in the long run have been disproven repeatedly.

What are the results of the two approaches? The outcome of conventional orthodoxy in Latin America is well known: quasistagnation. Since 1990, at least, the truth from Washington, D.C., and New York became hegemonic in this region, which is marked by dependence. Reforms and adjustments of all sorts have taken place, but no development has ensued. The results of new developmentalism in Latin America, in turn, cannot be measured. Chile has used it, but it is a small country, and its policies are halfway between the two strategies. The Argentina of the Kirschners and of former finance minister Roberto Lavagna is the only concrete experiment, but having begun in 2002, it is much too soon for an objective appraisal. Still, new developmentalism is more than proven because it is none other than the strategy that Asia's dynamic countries have been following.

Can new developmentalism become hegemonic in Latin America, as old developmentalism was in the past? The failure of conventional orthodoxy assures me that indeed, it can. Argentina's 2001 crisis was a turning point: the requiem of conventional orthodoxy. No country was more faithful in the adoption of its prescriptions; no president was ever more dedicated to confidence building than Carlos Menem. The results are common knowledge. On the other hand, new developmentalist thinking is renewing itself. It has available a younger generation of development macroeconomists, who are able to think on their own account, instead of just accepting the recommendations of the international financial institutions. There is, however, an issue of ideological hegemony to resolve. Latin American countries will resume sustained development only if their economists, businesspeople, and state bureaucracies recall the successful experience that old developmentalism was and reveal that they are capable of taking a step forward. They have already criticized the former mistakes and realized the new historical facts that affect them. They must now acknowledge that the national revolution that was under way, adopting old developmentalism as the national strategy, was interrupted by the great crisis of the 1980s and by the neoliberal ideological wave from the North. They must perform an in-depth diagnosis of the quasistagnation that conventional orthodoxy caused. They should consider that the key policies in need of change are the macroeconomic ones, particularly those related to the interest rate and the exchange rate. They must turn an attentive eye toward the national development strategies of the dynamic Asian countries. They must become involved in the great collective national endeavor of rejecting the macroeconomics of stagnation that conventional orthodoxy implies and of formulating a new national development strategy for their countries. I believe that this resumption of awareness is fully under way. Latin America's development has always been national-dependent because its elites were always in conflict and ambivalent – now affirming themselves as national leaders, now yielding to foreign ideological hegemony. There is a cyclical element to this process, however, and everything seems to indicate that the era of neoliberalism and conventional orthodoxy has passed and that new perspectives are opening up to the region.

APPENDIX: REGRESSION EQUATION

The equation used in the test and the econometric results of the regression is as follows:

$$d.\text{PIBk}_{i,t} = \beta_0 + \beta_1 d.\text{Defpub}_{i,t} + \beta_2 \text{ldInvest}_{i,t}$$
$$+ \beta_3 \text{ldContcorr}_{i,t} + \varepsilon_{i,t},$$

where $d.\text{PIBk}$ is GDP per capita (first difference), $d.\text{Defpub}$ is the public sector result divided by GDP (first difference), ldInvest is the rate of investment (gross formation of fixed capital divided by GDP; first difference lagging by one period), ldContcorr is the current account balance divided by GDP (first difference lagging by one period), i is country, and t is period.

Results of the panel analysis

Random effects of generalized least squares regression	
Group variable (i): paisnum	
R^2:	
Within	0.0738
Between	0.0137
Overall	0.0301
Random effects u_i	$\sim$ Gaussian
corr(u_i, X)	0 (assumed)
Number of observations	224
Number of groups	16
Observations per group:	
Minimum	14
Average	14
Maximum	14
Wald $\chi^2(4)$	38.37
Probabiliy $> \chi^2$	0.00

d.PIBk	Coefficient	Robust standard error	z	$P > |z|$	95% Confidence interval
d.Defpub	36.86118	19.69917	1.87	0.06	−1.748483–75.47085
ldInvest	36.57935	15.33271	2.39	0.02	6.527793–66.63091
ldContcorr	20.08072	12.30499	1.63	0.10	−4.036613–44.19805
_cons	354.9966	74.5847	4.76	0.00	208.8133–501.18

Part II

DEVELOPMENT
MACROECONOMICS

4

The Tendency of the Exchange Rate toward Overvaluation

Economic theory and common sense tell us that middle-income countries are supposed to gradually catch up, that is, to achieve the level of development of rich countries. In the past thirty years, several countries, particularly fast-growing Asian countries, have borne out this prediction, but to achieve such an outcome, they adopted national development strategies that I have called, in the previous chapter, *new developmentalism* and compared with the policies that characterize conventional orthodoxy or the Washington Consensus. The question that then arose for me was which among the policies forming new developmentalism are the strategic ones: those that will more effectively and rapidly bring about fast growth. Although not playing down the importance of the main supply variables affecting the rate of growth (education, technological progress, and infrastructure investment), I understand that the decision to grow with domestic savings and that the macroeconomic policy variables on the demand side – a strict fiscal policy, a moderate interest rate, and a competitive exchange rate – are the key ones. To come to this conclusion, I observed what was happening in the dynamic Asian countries – which policies were strategic in their growth process. The observation did not leave any doubt. On the other hand, institutional reforms are not so urgent as people usually presuppose. Long-term institutions are correlated to the *level*, but not to the *rate*, of economic development; the rich countries are also those with more elaborate and well-regarded institutions, but it is impossible to link institutional reforms to the rate of growth. Institutional reforms are always necessary, but they rarely precede economic growth: they take time to mature, to be transformed into law, and to be enforced. Actually, the key institution for growth is the national development strategy, that is, the sum of formal and informal objectives, norms and policies, that a nation adopts to orient economic growth and international competition.

By identifying macroeconomic policies as the strategic ones in the growth process, I adopted a development macroeconomics approach. My next step was to pin down, among the macroeconomic policies, the exchange rate as the most strategic. Three factors explain this choice: the role of the exchange rate in economic growth is strategic; the literature on the subject is poor; and the idea that there is, in developing countries, a tendency of the exchange rate to become overvalued is new. Other macroeconomic variables, such as inflation, and other policy tools, such as the interest rate and fiscal policy, are obviously relevant, but I do not discuss them systematically. In this chapter, I argue that there is, in developing countries, a structural tendency of the exchange rate toward overvaluation. Thus, the exchange rate does not vary around an equilibrium rate, as economic theory assumes. If the economic authorities fail to neutralize this tendency, the exchange rate will appreciate, first, because of the Dutch disease, and second, because of the attraction that developing countries exert on foreign capital. Policies seeking to attract foreign capital will further appreciate the national currency. In the absence of policies aiming to neutralize the tendency toward overvaluation, the national currency will appreciate to the point where a balance-of-payment crisis breaks. Given that capitalism is essentially dynamic, the country will not stop growing, but it will grow slowly, and it will not catch up.

The Tendency of the Exchange Rate toward Overvaluation

The previous three chapters offered a political economy approach to economic development; this and the remaining three chapters provide a development macroeconomics approach. In this chapter, I argue that in all developing countries, there is a structural tendency of the exchange rate to overappreciate. I first discuss the relation between the exchange rate and economic growth. The Dutch disease and the policy of growth with foreign savings cause exchange rate overappreciation, the former in the long term, the latter in the short term; the first is a major obstacle to industrialization or diversification of the economy, whereas the second causes the exchange rate to appreciate, then consequently the substitution of foreign for domestic savings, and often balance-of-payment crises.

EXCHANGE RATES AND GROWTH

To develop, a country should keep its public budget in balance, its interest rate moderate, and its exchange rate competitive. For long I knew this, and also that among these three policy variables, the most strategic was the exchange rate as it is a powerful determinant not only of exports and imports but also of salaries, consumption, investment, and saving. Thus, a competitive exchange rate – an exchange rate that is neither overvalued nor depreciated – plays a major role in economic development. Yet this fact was not acknowledged by growth theory; economists concerned with economic growth did not view the exchange rate as a legitimate subject of study. Only a few empirical works challenged this view, but they were not sufficiently focused and clear to change the dominant opinion. Research on this matter began with a major study by Dollar (1992) relating the exchange rate to growth, which was followed by works by Sachs and Warner (1999) and Razin and Collins (1997). Dollar assumed that Latin American and African countries tend to have higher exchange rates than Asian countries and concluded that if they had adopted Asian exchange rate standards, their yearly average growth in the period 1976–85 would

Development Macroeconomics

have been 1.5 and 2.1 percentage points higher, respectively, than they effectively have been. According to Dollar (1992: 535), "these results strongly imply that trade liberalization, devaluation of the real exchange rate, and maintenance of a stable real exchange rate could dramatically improve growth performance in many poor countries." Other studies (Benaroya and Janci 1999; Easterly 2001; Bresser Pereira and Nakano 2002b; Fajnzylber et al. 2004; Gala 2006; Johnson et al. 2007; Levy-Yeyati and Sturzenegger 2007; Rodrik 2007) also showed that a lower exchange rate would ensure developing countries higher growth rates. Using the Dollar data basis, Easterly studied the period 1960–99; his objective was to explain why market-oriented reforms effected in the 1980s and 1990s did not cause the expected results in growth terms. One of the explanations he found was that certain currencies, such as the Mexican peso, appreciated in real terms; others, like the Brazilian real and the Argentinean peso, remained constant; and some Asian currencies depreciated up to 1990 and then appreciated until the 1997 balance-of-payment crisis. Gala (2006) completed Dollar's and Easterly's data and corrected them by considering the different rates of productivity of the countries under study and the consequence that they should have on the relative real exchange rates. The currencies of the Asian countries experiencing above-average increases in productivity, such as Korea or Taiwan, should have appreciated relative to the others, as the Harrod–Balassa–Samuelson rule predicts. Yet this did not happen. The conclusion from Gala's econometric study was clear: the Asian countries showed clearly more competitive exchange rates than the Latin American countries, and for that reason, they grew faster.

The relation between a competitive exchange rate and economic development is now clear, and it is also clear how strategic exchange rate policy is. But we cannot just assume that the exchange rate tends to equilibrium and, so, is competitive. If it is difficult to keep the public budget in reasonable balance and the interest rate at an overall moderate level, it is considerably more difficult to keep the exchange rate competitive because policy makers are not supposed only to behave moderately and reasonably; they must also proactively neutralize a structural tendency: the tendency of the exchange rate toward overvaluation.

Although compelling from an econometric point of view, the recent literature on the subject presents two problems: it confounds competitive and depreciated exchange rates, and it lacks a theory or a transmission mechanism to explain why a merely competitive exchange rate causes economic growth in middle-income countries. The confusion between a competitive and a depreciated exchange rate was a mistake for which I, too, am to blame. For many years, since the 1970s, I was persuaded that a relatively depreciated currency was a central explanation of fast economic growth. Thus, I acknowledged the central role that the exchange rate plays in economic development but suggested that its average level was an artificial outcome of intervention in the money market. In other words, I was saying that this relatively depreciated exchange rate was the outcome of a developmentalist intervention in the market that could be indicted for being neomercantilist or for "begging thy neighbor." Since 2007, however, after I developed my model on the Dutch disease (Bresser Pereira 2008), I realized first that this disease, and also the higher profit and interest rates that tend to prevail in developing countries, were two structural causes for the tendency of the exchange rate toward overvaluation. Second, I realized that neutralizing such a tendency was a condition for fast growth in middle-income countries and that the resulting exchange rate was not relatively depreciated, but just competitive. Third, given the model of the Dutch disease that I developed, distinguishing a current equilibrium exchange rate that corresponds to the market rate from an industrial equilibrium that makes competitive business enterprises using the best technology available in the world and so corresponds to what I call a competitive exchange rate it became clear that the market does not tend to this rate but rather tends to an overvalued one: the current equilibrium exchange rate.

A competitive exchange rate is a condition for economic growth. Yet, since the 1990s, this condition has not been present in most developing countries, particularly Latin American and African countries. They do not have the required relatively devalued exchange rates, or, as I prefer to call it today, competitive exchange rates. Before the 1990s, Latin American countries were able to keep their exchange rates competitive insofar as the developmentalist policies that they adopted implied tightly managed currencies. To avoid overvaluation, their nominal exchange rates were modified by import taxes and export subsidies. In the case of Brazil, for instance, in the 1970s, given that import taxes were around 50 percent and export subsidies for almost all goods, except coffee, were also 50 percent, the effective exchange rate was 33 percent less than the nominal rate; coffee exporters paid a 33 percent tax.

Around the exchange rate, there are obvious interests. We cannot escape from the political economy involved. No country accepts that its competitors artificially depreciate their currencies. This is viewed as unfair – as a neomercantilist form of "beggar thy neighbor." According to conventional economic theory, Asian countries, particularly China, are growing at the expense of their competitors by artificially keeping their exchange rates depreciated. Yet, while these countries are just neutralizing the tendency of the exchange rate toward overappreciation or are just neutralizing the Dutch disease and rejecting the policy of growth with foreign savings that floods their countries with foreign currency they do not need, the neomercantilist argument ceases to make sense.

In this chapter, I offer a general explanation for this tendency and for the basic relation between economic growth and the exchange rate; in the three last chapters, I discuss two main factors leading to this overvaluation: the Dutch disease and the policy of growth with foreign savings. I suppose that countries have a floating exchange rate, but even if they have a fixed one, it makes little difference. In practice, the exchange rate regimes in developing as well as in developed countries are neither fully floating nor fully fixed but rather are always, to some degree, managed; they are a mixture of the two types. In other words, I reject the "fix or float" alternatives and assume that all countries manage, or try to manage, their exchange rates. On the other hand, I am not interested in the volatility of the exchange rate but rather in its general level and in its tendency toward overvaluation followed by balance-of-payment crises. On the volatility issue, there is a large body of literature that, although relevant, diverts our attention from the far more important problem represented by a chronically and cyclically noncompetitive exchange rate.

When we study economic development, we must always take into consideration its two sides: the supply side and the demand side. Conventional economics tends to analyze economic growth merely in terms of supply, focusing on education, on the broader improvement of human capital, on scientific and particularly technological development, on innovation, and on investments in infrastructure and in machines that increase workers' productivity. Yet, as Keynes and Kalecki classically demonstrated, demand is not automatically created by supply, and therefore insufficiency of demand may become an essential obstacle to economic growth. Although developing countries are characterized by low levels of education, limited command of technological progress, and deficient investment in energy production and transportation, the huge unemployment of human resources in low-growth, medium-income countries leaves no doubt that the main problem is often on the demand side rather than the supply side. Demand is formed by consumption, investments, public expenditure, and exports minus imports or the trade surplus. Among these components of aggregate demand, exports are key. Neoclassical economists just ignore the demand side. As for the Keynesian economists, who attribute a major role to demand, the problem is that they often forget the role of exports in sustained aggregate demand, for three reasons: first, because they focus on the short-run macroeconomic equilibrium; second, because they often presuppose closed systems; and third, because many Keynesian economists in developing countries continue to give priority to the domestic market and to mass consumption and are distrustful of export-led growth.

These are mistaken views that ignore the central role of the exchange rate and of exports in economic development. Exports are key to developing countries in any circumstance, and there is no conflict between the development of the domestic market and an export-led growth strategy. When the country is still poor, that is, when it has not completed its industrial revolution and does not have investment capacity or a class of entrepreneurs and middle-class professionals to conduct investments, it usually escapes the poverty trap by combining two strategies: by exporting some mineral or agricultural commodity with which the country is particularly endowed, and by a systematic and planned state intervention oriented toward forced savings and toward increasing the country's investment rate. The combination of these two strategies will vary from country to country (Brazil and Australia on one side, Japan, Russia, and China on the other), but exports are always important. It usually follows an import-substitution phase that should be short – an industrialization strategy that is only valid while we can assume that the manufacturing industry is still infant (a problem with Latin American growth was that the import-substitution strategy was artificially overextended). In this phase, exports apparently have been given a secondary role, but this is only partially true. Immediately after the import-substitution strategy is exhausted, the country will have to resort to exports to grow, now using its relatively low-cost labor to export manufactured goods.

As we see in the discussion of the Dutch disease, while the country is just exporting commodities, the neutralization of this disease is not a major problem because the country does not yet have to industrialize. At the moment that some entrepreneurial and technical capacity is acquired, however, the challenge will be to industrialize and export; it makes no sense to the now middle-income country to renounce diversification into high–per capita income industries, but for that, a competitive exchange rate is a necessary condition. To be sure, we could ask two questions: first, is it really necessary to industrialize to grow? Second, is it necessary to increase exports to sustain aggregate demand? Could not the country sustain it just by managing the internal variables, that is, investment and consumption?

I do not go over the first question. This is a problem that was resolved in the 1940s and 1950s by development economics and the Economic Commission for Latin America and the Caribbean and revisited by Nicholas Kaldor in the 1970s (see Prebisch 1950; Kaldor 1978). Economic development is a process of increasing productivity that takes place within industries and, principally, through the transfer of labor from low value-added industries to high value-added industries – industries that use sophisticated technology and pay high average wages and salaries. We know that primary goods industries are becoming increasingly technology-intensive, and thus we could imagine a developed country based entirely on primary industries. But for that, the country would have to be small, like New Zealand or Chile. And even these countries do not limit their production of tradable goods to primary goods. Economic development requires that the country that becomes technologically capable be able to transfer its labor to industries with the highest per capita value added. It makes no sense for a country to be limited in relation to industries in which it could specialize and gain knowledge because its exchange rate is structurally overvalued.

As to the question why a country should not sustain aggregate domestic demand just by managing it, the answer is that this is theoretically possible, but it is evident that the possibility of counting also on external demand makes things much easier for the country. If the economy is closed – or if policy makers act as if it were – it is difficult to increase investment and the savings rate without reducing short-term domestic consumption. Within the domestic market, the policy maker and the entrepreneur face a classic chicken-and-egg dilemma: investment opportunities depend on strong domestic demand, which, in turn, depends on investment. If the country begins by increasing demand, inflation can follow; if the idea is to start by increasing investment, what would be the incentive to invest? These problems disappear, however, if we assume that the economy is open and that growth should be export-led. In this case, when the developing country enjoys technological capacity and a competitive exchange rate, it will able to take advantage of its relatively cheap-labor export. Demand ceases to be just domestic demand and expands to become world demand. This was what the Asian Tigers, Brazil, and Mexico did successfully in the 1970s. This is what the latter two Latin American countries ceased to do after the debt crisis of the 1980s because they agreed to open their financial external accounts and ceased to neutralize the tendency of their exchange rates toward overvaluation. Exports based on a competitive exchange rate not only represent demand when there is a positive balance in commercial transactions; in addition, they encourage demand's main variable – investments – which operate as much on the supply side as on the demand side.[1] Exports are therefore strategic to solve the problem of unemployment or insufficient demand. In the era of globalization, export-led growth is the only sensible strategy for developing countries while they have the competitive advantage of cheap labor. The argument that an export-led growth model is inconsistent with income distribution and mass domestic consumption makes no sense. Exports increase employment, wages, and domestic consumption. Often export-led growth temporarily increases inequality, but still more often, import-substitution growth leads to the same outcome.

Most economists who acknowledge the positive relation between a competitive exchange rate and faster growth explain it by reference

---

[1] Investment expenditure evidently also depends on other variables, besides increased exports, such as the interest rate and, particularly, profit expectations, but these latter would be substantially better should the entrepreneurs rely on an exchange rate that encourages them to export.

to either financial crises or rent seeking, which usually derive from an overvalued currency. This is correct, but obvious. Recently, Rodrik (2007: 20–6) has written on a more elaborate explanation. Because real currency devaluation is, by definition, an increase in the relative prices of tradable goods in relation to nontradable goods, he argues that an "undervalued" currency would "enhance the relative profitability of the traded-goods sectors and cause it to expand (at the expense of the non-traded sector)." Yet he recognizes that this is not a theory because "such theory would have to explain why tradable goods are 'special' from the standpoint of growth." He resorts to two explanations for this. One explanation is not really in the realm of economics: weak institutions and their associated corruption would impose "a higher tax on tradable goods"; the other explanation is that "market failures predominate in tradables." These explanations are not satisfactory and wrongly insist on the idea of an undervalued, rather than a competitive, exchange rate (see the next section). Levy-Yeyati and Sturzenegger (2007: 22) make the same mistake but come closer to the real explanation. They find that the mechanism that makes an "undervalued" exchange rate cause faster growth "is associated with an increase in aggregate savings and investment, and a decline in unemployment and labor relative to capital compensation." Yet they do not explain why a competitive exchange rate is associated with higher savings and investment rates.

I have been arguing for some time that the transmission mechanism between a competitive exchange rate and economic growth is simple. On the demand side, given the existence of technological capacity and of idle or unemployed resources, growth depends on the rate of savings, which depends on the rate of investment, which depends on the existence of profit opportunities, which in turn depends on export opportunities, which finally will exist only if the exchange rate is not overvalued but rather is competitive. The exchange rate is, in fact, the main variable to be studied by development macroeconomics because it plays a strategic role in economic growth. According to the classical or political economy model, growth depends essentially on the rate of capital accumulation, which depends on expected profits or, more precisely, on the difference between expected profits and the interest rate, but which also depends on savings. According to the Keynesian view, however, savings depend on investments – which makes profit expectations the key economic growth variable. Although profit expectations depend on domestic demand, they depend also and more strongly on exports and so on a competitive exchange rate. In other words, if conditions exist on the supply side – and we should not overlook them – a competitive exchange rate is necessary for export-oriented investments to materialize. The central mechanism that links the exchange rate to growth is on the demand side, but it also may be thought of as being on the supply side – as a factor that increases domestic savings. The exchange rate has a strong effect on real wages and salaries. When the exchange rate is overvalued, wages will be artificially high; wages and salaries will be equally high; and, given the high marginal propensity to consume, principally among workers, domestic consumption will also be artificially high. Thus, when economic policy brings the exchange rate to the competitive or equilibrium level, real wages will fall and domestic consumption will decrease, creating space for an increase in domestic savings (insofar as this change in the supply side is completed by the increase in the investment rate on the demand side).

This theory assumes that policy makers are able to manage the long-term exchange rate. Thus, it rejects the neoclassical assumption that the exchange rate is endogenous. And naturally, it also rejects the neoclassical inversion that makes the exchange rate dependent on the savings rate. This is what Pastore et al. (2008) argue, for instance. They agree that a competitive exchange rate is associated with economic growth but expressly reject my model, in which a nonneutralized Dutch disease and the policy of growth with foreign savings plus a high interest rate policy (and exchange rate populism) determine the overvaluation of the real exchange rate, which, in turn, reduces the saving and investment rates.

Instead, Pastore et al. (2008: 296) assume that the exchange rate is "an endogenous variable" and conclude that "countries having high savings in relation to investments present current account surpluses, a more depreciated real exchange rate, and grow fast. But this is the outcome of their high savings, not of their deliberate policy of determining a more depreciated real exchange rate." In doing so, they make the real exchange rate, a short-term macroeconomic variable, dependent on the savings rate, a long-term structural variable – which makes little sense.

If we admit that the exchange rate may be systematically managed by a country in the context of a national development strategy – something for which there is strong historical evidence, not only in Asia, but also in Latin America between 1930 and 1980 – it makes more sense to say that a macroeconomic policy aiming at a competitive exchange rate is able to gradually bring about an increase in the savings rate, which, in turn, insofar as it increases, reinforces the competitive exchange rate policy. Today, the policy of managing the exchange rate to prevent its appreciation is more effective in the dynamic Asian countries than in Middle Eastern, African, and Latin American countries. The Latin American countries extensively used exchange rate management up to the 1980s and grew fast, but lost this capacity after the debt crisis and their submission to the North. The fast-growing Asian countries' capacity to manage their exchange rates is the central explanation of their success. It originates in their greater national autonomy in relation to the North and in their firm rejection of economic populism. These are two essential conditions for a national development strategy. A third explanation could be that Asian countries have relatively scarce natural resources and therefore are less subject to the Dutch disease. Yet it is significant that the countries that do have abundant natural resources, such as Thailand and Malaysia, do not base their growth on their exploitation.[2]

---

[2] They are subject only to the extended Dutch disease, derived from the existence of cheap labor, the concept of which I discuss in Chapter 5.

THE TENDENCY TOWARD OVERVALUATION

I am now ready to present the central theoretical claim of this book. The main reason why some medium-income or emerging countries grow fast and catch up, while others fall behind, is that the former neutralize and the latter fail to neutralize the tendency of the exchange rate toward overvaluation. After several years of studying the relation between the exchange rate and economic growth, my more general conclusion is that the fundamental obstacle that middle-income countries face in catching up is this tendency of the national currency to chronic and cyclical overvaluation. Although a competitive exchange rate is associated with faster growth, its tendency toward overvaluation is still a topic of scientific inquiry and may be viewed as a hypothesis to be demonstrated. Yet the almost permanent state of financial fragility and the recurrent balance-of-payment crises that we observe in developing countries amount to strong evidence supporting the hypothesis. The tendency of the exchange rate toward overvaluation has two main structural causes: (1) the Dutch disease and (2) the attraction that the higher rates of profit and interest existing in developing countries exert over abundant international capital as a result of the prevailing relative scarcity of capital. They are *structural* causes because they are independent of economic policies or human intervention. The second cause, however, is *augmented* by three policies, two of which are recommended by conventional orthodoxy (the policy of growth with foreign savings and capital deepening) and the third of which originates within developing countries as exchange rate populism.

The role played by the Dutch disease is different from the roles played by the other causes because it exerts a powerful upward pressure on the exchange rate but does not lead a country to experience current account deficits and high foreign indebtedness. As we see in Chapter 5, the Dutch disease is the outcome of Ricardian rents arising from the exports of a commodity using abundant natural resources that lead to an exchange rate consistent with long-term equilibrium of the current account but inconsistent with the international competitiveness of all other tradable industries, although using the best technology available in the world. Thus, as we see in Chapter 5, a country benefiting from the existence of precious natural resources is cursed because it has not one, but two, exchange rate equilibria: the current equilibrium, which balances the exchange rate intertemporally, and the industrial equilibrium, which makes tradable industries utilizing state-of-the-art technology economically viable. The larger the difference between these two equilibria, the more serious the disease will be. Thus, the Dutch disease appreciates the national currency, taking it from the industrial exchange rate equilibrium to the current one. A competitive exchange rate is one that corresponds not to the current equilibrium but to the industrial equilibrium. The former equilibrium is the one that markets offer to all countries, although imperfectly (given the well-known volatility of the exchange rate); the latter is the one that economists assume to be equal to the former, when they expect markets to define the right prices and therefore well coordinate the economy but also to be more appreciated than the current equilibrium when the country faces the Dutch disease.

Yet, because the Dutch disease stops depressing the exchange rate when it reaches the current equilibrium, we need another explanation of why the exchange rate falls behind the current equilibrium and the country falls into current account deficit. The other main cause of the tendency of the exchange rate toward overvaluation is related to capital inflows. They are the outcome of the structural attraction that higher rates of profit and interest exert on international capital. But they are also the outcome of a persistent policy of growth with foreign savings that conventional orthodoxy recommends. Because business enterprise investments require finance, conventional economists conclude that the country as a whole will also need foreign finance. Yet this is a classical situation in which microeconomic logic (the need for finance on the part of entrepreneurs) cannot be transferred to macroeconomic logic. In some cases, foreign finance may be positive, but as I show Chapter 6, in most cases, the attempt to grow with foreign savings fails: instead of increasing investment, foreign savings increase consumption, and a high rate of substitution of foreign for domestic savings materializes. Countries that engage in the policy of growth with foreign savings pass through three perverse stages: in the first stage, they experience substitution of foreign for domestic savings; in the second, external financial fragility; and in the last, a balance-of-payment crisis. In Chapter 6, I limit my analysis to the first stage, in which the country has not yet suspended international payments or even gotten deep enough into debt to become dependent on creditors and therefore compelled to adopt the alienating practice of confidence building, but has fallen victim to the perverse process of substituting foreign savings for domestic savings because, through the appreciation of the exchange rate, a sizable share of the foreign funds, which should hypothetically increase investment, ends up increasing consumption.[3] As Alexandre Barbosa Lima Sobrinho (1973), following Ragnar Nurkse (1953), puts in the title of one of his books, "capital is made at home." Only at particular moments when a country is growing at an extraordinary pace and expected profit rates are high, may foreign savings or current account deficits be positive in causing growth because at such moments, the increase in real wages caused by exchange rate appreciation will flow mostly not to consumption but to investment. In Chapter 7, I reject the conventional view that balance-of-payment crises derive from expansive fiscal policy and show how they are the consequence of current account deficits that, contrary to the twin-deficits hypothesis, are not necessarily tied to fiscal deficits: there are other factors causing exchange rate misalignment – particularly the overappreciation of the exchange rate.

---

[3] For a discussion of balance-of-payment crises or foreign exchange crises, see Alves et al. (2004). The authors distinguish first-, second-, and third-generation models; these models invariably cast the public deficit in a leading role in explaining these crises. A doctoral student of mine, Lauro Gonzalez (2007), wrote a thesis to show that the roles of the policy of growth with foreign savings and therefore current account deficits are truly the deciding factors.

The Tendency of the Exchange Rate toward Overvaluation

While the Dutch disease stops pushing up the exchange rate when it reaches the current equilibrium, the capital inflows resulting from the policy of growth with foreign savings have a continuing effect on the appreciation of the currency over and above that equilibrium. The exchange rate appreciates gradually, as capital inflows finance the current account deficit and increase foreign debt. If such inflows are not stopped, sooner or later, they will lead to a balance-of-payment crisis. The crisis will arrive sooner the stronger the process of appreciation is and the less the local government neutralizes it.

It is easy to understand this overappreciation if the exchange rate is fixed. It is a mistake, however, to believe that the problem will be solved if the exchange rate floats. It will not be because exchange rate markets are highly inefficient, principally in relation to developing countries. They do not react by depreciating the currency as soon as a deficit appears in the current account. In today's financial markets, the exchange rate depends less and less on commercial flows and increasingly on capital flows. While investors continue to believe that the country is sound – and they will be tempted to believe that, as long as they are being well remunerated – they will continue to pour capital into the country, and the exchange rate will remain overappreciated.

The pressure of the Dutch disease on the overvaluation of national currencies varies according to its gravity. This major market failure exists at different levels in the countries where abundant and cheap resources generate Ricardian rents. Such rents make the economic exploitation of resources viable at a more appreciated exchange rate than is consistent with the international competitiveness of industries using state-of-the-art technology. The consequence is that the only tradable goods that the country is able to produce are those that generate the Dutch disease. A national development strategy will materialize only if the country is capable of neutralizing the effects of the Dutch disease through the imposition of an export tax on the commodities that generate it.

141

The policy of growth with foreign savings has capital deepening as a complementary policy. *Capital deepening* is simply an elegant term to justify high interest rates that will attract capital inflows; McKinnon (1973) and Shaw (1973) introduced it in the 1970s, when many developing countries controlled interest rates and often kept their basic interest rates negative (as rich countries still do today). Besides, capital deepening should also convey earnestness in terms of economic policy, while administered interest rates and economic populism suggest the opposite. Another complement to the policy of growth with foreign savings is the use of the exchange rate, and particularly of an exchange rate anchor, to control inflation. This policy became popular in the 1990s, after Argentina, in 1991, controlled hyperinflation by pegging the exchange rate to the U.S. dollar. The disastrous consequences of this policy are well known even by conventional orthodoxy, which, after the late 1990s, abandoned it in favor of a floating exchange rate. Yet the practice of using exchange rate appreciation to control inflation remains central to conventional orthodoxy. The success of Brazil in reducing inflation since 2002, for instance, is due to the subsequent strong appreciation of the real. On the other hand, when the exchange rate becomes over-appreciated, the acceleration of inflation that the required depreciation would entail forms a big obstacle to such a depreciation. This acceleration of inflation is temporary in an open, competitive, and nonindexed economy; the inflation bubble will soon subside. But the stigma of high inflation can be significant, as it is in Brazil, so that faced with any acceleration of inflation rates, however temporary, people fear the return of high inflation, which legitimizes the Central Bank's policy of increasing the interest rate, even in the absence of excessive inflation, simply to appreciate the exchange rate and to lower the inflation rate.

Yet the justification of growth with foreign savings originates also with the pioneers of development economics. Rosenstein-Rodan's (1943) founding paper on the big push assumed that foreign savings would finance the beginning of development. The well-known two-gap model is generally associated with one of the pioneers of development economics, Hollys B. Chenery, who was the World Bank's vice president for development policy from 1972 to 1982 – just before the bank turned to the Washington Consensus (Bresser Pereira 1995). According to the model, there would be a structural gap between a country's own provision of resources and its absorptive capacity: the savings gap and the foreign exchange gap. Whichever of the two gaps is binding (or is the greater) will constrain the amount of investment and capital formation that can be undertaken. Usually, the second gap was considered the constraining one – and the solution would be increased access of developing countries to the World Bank and to international financial markets.

Finally, exchange rate populism – one of the two forms of economic populism – is also a cause of the tendency of the exchange rate toward overvaluation. While political populism is a political practice whereby political leaders become directly connected with the people, without the intermediation of political parties and ideologies, economic populism is simply to spend irresponsibly more than one's income. Whereas with fiscal populism, the state organization or apparatus spends more than it collects in revenues, incurring chronic and irresponsible public deficits, with exchange rate populism, it is the nation-state or country that spends more than it collects, incurring chronic current account deficits.[4] An appreciated exchange rate is attractive in the short run as it implies higher real wages and higher profits than a competitive rate will provide. The rich, who measure their wealth in dollars, see it grow every time the local currency appreciates. The wages of the middle class, with its relatively high component of imported consumption, rise when the local currency gains value. Even the poorest benefit from real wage increases with noncompetitive exchange rates, as a share of the products

---

[4] On economic populism, see Dornbusch and Edwards (1991) and Bresser Pereira, ed. (1991b) where are reproduced the classical studies on economic populism, including fiscal and exchange rate populism, written by Adolfo Canitrot (1975), Carlos Diaz-Alejandro (1981), and Jeffrey Sachs (1989).

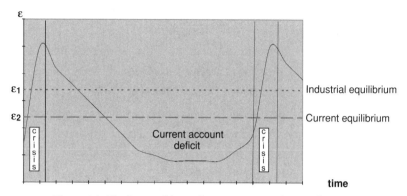

Figure 4.1: Tendency of the exchange rate toward overvaluation.

in their consumption basket becomes cheaper. Government ministers have an interest in an appreciated exchange rate because it pleases voters, and as a result, they do not hesitate to practice what I have been calling *foreign exchange populism*. And the government's economists who accept conventional orthodoxy's single mandate for the Central Bank – controlling inflation – also have an interest in an appreciated exchange rate because they can say, as has become common in Brazil recently, that the appreciation of the real was "a good thing" because it increased wages. Conventional orthodoxy criticizes fiscal populism but is sympathetic to exchange rate populism because exchange rate appreciation is consistent with its central proposal to developing countries: growth with foreign savings.

The tendency of the exchange rate toward overvaluation may be illustrated with a simple graphic. In Figure 4.1, the exchange rate is defined as the price in national currency terms of the foreign currency or basket of currencies[5] so that the lower the exchange rate curve is, the more appreciated the national currency or the exchange rate will be. The exchange rate is depicted on the vertical axis, and ε_1 and ε_2

---

[5] Thus, in Figure 4.1, we do not have the price of a country's own currency in terms of others' currencies, as usually U.S. or British citizens do; rather, we see the inverse.

144

are, respectively, the industrial exchange rate equilibrium (the exchange rate required to make industries utilizing state-of-the-art technology competitive internationally) and the current exchange rate equilibrium (the rate the market rate tends to because it is the rate that equilibrates the current account intertemporally). If we take as a starting point a financial crisis and the respective fast and large depreciation of the local currency (an almost vertical rise of the exchange rate in Figure 4.1), a gradual process of appreciation of the exchange rate will follow, driven by the several factors or causes just discussed. In the overvaluation process, the exchange rate, under the pressure of the Dutch disease, first crosses the horizontal line representing the industrial equilibrium exchange rate (ε_1), continues to appreciate (i.e., to fall in the graphic), and crosses the horizontal line representing the current equilibrium exchange rate (ε_2). From this point on, the Dutch disease ceases to push down the exchange rate, but its appreciation continues, and the country enters into the current account deficit area under the pressure of the policy of growth with external saving and exchange rate populism. Finally, as the deficit grows and erodes the confidence of international creditors, a balance-of-payment crisis materializes, and the exchange rate again vertically depreciates. How much time does this cycle require for completion? If the country does not have a policy of neutralizing the tendency of its exchange rate toward overvaluation, the gap between crises may be short (say, eight years). The assumption that a floating exchange rate regime will automatically correct the exchange rate is not realistic because capital flows, not commercial flows, are today the main determinants of the market exchange rate. While foreign investors remain confident and are attracted by high interest and profit rates, they will continue to finance the country. At a given moment, however, they will realize the risk, and the herd effect will lead the country to default. Insofar, however, as the country is able to neutralize partially the tendency of the exchange rate toward overvaluation, the crisis may never happen – only reduced growth rates will follow.

This simple theory explains why developing countries are so subject to balance-of-payment crises. Contrary to what conventional economists believe, they are not just caused by exchange rate volatility, nor do they indicate the existence of exchange rate misalignment; rather, they are a consequence of a structural tendency magnified by mistaken policies. Exchange rates are effectively volatile, and they are often misaligned, but they are the outcome neither of random shocks nor of the psychological instability of economic agents, despite the fact that some shocks are difficult to predict and economic behavior often falls short of rationality. These factors may play a role, but the essential thing is a tendency toward overvaluation that lies behind Ricardian rents, giving rise to the Dutch disease and the attraction that higher profit and interest rates characteristic of developing countries exert on foreign capital. Because of these structural factors and the mistaken policies that deepen them – the growth with foreign savings strategy, the practice of using nominal anchors to control inflation, the police of capital deepening and exchange rate populism – local currencies in developing countries tend to become cyclically overappreciated to the point that a balance-of-payment crisis is triggered.

The theory is simple, but its consequences are huge: if the country is not able to neutralize the tendency of the exchange rate toward overvaluation, it will not grow, or it will grow slowly. Because I am not offering empirical evidence that such an assertion is true, we should consider it a hypothesis, albeit a strong one, because it explains the recurrent balance-of-payment crises to which developing countries are subject. These crises are not principally the outcome of economic populism, as is often said, but rather, of a tendency that has, as one of its causes, a particular kind of economic populism – exchange rate populism. Countries are not always financially fragile because the inflow of foreign capital in the form of loans or direct investment is a condition for their development but rather because they fail to neutralize this tendency. To find econometric evidence of this tendency and to discover how to neutralize it – which is the role of the decision to grow with domestic savings, to impose taxes on the exports of goods causing the Dutch disease, and more generally, to manage a floating exchange rate – is a task for further study.

5

The Dutch Disease

The main reason why medium-income countries tend to have over-valued exchange rates is the Dutch disease; the main reason why some nevertheless grow fast, while others fall behind, is that the former are able to neutralize this disease. The *Dutch disease* is a market failure or market syndrome resulting from the existence of cheap and abundant natural resources used to produce commodities whose exports are compatible with a more appreciated exchange rate than would be needed to make the other tradable industries competitive. By using cheap resources, the respective commodities cause the appreciation of the exchange rate because they can be profitable at a rate incompatible with the rate that other goods, using the best technology available worldwide, require. Resources are cheap because they generate Ricardian rents for the country; in other words, they are cheap because their costs and corresponding prices are less than those prevailing on the international market, which are determined by the less efficient marginal producers admitted to this market.

The Dutch disease is a market failure that affects almost all developing countries and may permanently obstruct their industrialization because the market converges on a long-term equilibrium exchange rate that is caused by this disease. It is consistent, in the long run, with the equilibrium of a country's foreign accounts, that is, with a balanced current account – something that does not occur with the policy of growth with foreign savings, which usually ends with a balance-of-payment crisis. To discuss the Dutch disease, I first define it in a conventional way as related to the abundance of cheap natural resources; second, I point to the circumstances that allow us to diagnose the Dutch disease; third, I show that it is not limited to oil-producing countries because countries like Brazil have achieved industrialization only as long as they were able to neutralize its effects, nor is it the case that production of the commodities represents low value added per capita. Next, I discuss the extended concept of the Dutch disease, which equally applies to countries, such as China, that, even though lacking many natural resources or not using them as intensely in their growth processes, nevertheless have cheap labor.

THE CONCEPT OF THE DUTCH DISEASE

The Dutch disease is an old problem, essential to an understanding of development and underdevelopment. Yet it was identified only in the 1960s, in the Netherlands, where the discovery and export of natural gas appreciated the exchange rate and threatened to destroy the country's entire manufacturing industry. In the 1980s, the first academic studies of the subject appeared (Corden and Neary 1982; Corden 1984). Even today, the literature on the subject is scarce and insufficient. The Dutch disease, or the curse of natural resources, is the chronic overvaluation of a country's exchange rate caused by the exploitation of abundant and cheap resources whose commercial production is consistent with an exchange rate clearly more appreciated than the average exchange rate that makes tradable goods industries economically viable using state-of-the-art technology. It is a structural phenomenon that obstructs

149

industrialization or, if it has been neutralized but ceases to be so, provokes deindustrialization.

The Dutch disease is consistent with the intertemporal equilibrium of foreign accounts and may therefore produce negative effects indefinitely. It is a market failure because the sector producing natural resource–intensive goods generates a negative externality[1] on the economy's other sectors, preventing those sectors from developing despite their use of state-of-the-art technology. It is a market failure that implies the existence of a difference between the exchange rate that balances the current account (which is the market rate) and the exchange rate that enables efficient and technologically sophisticated economic sectors (which is the rate at which economics predicts that efficient industries will be viable in competitive markets). Only when the Dutch disease is neutralized will the market be able to play its role in effectively allocating resources and encouraging investment and innovation.

The Dutch disease leads to an exchange rate that prevents the production of tradable goods that do not use the resources that give rise to it. For this to occur, a sector that uses a country's natural resources must be substantially more productive than the corresponding sector in other countries so that it gives rise to Ricardian rents (i.e., the market price of the respective commodity is defined on the international market by the least efficient producer on the margin). In these terms, the Dutch disease is the market failure that derives from Ricardian rents associated with the production and export of a limited number of goods produced with those natural resources. In their model, Corden and Neary (1982) supposed an economy with three sectors, two of them related to tradable goods (the booming natural resources sector and the lagging manufacturing sector) and a third consisting of nontradable goods. Sachs

[1] The idea that the Dutch disease implies a negative externality was suggested to me by José Luiz Oreiro. It is thus easier to understand why it constitutes a market failure – a situation in which prices do not reflect the (marginal) social cost of the production of goods.

and Warner (2001), summarizing the literature on the Dutch disease, explain it by reference to a wealth shock in the natural resources sector, which creates excess demand in the nontradable goods sector, implying a change in relative prices. The appreciated exchange rate is defined by the change in relative prices favoring nontradable goods. In the model that I present here, the emphasis is placed directly on the exchange rate, and the change in relative prices that causes its appreciation is related to the Ricardian nature of the rents occurring in the sector that makes use of cheap resources – not only natural resources but also, as we shall see, labor itself. Whereas in Ricardo's model, Ricardian rents benefit only the owners of the most productive land, in the case of Dutch disease, they also benefit, in the short run, the country's consumers, who buy relatively cheaper tradable goods; and whereas in the classical model, the tendency of the economy is toward stagnation, in the case of Dutch disease, there will be quasistagnation in the country as a whole. Unlike in Ricardo's model, however, the overvaluation caused by Ricardian rents converted into Dutch disease can be neutralized. It must be stressed that in the model I am presenting, I refer to the country's Ricardian rents, and there is no difference in productivity among local producers but only a difference in the country's productivity in relation to the international price (i.e., between local producers' average and that of producers in other countries). If there is a difference in productivity, there will also be Ricardian rents among the producers, as long as the exchange rate tends to converge on the one that favors the most inefficient local producer.

AN ECONOMIC OR POLITICAL PROBLEM?

The Dutch disease is essentially an economic problem, a market failure insofar as it makes tradable industries utilizing the best existing technology economically unviable. It is a contradictory problem: on one hand, natural resources represent an enormous benefit to the country – their exploitation is often the way a developing country can begin to grow; on the other hand, natural resources are a curse because they prevent the country from industrializing and diversifying. Some economists (Baland and François 2000; Sachs and Warner 1999, 2001; Torvik 2001; Larsen 2004) make a distinction between the Dutch disease and the curse of natural resources: whereas the Dutch disease would be a market failure, the curse of natural resources would result from corruption or rent seeking – two problems that derive from the abundance of such resources in countries with a backward society and weak institutions. In a similar vein, a distinguished political scientist, Terry Karl (1997: xv, 6) asked herself, "After benefiting from the largest transfer of wealth ever to occur without war, why have most oil exporting developing countries suffered from economic deterioration and political decay?" What answer did she give for this puzzle? She attributed the problem to poor institutions. Showing a clear awareness of the contradictory character of the relations between economic development and institutional change, she nevertheless transformed the Dutch disease into a consequence of poor institutions: "because the causal arrow between economic development and institutional change constantly runs in both directions, the accumulated outcomes give form to divergent long run national trajectories. Viewed in this vein, economic effects like the Dutch disease become outcomes of particular institutional arrangements and not simply causes of economic decline." This reasoning makes no sense because the disease has strictly economic causes: it is definitely not caused by poor institutions. It could make sense if we assumed that the role of institutions and government was to face and resolve any economic problem that emerges, no matter how serious it is. Yet this kind of counterfactual argument likewise makes no sense. The Dutch disease is a serious illness in the midst of plenty. In most countries, it arises when the country is still very poor, its society shows little cohesiveness, and its institutions are weak. In the beginning, it appears like manna from heaven: its negative aspects are not yet evident because the country has no possibility of diversifying its economy. As times go on, however, the country gradually sees itself in a trap. Instead of its natural resources causing growth, they overvalue the local currency, which then turns into a major obstacle to growth: an obstacle that, as we will see, is very difficult to overcome, given the economic and political problems involved. Thus, instead of causing growth, the new wealth causes rent seeking and becomes a major source of and stimulus to corruption. The problem is different when a rich country like the Netherlands or Norway discovers natural resources as such countries have more political resources to tackle the problem and neutralize it, so that the currency does not become overvalued or wages artificially high. This fact, however, does not justify the claim that the Dutch disease is a political problem. Although the problem of corruption exists in all countries and is more serious in poor countries rich in natural resources, I do not discuss this issue further here and do not recognize any difference between the Dutch disease and the natural resources curse because I wish to emphasize the purely economic nature of the Dutch disease. It is well known that in poor countries, the state and other institutions are weak and governments are much more likely to face political instability. It is also well known that when a poor country is rich in mineral resources, it is more likely to become trapped by corruption and civil war increases. The studies by Collier (2007) and Collier and Hoeffler (2004) are conclusive in this respect. The basic cause of political instability, civil war, corruption, and the lack of democracy in poor countries is that they are precapitalist countries, where the control of the state is a necessary condition for the appropriation of an economic surplus. Thus, governments will tend to be authoritarian and corrupt and will be permanently under siege by rebel groups, which are sometimes composed of republican rebels but, more often, are just other political and social groups aiming to replace the governing group in appropriating the economic surplus. It is for that reason that poor countries face the so-called poverty trap. Yet the way conventional orthodoxy usually treats the Dutch disease is unacceptable. It either does not focus on the exchange rate overvaluation and downplays the disease aspect implied in the veto to industrialization, as, for instance, we see in Lederman and Maloney (2007), or, as we have already seen, it reduces the Dutch disease to a political problem by emphasizing the corruption aspect and playing down the purely economic aspect. Although Sachs and Warner (1999) were able to demonstrate the disease econometrically, other authors have developed other tests aiming to demonstrate that the disease or the curse does not exist, as do Lederman and Maloney (2007). This chapter does not discuss these findings and counterfindings. It is a theoretical chapter that has as background the history principally of oil-exporting countries that, on one hand, are blessed by their natural wealth but, on the other, are cursed by it to the extent that they are unable to genuinely industrialize and develop a diversified economic and social structure. In opting for a theoretical approach, I am not disregarding research but just saying that in this case, econometric research has a secondary role: on one hand, because the disease is obvious and, on the other, because many countries neutralize it partially or fully. I know that the Dutch disease creates scope for corruption, but I likewise avoid discussing this (also obvious) problem because I do not want to divert my attention from the crucial market failure involved, and I wish to emphasize the serious economic consequences of the Dutch disease. The existence of natural resources is essentially a benefit, but if the central consequence of the disease – the overvaluation of the currency – is not neutralized, the benefit turns into a curse.

TWO EQUILIBRIUM EXCHANGE RATES

The central idea in this chapter is that when the Dutch disease exists, even the goods produced with state-of-the-art technology are not viable economically in a competitive market. If a high-tech company sets up in a country affected by this disease (all the other factors of competitiveness being equal), it will be viable only if its productivity is greater than that achieved by competing countries, at the same or greater degree than the appreciation caused by the disease. This fact leads to the conclusion that in countries suffering from the Dutch disease, there are two equilibrium exchange rates: the current equilibrium exchange rate – the one that balances intertemporally a country's current account and is therefore also the market rate, the rate on which the market converges – and the industrial equilibrium exchange rate, which is the one that enables the production of tradable goods in the country without the need for duties and subsidies (we presume here that the other external determinants of companies' productivity are equal); in other words, it is the exchange rate that, on average, allows companies using state-of-the-art technology to be profitable or competitive. In this chapter, these two rates are always conceived in nominal terms: there is no need to talk about a real exchange rate because only the difference or the relationship between the two equilibrium rates is of significance. Yet we have to distinguish the nominal exchange rate from the *effective-effective* exchange rate, the latter being understood not only as the result of using a currency basket instead of a single hard or reserve currency to calculate it (which would attract just one adjective, *effective*) but also as the average exchange rate that results from taking into account the import duties and export subsidies to which the goods are subject.

If we name ε_c the current equilibrium exchange rate and ε_i the industrial equilibrium exchange rate, in a country without the Dutch disease, the two rates will be identical:

$$\varepsilon_c = \varepsilon_i,$$

whereas in a country with the Dutch disease, the current equilibrium exchange rate will be more appreciated than the industrial equilibrium exchange rate. If we measure the exchange rate as the price of the local currency in terms of the reserve currency, the more competitive it is, the higher the rate will be; the more appreciated it is, the lower the exchange rate will be.[2] Accordingly, in the presence of the Dutch disease, the current equilibrium exchange rate will be less than the industrial equilibrium exchange rate:

$$\varepsilon_c < \varepsilon_i.$$

The current equilibrium exchange rate in a country affected by the Dutch disease is determined by the marginal cost in domestic currency of the good that gives rise to it (marginal cost is here understood as the cost of the least efficient producers that manage to export). This cost is equal to the price in domestic currency that all producers, including the marginal or least effective producer that manages to export, accept to be able to export. When the Dutch disease occurs, this price is substantially less than the necessary price, that is, the price that makes it economically profitable to produce other tradable goods using state-of-the-art technology. It is therefore a lower price than the one that would be necessary for the current equilibrium exchange rate to be identical to the industrial equilibrium exchange rate. As long as this domestic marginal cost is less than the necessary price, as defined previously, and as long as the participation of that commodity in the country's export portfolio is relevant, the market's exchange rate (which is also the current equilibrium exchange rate) converges on a level consistent with the profitability of that commodity and not on a level compatible with the competitiveness of any industrial sector using state-of-the-art technology. The lower the marginal cost, and thus the market price, of the exported good as compared with the necessary price, the higher the Ricardian rent is, and the more appreciated the country's currency will be. Because the Ricardian rents obtained differ from country to country, depending on the productivity provided by their natural resources,

---

[2] We are here defining the exchange rate as the price in national currency of the basket of currencies.

the Dutch disease affects countries to different degrees or intensities. The greater the difference in productivity of every product that gives rise to the disease as compared with its necessary price, the greater the currency's overvaluation will be, and thus the more serious the Dutch disease will be.

The factors determining the necessary price of that commodity (always in domestic currency) are, on one hand, the average productivity of the tradable goods using state-of-the-art technology but not benefiting from natural resources, which defines the industrial equilibrium exchange rate, and, on the other hand, the variations in the international price of such goods. If there is a Ricardian rent (resulting from differences in productivity and from the existence of an international market price corresponding to the least efficient producer), the necessary price will be higher than the market price, or in other words, the current equilibrium exchange rate will be more appreciated than the industrial equilibrium exchange rate. The Ricardian rents that each country earns by making the market price lower than the necessary price determine the intensity or the severity of its Dutch disease. We must emphasize that the difference between the real price and the necessary price should be large and constant enough so that we can talk about a Dutch disease. Otherwise, it would be present whenever there was a comparative advantage and therefore whenever there was trade.

As defined previously, the market price, p_m, of the commodity will be proportional to the current equilibrium exchange rate, whereas the necessary price, p_n, will be proportional to the industrial equilibrium exchange rate:

$$p_m :: \varepsilon_c$$
$$p_n :: \varepsilon_i.$$

Given a marginal cost or market price, $p_m p_m$, in domestic currency, and an international price, p_x, the current equilibrium exchange rate, in countries where there is no Dutch disease, ε_c, will be identical to p_m/p_x, or simply equal to ε_i:

$$\varepsilon_c = \varepsilon_i.$$

The intensity of the Dutch disease can be measured by the ratio between this country's current equilibrium exchange rate and its industrial equilibrium exchange rate as well as by the ratio between the market price and the necessary price. Let us take the second one. In this case, the intensity of the Dutch disease, dh, will be

$$dh = [1 - (p_m/p_n)] \times 100.$$

The intensity of the Dutch disease, therefore, is always

$$0 \leq dh \leq 1.$$

Let us assume three countries: country Z_1, which exploits oil at a marginal cost or at a market price corresponding to 20 percent of the price the product should have if the exchange rate corresponded to the industrial equilibrium exchange rate, that is, the necessary price; country Z_2, which still exploits oil, but whose marginal cost is 50 percent of the necessary price; and country Z_3, which exports a combination of products such as iron, oil, ethanol, wood, orange juice, and soybean at a cost equivalent to 80 percent of the average necessary price. In these three cases, the intensity of the Dutch disease is, respectively, 80 percent, 50 percent, and 20 percent.

In Z_1 as much as in Z_2, the intensity of the Dutch disease is so high that there will be no room for the production of any other internationally tradable good. Yet Z_3 can keep the domestic market, and even export, if it has very efficient enterprises.

However, the intensity of the Dutch disease, besides being different from country to country, will be different within each country, depending on the international price of the good or goods that give rise to it.

The higher the international prices of a commodity, the more appreciated the current equilibrium exchange rate will be and the more serious the Dutch disease will be. For the goods exported by Z_3, there may be a huge increase in international prices because of, for instance, an increase in the demand for those goods. In this case, let us assume that the current equilibrium exchange rate in that country was 2.20 and falls to 1.90 units of local currency per reserve currency, that is, that it represents not 80 percent but 69.1 percent of the industrial equilibrium exchange rate. In this case, the Dutch disease worsens, going from 20 percent to 30.9 percent.

Briefly, if we assume that for all countries, the industrial equilibrium exchange rate is equal to 100, the lower the current equilibrium exchange rate is compared with this level, the more serious the Dutch disease will be. This severity or intensity will depend on Ricardian rents, which, in turn, will depend on the difference in productivity and on the variations in the goods' international price.

Neutralization

If we take into account not the possession but the exploitation of natural resources, the countries that commercially exploited their natural resources more were those that developed less. Since World War II, Asian non-oil-exporting countries grew more than Latin American non-oil-exporting countries, and these latter grew more than all the oil-exporting developing countries. Mineral-rich African countries, in effect, did not grow. Many factors have certainly contributed to this outcome, but given the weight of the Dutch disease in hindering industrialization and growth, we may generalize and assert that the richer the country in natural resources, the smaller the probability is that it will be able to successfully neutralize it. Evidently, it was easier to neutralize the Dutch disease in Asia than in Latin America and Africa and easier in non-oil-producing countries than in oil-producing ones.

The neutralization of the Dutch disease always involves managing the exchange rate – which is not incompatible with a floating exchange rate. In terms of exchange rate regime, there is a reasonable consensus nowadays in favor of a floating but managed exchange rate. The fixed exchange rate alternative has been discarded, but this does not mean that the exchange rate should or could be left to the market's whim, or that a managed exchange rate (which is widely practiced) should be called a "dirty exchange rate." The pragmatic solution is to reject the "fix or float" alternatives and to manage the exchange rate to prevent its appreciation, whether by keeping the domestic interest rate at a low level, by acquiring international reserves, by levying taxes on the goods that cause the Dutch disease, or during temporary periods by imposing controls on capital inflows. The first two of these four mechanisms are adopted by virtually all countries, even though they do not admit that they are managing their exchange rates. The third is necessary only for countries that face the Dutch disease. The fourth is a measure to be adopted only in situations of excessive pressure on the local currency to appreciate. Conventional economics naturally rejects the idea of managing the exchange rate. The countries that have international reserve currencies are those that are less able to manage their exchange rates because this would reduce the confidence of financial agents. Probably for this reason, conventional economics attaches much less significance to the exchange rate than it actually has and denies the possibility of managing the exchange rate in the medium term, despite all the historical evidence to the contrary.

The neutralization of the Dutch disease can be achieved in full by adopting two measures. First, a tax or contribution should be imposed on the sale of the goods that give rise to it.[3] This tax should correspond to the difference between the current equilibrium exchange rate and the industrial equilibrium exchange rate so that the supply curve of the

---

[3] The tax cannot be imposed only on exports because this would imply an artificial diversion of production to the domestic market.

product shifts up to the level of industrial equilibrium. Second, neutralization is completed by the creation of an international fund with the revenues derived from this tax; the fund will prevent the inflow of tax revenues reappreciating the exchange rate. This is essentially what Norway did after it discovered and began to export oil from the North Sea. Britain, which discovered oil at the same time, did not neutralize the Dutch disease, and its economy suffered the consequences (Chatterji and Price 1988). Chile also adequately neutralizes the Dutch disease by heavily taxing copper exports, but this is a partial neutralization because the revenue from the tax is not directed to the establishment of an international fund. Every oil-producing country taxes its exports, but usually at a level that is unable to neutralize the Dutch disease. Usui (1998) studied the cases of Indonesia and Mexico and showed that whereas Indonesia adequately neutralized the Dutch disease, Mexico did not. Greater fiscal discipline in Indonesia made it possible for this country to buy and sterilize reserves to prevent an exchange rate appreciation, paying a very low interest rate for such acquisitions.

The direct way of neutralizing the Dutch disease is through a tax on sales and exports. The desired effect of the tax is microeconomic: it shifts upward the supply curve of the good, causing the disease to raise its marginal cost approximately to the level of that of other goods. I say approximately because there is no simple way of estimating the necessary rate of this tax. The tax rate, m, must be enough to cancel or eliminate the Dutch disease. Therefore, it must be equal to the intensity of the Dutch disease divided by the ratio between the current equilibrium exchange rate and the industrial equilibrium exchange rate of this product:

$$m = dh/[e_c/e_i].$$

For country Z_3, for instance, at the initial situation in which e_c/e_i is equal to 0.8, the tax rate must be 25 percent.

The tax or contribution on sales should therefore be different for each product, according to the intensity of the Dutch disease it causes.

Thus, to determine the tax q_i for each product i, we should use the ratio between the market price and the necessary price of each good, which, as we have already seen, are proportional to the two exchange rates. We have therefore

$$q_i = dh/[p_{mi}/p_{ni}].$$

Besides, it should vary over time because the intensity of the Dutch disease will increase or decrease depending on the international price of the good. The law that imposes the tax should leave the tasks of defining this rate and varying it over time to the economic authorities who manage the tax.

According to the terms defined previously, neutralizing the Dutch disease appears to be a simple task, but in practice, it can be very difficult, first of all because the government will have to face the resistance of exporters of the commodities giving rise to the Dutch disease. This resistance is usually great, although it is irrational because the purpose of the tax is not to reduce the sector's profitability but rather to maintain it and eventually make it even more stable, as long as the revenues from the tax, besides constituting an international fund so that their inflow to the country does not put pressure on the exchange rate, should also be used as an exchange rate stabilization fund. To maintain profitability, the tax can be only marginal: it should be applied only to gains resulting from the depreciation achieved by the tax or, preferably, by temporary measures of control inflow. When the tax is created and the product's supply curve in local currency shifts upward, this movement causes depreciation so that the amount the exporter pays in tax is returned as an increase in revenue in local currency. On the assumption that this depreciation is obtained mainly by a transitory imposition of inflow controls, the export tax will later ensure that the exchange rate stabilizes at the industrial equilibrium level. Of course, there is a problem here of transition costs from one position to another, which must be taken into account and offset by the government. On the other hand, if the country has a significant weight (market share) in the international supply of the good, the tax can also have the effect of increasing its international price. This effect would probably be small but cannot be neglected because the increase in international prices due to the tax worsens the Dutch disease that the tax aims to neutralize.

Second, the tax faces a macroeconomic difficulty because it implies a transitory rise in inflation. However, provided that there is no formal or informal indexation of the economy, the prices will subsequently stabilize. A cooling down of the economy during transition may reduce this transitory increase in inflation but will not eliminate it.

A third and fundamental problem is the decrease in wages caused by the depreciation of the local currency. Effective depreciation minus inflation or real depreciation is, by definition, a change in relative prices in favor of tradable goods, whose prices increase as compared with the prices of nontradable goods. Whereas the currency is overvalued because of the Dutch disease, wages are artificially high because people directly benefit from the Ricardian rent.[4] The creation of a tax that neutralizes the Dutch disease by appreciating the domestic currency implies, therefore, a decrease in the actual returns on labor and on real property rents, even after they are corrected for inflation. It also implies a relative decrease in the revenues of the producers of nontradable goods, such as the hotel industry and the building industry, which gain smaller shares in the national income. In other words, while the Dutch disease was operating, the country's Ricardian rents were not only being captured by commodity producers but were benefiting all local consumers, who were buying tradable goods at lower prices. When the tax is imposed,

---

[4] One can naturally argue that by keeping the exchange rate depreciated, the country is internally producing sophisticated goods that could be imported at a lower price, hence the consumer surplus, but this is not the case. The country is producing all the goods with state-of-the-art technology, and there is no protection. Wage earners or consumers, however, lose in the short run in terms of well-being because this is the condition for neutralizing the Dutch disease.

the Ricardian rents remain in the country, but they now become state revenue. We understand, therefore, that from a political point of view, it is not easy to impose this tax.

In the fourth place, not many countries have, as Norway and the United Arab Emirates[5] do, the political conditions for allocating the whole revenue from the tax to offshore funds as well to a stabilization fund of exported commodities. In less developed countries, the tax is generally used for fiscal purposes because its existence reduces the government's ability to finance its expenses with the direct and indirect taxes used by all countries. This is the case with Chile, for instance. However, although we should not confuse this fund with reserves obtained by countries with domestic indebtedness, the formation of those reserves is an indication that, after all, the creation of neutralizing funds is not as difficult as we might imagine.

It is understandable, therefore, that countries severely affected by the Dutch disease, such as Saudi Arabia or Venezuela, have difficulty neutralizing it. All the oil-exporting countries encumber oil exports with taxes, but usually the tax has merely fiscal purposes, and the tax rate is unable to compensate for the overvaluation caused by the disease. The state lacks the power to levy a higher tax, whether because even the exporting companies of the goods resist it or because the population as a whole resists the increase in the prices of all tradable goods, both imported and locally produced, caused by the depreciation. Besides, the state ends up using the resources to finance its current expenses, rather than to set up an offshore financial fund, on account of the economic agents' resistance to paying taxes.

Once the Dutch disease is neutralized by the tax and the creation of the international fund, the two equilibrium exchange rates become

---

[5] The United Arab Emirates is the country that imposes the highest tax on oil production: 98%. Only this explains why it is so able to build financial and, principally, tourism industries (tradable industries).

reasonably identical. The country will be living its everyday life as any other country and will be using its Ricardian rents to build up an offshore fund that will yield future benefits.

We may identify two incidences of the Dutch disease. In the one case, it has always existed and prevented industrialization, as in oil-producing countries; in the other, a country has for a while succeeded in neutralizing the disease and therefore developed but, at a certain time, in the name of a radical liberalism, eliminated the mechanisms of neutralization and began to grow at very slow rates, as in Latin American countries that underwent liberalizing reforms without replacing the old system of duties and subsidies by a more rational system of taxes on sales of commodities giving rise to the disease.

The most important symptoms of the Dutch disease are exchange rate overvaluation, slow growth of the manufacturing sector, fast increase in the services sector, high average wages, and unemployment (Oomes and Kalcheva 2007). As the Dutch disease is a market failure on the demand side, limiting investment opportunities in the manufacturing industry, it exists only when there is unemployment of a country's human resources, or in other words when a country meets the technical and administrative conditions for investing in the production of goods with more sophisticated technology and higher wages but the prevailing exchange rate prevents those investments from being made. Notwithstanding unemployment, the Dutch disease implies artificially high wages. However, wages may also be low because the national work force is abundant and unorganized. The distribution of Ricardian rents involved in the Dutch disease will vary from country to country, depending therefore on the rent-seeking ability of the various groups.

Countries affected by the Dutch disease either have been exporting a natural resource for a long time but never achieved industrialization or achieved industrialization for some time but later engaged in a process of premature deindustrialization. In the first case, the country has never neutralized the Dutch disease, which takes on a relatively permanent quality. The obvious symptom is the fact that this country does not produce tradable goods other than those that benefit from the Ricardian rents of the Dutch disease. This is certainly the case with country Z_1 and probably Z_2. If the country already is a significant producer and exporter of natural resources, which has allowed it to accumulate capital and to have a significant entrepreneurial class, but does not have a tradable industry sector, this is a sign that it is severely affected by the Dutch disease. Saudi Arabia and Venezuela are good examples.

In the second case, the country has abundant natural resources and exports them, but even so, it has achieved industrialization and therefore neutralized the Dutch disease – usually making use of import duties and export subsidies. However, under international pressure, accused of protectionism, this country has abandoned neutralization in the name of trade liberalization despite the fact that there was, in fact, no protectionism in those duties, but rather, mere neutralization of a market failure. As a consequence of liberalization, the effective-effective exchange rate actually appreciates, if when measuring the exchange rate before liberalization we take into account the duties and subsidies that actually made it more depreciated. The appreciation is not immediately perceived because it is disguised by the fact that part of the appreciation results from the elimination of duties and subsidies. Yet the country's manufacturing sector soon begins to suffer the effects of the appreciation, and premature deindustrialization is under way. If the disease is not very intense, as in the case of country Z_3, the symptoms of deindustrialization will not be clear, although they would be reflected in the decreased participation of the manufacturing sector in the domestic product and net exports (in terms of value added).

If the country abandons neutralization with or without an increase in international prices, it will be able to maintain manufacturing sectors and tradable services only with a zero import duty if the severity of the Dutch disease is low enough to be compensated by the country's possible productivity edge over its international competitors. Generally, however, the now overvalued exchange rate will gradually compromise the tradable sectors, one by one. Faced with the facts that their foreign sales are no longer lucrative and that the importation of competing goods is growing, enterprises will first redouble their efforts to increase productivity, then they will reduce or suspend exports or increase the share of imported components in their production to reduce costs; ultimately, as this process continues, they will become mere importers and manufacturers of the good they reexport or sell on the domestic market. In other words, the country's manufacturing industry gradually becomes a maquiladora, or just a maquila industry.[6] Deindustrialization is under way. The sales of manufacturing companies, and even of their exports, may continue to earn high values, but their value added will decrease, as will their value added per capita, as we see later, because the components with greater technological content will be increasingly imported.

At this point, conventional economists and people associated with short-term interests in maintaining the system refuse to accept the diagnosis that deindustrialization is taking place and that its cause is the Dutch disease, and this predictable refusal constitutes another symptom of the Dutch disease. They then begin to develop empirical refutations of the diagnosis. More radical economists will declare that even if deindustrialization is taking place, it does not prevent economic growth. Yet not only the data but also the very logic of exchange rate appreciation without a decrease in the foreign trade surplus indicate that the Dutch disease is present and having an effect.

---

[6] The maquiladoras are originally the manufacturing enterprises that were created on the United States–Mexico border to profit from cheap labor. The production processes transferred to Mexico were very simple, not requiring skilled labor nor contributing to technological development.

Another symptom of the Dutch disease and of premature deindustrialization, besides the decreased share of the manufacturing sector in the national product, the increase in the imported components in production, and the relative decrease in exports of manufactured goods measured in terms of value added, is the gradual decrease in the export of high value-added goods. As in the participation of exports of manufactured goods in general, the participation of manufactured goods with high technological content in imports is misleading because gross exports (not including imports of inputs) of companies in the process of transformation into maquilas remain high; what decreases is their participation in terms of value added, the data for which are not always available. The reason why goods with high technological content are more affected by the Dutch disease, however, will become clear only in light of the concept of the extended Dutch disease. Yet, even though it has the same outcome, we must not to confuse this process of transformation of the country's manufacturing industry into a maquila industry as a consequence of the Dutch disease with a more general process, which is the division of labor at the international level, which I discussed in Chapter 1. Through this process, tasks with more value added per capita and demanding more skilled labor, acquired mainly by managers and communicators, are performed in rich countries, which have plenty of this kind of labor, whereas standardized or codified tasks are transferred to low-wage workers in developing countries. This process of the division of labor that gives birth to maquila business enterprises, such as those that have long been installed on the Mexican–United States border, results from the quantity of low-skilled labor available in the country. However, when the country begins to raise the quality of its labor, if the exchange rate becomes overvalued on account of the Dutch disease, this work force will not find employment. And if the country, as was the case with Mexico and the remainder of its manufacturing industry, was already industrialized but renounced the mechanisms for neutralizing the Dutch disease, the result is that this large group of enterprises will also gradually become maquila companies. As it usually turns out, the developing country already has the necessary technological conditions to perform more complex activities in its territory but does not achieve them or fails to achieve them because the Dutch disease is causing an overvaluation of its exchange rate. In this case, the country is limited to low-technological-content processes. Work processes that require higher skills are reserved for rich countries on the assumption that developing countries lack this kind of labor, but this is often not the case, and high unemployment rates of skilled personnel are observed in those countries.

STAGES

The Dutch disease has existed since the commercial revolution and the emergence of an international market. Spain's backwardness from the seventeenth century was certainly caused by the gold it collected from its colonies. Yet this cause was identified only in the 1960s, and only lately has it begun to be discussed. How can we explain, then, that countries that were victims of the Dutch disease have been able to industrialize, when economists and politicians were not aware of it? To answer this question, we must distinguish the roles of the natural resources that give rise to it in two stages. In a first stage, the exploitation of natural resources is a blessing because it enables the country to take part in international trade, to promote early capital accumulation, to establish a minimum economic infrastructure, and to foster the emergence of a capitalist entrepreneurial class. It is the existence of these resources that makes it possible for a precapitalist economy or for an economy that is incipiently a mercantile capitalist one to become a true capitalist economy. It is usually with those resources that the country penetrates world markets, performs its primitive capital accumulation, and creates an entrepreneurial class. Even in this condition, the country is supposed to tax the Ricardian rents so that these rents do not accrue just to the commodities' producers and to local consumers (whose wages

169

increase artificially with the overvalued currency) but may be used to develop strategic industries. Yet, as the country develops the conditions for industrialization on the supply side, and thus potential conditions for the efficient production of manufactured goods, the Dutch disease becomes a fundamental obstacle. In this second stage, the country faces the challenge of industrializing or, more generally, of developing a broad range of internationally tradable products with increasingly more value added per capita, and the Ricardian rents derived from goods based on natural resources become the Dutch disease, as I have described it.

If we abandon this oversimplified concept of two stages and imagine that when a country begins to develop, it will gradually achieve technical competence, we may also reduce the requirements to characterize the Dutch disease. The Dutch disease will exist whenever a country has at least one manufacturing industry with state-of-the-art technology. On the other hand, we may presume that the more technologically advanced a sector is, the more obvious the need to neutralize the Dutch disease will be. Once we define the Dutch disease in these terms, we accept the assumption that the transition of a purely commodity-producing economy using abundant and cheap resources to a more advanced economy implies the recognition of the Dutch disease and the gradual adoption of mechanisms to neutralize it. It also implies admitting that instead of two stages, as in Lewis's (1954) model, we have several stages that are characterized by the degree of technological sophistication. In each of them, the neutralization of the Dutch disease through the imposition of a tax will be necessary, but the method of using the tax revenues will be different. In the first stages, the government will use the tax to set up the country's infrastructure and public education system and to create a stabilization fund for the taxed commodities – that is, it will try to promote economic development on the supply side and to stabilize the production of the export good. In more advanced stages, when serious problems no longer exist on the supply side and government prefers to reduce its degree of intervention in the economy, as in Norway, it will experience fiscal surpluses that will enable it to create an international or sovereign fund to avoid additional pressures on the exchange rate. Some countries, such as Chile and the United Arab Emirates, adopt middle-of-the-road policies in this matter.[7]

When the country starts industrializing, economic growth will depend on the neutralization of the disease. This is what happened in all the countries in Latin America and Asia that industrialized in the twentieth century. Latin American countries, for instance, have abundant natural resources, both mineral and agricultural, that allowed them to set up sectors to produce and export primary goods. However, from 1930 onward, when this approach had exhausted its possibilities and the challenge was industrialization, these countries were successful in meeting that challenge. Between 1930 and 1980, Mexico and Brazil, in particular, industrialized and grew extraordinarily fast because they adopted policies that neutralized the Dutch disease (Palma 2005). Their politicians and economists ignored the existence of the Dutch disease but, at several moments, made use of multiple exchange rates or complex systems of import duties combined with export subsidies, which addressed the problem by depreciating the currency for the producers of industrial goods. First, they imposed import duties based on the Hamilton–List theory of infant industry and considering also the Prebisch–Singer–Furtado theory of the tendency of the terms of trade to deteriorate. In fact, the import duty is a partial but effective way of neutralizing the Dutch disease: it merely protects manufacturing industry against foreign imports but does not allow it to export; in other words, the import duty neutralizes the Dutch disease for the purposes of the domestic market, not of exports. When the Dutch disease exists, the import duty can be considered as a manifestation of a country's protectionism only if the

---

[7] In Argentina, there is a tax on the goods that cause the Dutch disease, but in addition to the money being used to finance current state expenditures, the tax is only on exports; domestic consumption is exempted, which makes it politically more acceptable but creates imbalances between relative prices.

tax rate is higher than the rate necessary to neutralize this market failure; if this is not the case, the tariff is just partially correcting a market failure.

Second, many countries have subsidized the export of manufactured goods. When they had already reached a reasonable degree of industrialization, Brazil and Mexico, for instance, realized that they could compete internationally if they established subsidies for exports of manufactured goods. In fact, they were not subsidizing exports but merely neutralizing the Dutch disease on the export side, just as import tariffs neutralize it on the import side. This way, once again, they were depreciating the effective exchange rate for export purposes to compensate for the appreciation caused by the Dutch disease. When a country levies import taxes on virtually all imported goods and establishes subsidies for the export of manufactured goods, it is, in practice, establishing a tax on the commodities that use natural resources and give rise to the Dutch disease. It is a disguised way (actually poorly disguised) of taxing those goods and therefore of neutralizing the Dutch disease, but it is often the only feasible way from a political point of view. In Brazil, for instance, in the 1970s, when there was considerable economic growth and a huge increase in exports of manufactured goods, the exchange rate system was roughly as follows: all goods paid nearly 50 percent of import duty and all manufactured goods received an export subsidy of nearly 50 percent, whereas export commodities continued to have the nominal exchange rate appreciated by the Dutch disease. On the assumption that this nominal exchange rate, which was also the current equilibrium exchange rate, was 66.66 and that the industrial equilibrium exchange rate was 100, the tax implicit in the system of duties and subsidies that raised the real exchange rate to 100 was 50 percent.

A duly negotiated and directly established export tax would be more rational because it would be much easier to manage, given the relatively small number of exported commodities, but an export tax faced, or seemed to face, more political difficulties than the adopted system. It only seemed to face them because this system never fooled anyone: coffee growers were always protesting against the so-called exchange rate confiscation.

THE EXTENDED CONCEPT OF THE DUTCH DISEASE

The Dutch disease does not affect only countries that exploit natural resources. Another source of the Dutch disease that is becoming significant is represented by remittances from immigrants; Central American countries are particularly affected by it (Acosta et al. 2007). Even foreign aid may also be generating the Dutch disease in the poorest countries. But besides these additional causes, there is one that dramatically increases its extension. I now argue that we may expand the concept of the Dutch disease to include as one of its causes the existence of cheap labor. If this is true, the Dutch disease becomes an even more general and more serious market failure. Countries like China or India would also have the Dutch disease and would develop only if they neutralized it by managing their exchange rates. This is exactly what those countries and, more broadly, the dynamic Asian countries do.

As for the extended Dutch disease, we must take into account the problem of economic growth effected by the transfer of labor from sectors with lower value added to sectors with higher value added. I have said that in the case of the restricted Dutch disease, this was not strictly necessary because the goods giving rise to the Dutch disease are not necessarily produced with less scientific and technological intensity than others. However, in the case of the extended Dutch disease, this problem exists by definition. Goods produced with cheap labor are basically goods that use low-skilled labor and therefore are products with less technological intensity.

The existence of cheap labor does not generate Ricardian rents, but its consequences are similar to those originating in cheap natural resources, provided that cheap labor is combined with a wide *wage spread*. The necessary condition for cheap labor as a cause of the Dutch disease is that the wage spread is substantially wider than in rich countries – a condition that is usually present because in developing countries the difference between the salaries of engineers and the wages of blue-collar workers tends to be very great.[8] Industries using mainly cheap labor have a lower marginal cost than more technologically sophisticated industries. As a consequence, the exchange rate tends to converge on the level that makes it profitable to export goods that use cheap labor. When this happens – and given that the wages of the more skilled workers and managers are disproportionally higher – goods using more sophisticated technology and more expensive labor will be economically compromised. Wages paid in more sophisticated industries shall be necessarily higher because they use more skilled labor. If the wage difference between an unskilled worker and an engineer, for instance, were approximately three to four times, as it is in rich countries, the country would produce, with cheap labor, all kinds of goods with no difficulties but technical and administrative ones. However, if this wage spread is wider, say, ten to twelve times, then the extended Dutch disease will exist and will become a serious obstacle to economic growth because industries with higher technological content need a higher exchange rate than the current equilibrium exchange rate determined by the market.

The extended concept of the Dutch disease is not the only reason but is certainly a fundamental one why dynamic Asian countries manage their exchange rates so rigorously, preventing its appreciation. China, for instance, would never be in the business of increasingly sophisticated exports without managing its exchange rate. By doing that, it keeps the exchange rate at the necessary level – that is, at the industrial equilibrium exchange rate level – that makes its sophisticated manufacturing industries economically viable.

[8] Thus, we can say that the people receiving the high wages are actually benefiting from a kind of Ricardian rent.

DAMAGE?

So far, I have assumed that specialization in the production of commodities that deliver substantial Ricardian rents is a disease. Yet, according to neoclassical thinking, it is not wrong for a country to specialize exclusively in the exploitation of its natural resources. It is just benefiting from its comparative advantage and allocating its resources where they are most profitable. In these terms, industrialization would not be necessary for economic growth. Here I do not discuss this argument, which already has a long history in economic theory – particularly in the Latin American structuralist school and in the development economics school. I merely observe that a developed country, such as the Netherlands, does not seem to have reasoned along these lines because it identified the problem as a disease that was killing its manufacturing industry. I also do not believe that this was Norwegians' view when they decided to competently neutralize this disease.

The Dutch disease is an obstacle to economic development on the demand side insofar as an overvalued currency precludes investment. When a medium-income country is threatened by the Dutch disease, it is demand for the entire local manufacturing industry that is under threat. To assume that the country can incur premature deindustrialization and fall back to the condition of specialization in natural-resource-intensive industries without major costs is not realistic. Second, when specialization in natural resources takes place in a country because it is economically unfeasible to implement economic activities other than those involving nontradable goods and services, we are in the presence of a disease because, in this situation, the country is limiting its ability to create jobs and giving up the production of any goods with more value added per capita than those existing in the commodities that it produces and exports.

Before my basic article on the Dutch disease (Bresser Pereira 2008), I argued that the Dutch disease precluded an increase in productivity because it barred the transfer of members of the work force to sectors with more value added per capita. This claim, however, wrongly presupposes that the value added per capita of the good that gives rise to the Dutch disease has a lower technological content than the average of industrial goods. Although the value added per capita of agricultural and mining production is traditionally less than that of industrial production and exportable services, this need not be the case. There is no reason for agricultural and mining production to be intrinsically less productive or less effective than manufacturing production. Besides, we have been observing, since the 1970s, huge worldwide growth in agricultural productivity, and at the same time, mining production has become increasingly technologically sophisticated. However, even if this exploitation involves high value added per capita, the country is renouncing other activities that it is already able to carry out with even more scientific and technological content, and – this is even more serious – it is renouncing all the other activities that it could carry out with greater value added per capita. Besides, the Dutch disease exists even if the alternative goods have a value added per capita nearly identical to that of the good that causes the Dutch disease, but their production is necessary to guarantee full employment of the available work force because the goods giving rise to the disease alone are not able to provide this volume of employment.[9]

In a country in which the Dutch disease arises mainly from agricultural commodities, supporters of these commodities argue that we must also take into account the industrial production that they generate. This is undoubtedly true. Given transportation costs, commodity-producing countries will tend to have an advantage in producing the industrialized good. However, the Dutch disease has an effect on this industrial production as well: although affecting this kind of manufacturing industry

---

[9] It should be noted, therefore, that I am not taking into account a number of other effects engendered by dependence on the commodity giving rise to the Dutch disease such as concentration of political and economic power, an increase in the economy's vulnerability, and distributive issues among the various sectors of society.

less intensely than the other kinds, it also triggers the regression of the production chain and tends to make profitable only the production of the raw commodity because it is its marginal cost that determines the exchange rate. In the case of mineral resources, it is also important to remember that they are exhaustible.

Thus, Ricardian rents that originate in cheap natural and human resources are a major source of growth for developing countries or, more precisely, for all countries deriving such rents from cheap natural and human resources, provided that they neutralize the Dutch disease. The rents are, in all circumstances, won by the country, but if a sales and export tax neutralizes the disease, this means that these rents will be captured by the state. The question, then, is whether governments will return the revenues to society. They may ideally create international investment funds, as Norway did; they may expend the resources on necessary public investment and in increasing social expenditures, as Argentina is doing; they may use the revenues to lower or keep low other taxes, as is the case in Mexico; and they may privately appropriate some of them, as is usual in the poorest countries, which sadly tend also to be the more corrupt, although corruption happens in any type of country – the difference is that the richer the country, the more active or originated in businesspeople is the corruption, and the poorer the country, the more passive or originated in bureaucrats it will be.

A last but not minor question is what will happen to countries without the Dutch disease if those countries with the disease neutralize it fully. The answer is that they will have no alternative but to experience chronic current account deficits that will be settled by the transference of assets to the countries that neutralized the Dutch disease. This does not mean, naturally, that the rich countries among them will face major problems. They will continue to be rich and grow, but catching up will be taking place. In relation to poor non–Dutch disease countries, the problem is more serious, and the global political system headed by the United Nations will have to face it. Why such chronic current account deficits? Because if the Dutch disease exists when the current exchange rate equilibrium is more appreciated than the industrial exchange rate equilibrium, and if the former equilibrates intertemporally the country's current account, this means that if it neutralizes the disease, depreciating the currency up to the point that the two equilibrium rates are equal, these countries will present large current account surpluses that will have to be compensated by current account deficits in non–Dutch disease countries. Despite the fact that, for the moment, the Dutch disease is only partially neutralized in most countries – many of them do not know about this disease and use export taxes only for fiscal reasons – we are already seeing, among the oil producers, major current account deficits and the formation of huge sovereign investment funds.

CONCLUSION

The Dutch disease is the fundamental component of the tendency toward exchange rate overvaluation that characterizes developing countries. In this chapter, I have tried to (1) define the Dutch disease as clearly and precisely as possible; (2) present the concept of the extended Dutch disease, which does not result from natural resources but rather from cheap labor; (3) show that it is a serious market failure; and (4) discuss how it can be neutralized. The best way to conclude the chapter is to summarize it briefly in a few points:

1. The Dutch disease occurs when there is a relatively permanent over-valuation of the exchange rate resulting from the country's abundant natural resources (restricted concept) or cheap labor (extended concept), whose low marginal cost is consistent with a market exchange rate substantially more appreciated than the industrial equilibrium exchange rate.

2. There are two equilibrium exchange rates: the current equilibrium exchange rate, which balances intertemporally the country's current

account and is therefore the rate the market tends to determine, and the industrial equilibrium exchange rate, which enables industrial sectors using state-of-the-art technology; the Dutch disease occurs when these two equilibria present conflicting values.

3. The symptoms of the Dutch disease in a country are permanent when the country has never produced industrial goods or they result from some new fact that led the already industrialized country to stop neutralizing the disease or, again, from a change in the terms of trade that increases commodities' market price; in the two latter cases, there will be an appreciation of the exchange rate without a reduction in the country's trade surplus, there will be deindustrialization, and the industrial goods–exporting companies will be increasing the imported component in their production to gradually transform the country's manufacturing industry into a maquila industry.

4. The Dutch disease should be neutralized through a tax on domestic sales and on commodity exports that will be different for each commodity, to be proportional to the difference between the current equilibrium exchange rate and the industrial equilibrium exchange rate that is necessary for industrial companies using state-of-the-art technology to be competitive.

5. The more serious the Dutch disease in a country is, the more difficult its neutralization will be, and the lower the probability that the country will industrialize and grow will be.

6. The revenues from the tax created to neutralize the Dutch disease should not be invested in the country (unless they are used to stabilize the prices of commodities on which the tax will be imposed), but rather they should be invested in an international financial fund so that the inflow of revenues does not entail the revaluation of the local currency.

7. Despite the fact that the tax should be imposed only on the marginal revenue obtained by the producers resulting from the depreciation assured by the tax, it is not easy to neutralize the Dutch disease in

view of the resistance to taxation by commodity exporters; on the other hand, depreciation faces resistance from the entire population because it causes temporary inflation and especially because it reduces real wages.

8. Although developing countries have always had the Dutch disease but did not realize it, many have industrialized; the reason is that, in practice, they have neutralized the Dutch disease through the use of multiple exchange rates and through import duties and export subsidies that implied a disguised tax on commodities. They justified these policies with infant industry theories and the deterioration of the terms of trade; however, there is no protectionism when duties merely compensate for the appreciation caused by the Dutch disease.

9. Dutch disease is a serious market failure because its nonneutralized existence implies negative externalities derived from cheap resources.

10. The Dutch disease exists even if the commodities that give rise to it have high technological content, as is currently the case with oil production and with an increasingly technologically sophisticated agriculture; it is an obstacle to growth because mining and agricultural activities are not able to employ the whole labor force and because it implies that the country renounces its opportunities to invest and to innovate in sectors with potentially still greater technological content and therefore with more value added per capita.

11. The Dutch disease may also stem simply from cheap labor; in this extended concept of the Dutch disease, the condition for it to occur is that the wage spread in the developing country is substantially wider than in the rich countries to which the goods would be exported.

12. As for the extended Dutch disease, there is an incompatibility, in principle, between this nonneutralized disease and economic growth because economic growth always depends on the possibility of transferring labor to sectors with more value added per capita – a transfer that is impossible in this case because the more sophisticated manufactured goods necessarily use a more skilled labor force

(whose salaries exceed those of nonskilled workers to a much greater degree than is the case in rich countries).

13. The distinction between the restricted and the extended Dutch disease is theoretical; in practice, both are so integrated that it is impossible to distinguish the effects of each; it is impossible, however, to ignore the dire effects of the Dutch disease on the economies of developing countries.

6

Foreign Savings and Slow Growth*

Economic development relies, on the supply side, on existing natural resources, on the available stock of physical capital, and on the human ability to produce. On the demand side, it relies on capital accumulation, on consumption, and on exports. Supply and demand should grow in a balanced way, but a universal characteristic of capitalist economies is that supply usually exceeds demand so that there is widespread unemployment of human resources. Keynes criticized Say's law, which presupposes an automatic equilibrium between supply and demand, by reference to the possibility of hoarding and the liquidity preference. In this chapter, even if we know that there are other factors determining the underutilization of resources in developing countries, I argue that the central problem is the insufficiency of opportunities for export-oriented investment opportunities, which, in turn, is mainly due to the existence of a tendency toward exchange rate overvaluation in those countries, which discourages investment in the production of tradable goods. This overvaluation stimulates imports and discourages exports, thus limiting new

---

* This chapter was written with Paulo Gala.

182

investments that are essential for sustained domestic aggregate demand. Theorists of economic development usually emphasize limitations on the supply side such as a lack of education, health care, and technical competence as well as a lack of available capital to hire individuals. However, when human resources are idle, it is evident that we need to search for the causes of the bottlenecks of economic growth mainly on the demand side.[1]

In Chapter 5, I discussed the Dutch disease; in this chapter, we show that a second fundamental origin of the insufficiency of demand in developing countries is exchange rate overvaluation caused by the policy of growth with foreign savings, that is, by rich countries' insistence on recommending growth with foreign savings. As a consequence of this policy, developing countries frequently go through three consecutive stages of increasingly worsening economic conditions: first, exchange rate appreciation; second, international financial fragility; and third, balance-of-payment crisis. There is no need to stress the damage resulting from the two latter stages as such damage is self-evident. We merely point out that this damage has been systematically underestimated by the economic policy recommended to developing countries, under the double assumption that the market will take care of the exchange rate and that capital-rich countries should transfer their capital to capital-poor countries. The latter assumption is in line with common sense, but, as we will see, is incorrect. It is not "natural" for capital to be transferred to developing countries, and it is also not true that financial fragility is inevitable in countries that need foreign capital. Developing countries that succeed in catching up are precisely those that do not make these mistakes – those that do not accept economic dependency as inevitable.

[1] A significant empirical contribution to this kind of analysis was recently made by Oreiro et al. (2007).

THE POLICY OF GROWTH WITH FOREIGN SAVINGS

Returning to the main argument of this chapter – the critique of the policy of growth with foreign savings – and leaving aside the two final stages of this policy (increased international financial fragility and balance-of-payment crisis) whose negative aspects are obvious, we limit ourselves to analyzing the first stage: exchange rate appreciation caused by capital flows that enter the countries to finance their current account deficits, that is to say, foreign savings received by them. If it remains clear that the policy of growth with foreign savings implies an exchange rate appreciation, that it causes a high rate of substitution of foreign for domestic savings, with little or no net gain for the country, and therefore that it limits investments destined for exports, it will become clear that the fundamental strategy that conventional orthodoxy offers to developing countries for their development should be abandoned. It is true that the overvalued exchange rate stimulates another component of aggregate demand – domestic consumption – but this incentive results from the artificial increase in real wages caused by the overvaluation and is served by an increase in imports. Unlike Keynes's criticism of markets' inability to ensure equilibrium between supply and aggregate demand – a criticism that is inherent in macroeconomic dynamics regardless of any policy – our analysis of the insufficiency of demand, which is to be added to Keynes's analysis, depends on the acceptance by the developing country of the strategy of growing with foreign savings or of incurring chronic current account deficits; if the country rejects this proposal, there will be no point in referring to insufficiency of demand. Although, in some brief moments, foreign savings could promote economic development, historical experience shows that all developed countries achieved development thanks to their own domestic savings. Yet this empirical observation lacked a theoretical explanation. It is this explanation that we offer in this chapter. Therefore, we criticize the assumption of conventional orthodoxy that economic growth is nothing but a huge

competition between developing countries to obtain rich countries' foreign savings; instead, it will become clear that economic development
should essentially be financed by domestic savings.

Although foreign indebtedness is an ancient problem, the policy
of growth with foreign savings, which implies financial or patrimonial
indebtedness,[2] took on a deliberate quality of a strategy and became
dominant in the 1990s. It was then followed by developing countries'
financial opening and by a huge increase in capital flows into them.
But this strategy was not challenged because the widespread belief that
"capital-rich countries should transfer their capital to poor countries"
was assumed to be true. The economics literature stressed only the
problems related to the opening of the capital account, such as the
high volatility of this kind of capital, or problems related to foreign
indebtedness, such as the concept of original sin, that is, the fact that those
countries cannot, as rich countries do, borrow in their own currency.[3] On
the other hand, in the economic journalistic literature, foreign savings
are usually confused with direct investments. It is not made clear that
direct investments do not necessarily finance current account deficits
(i.e., foreign savings); they may finance an increase in the international
reserves or be a counterpart to the direct investments made by the
country abroad.[4]

The consequences of the policy of growth with foreign savings for the
exchange rate, contributing to its appreciation, have not been challenged
in the economic literature for another reason, besides the assumption
that it is natural for capital-rich countries to transfer their capital to
capital-poor countries: because conventional orthodoxy presupposes

---

[2] We understand *financial indebtedness* as indebtedness that results from foreign loans
and *patrimonial indebtedness* as indebtedness that results from direct investments.

[3] Of this vast literature, I mention here only Calvo et al. (1995), Rodrik (1998), Eichengreen and Leblang (2002), and Eichengreen (2003).

[4] This is the case with fast-growing Asian countries that grow with current account
surpluses: direct investments entering the country are offset by direct investments that
the country's companies make abroad or by an increase in their international reserves.

that the exchange rate cannot be managed in the long run. According to this theory, the only thing that economic policy makers can do is to choose either the fixed exchange rate regime or the floating exchange rate regime. We see it differently: the "fix or float" alternative is a false one, as is the idea that in the long run, the real exchange rate cannot be managed; in practice, within certain limits, and over a reasonable amount of time,[5] countries manage their exchange rates more or less consciously.

In the model that we present in this chapter, this management unconsciously begins with the decision to adopt the policy of growth with foreign savings. When a country accepts this policy, it manages the exchange rate downward (appreciating) because the current account deficit necessarily implies results in a more appreciated exchange rate than the one that would exist in the absence of such a deficit and in the presence of current account equilibrium. On the opposite side, when a country grows with negative foreign savings, that is, with a current account surplus, it will be managing its exchange rate to keep it competitive. It is certain that in many cases, countries that accept the policy of growth with foreign savings do not realize that it implies an appreciated exchange rate, but this lack of awareness does not change the fact that they are managing their exchange rates downward, whether by keeping interest rates high or by accepting capital flows without restriction.

EXCHANGE RATE, WAGES, AND PROFITS

We begin our case with the relations of the national accounts in a stateless economy, in which the output is the sum of investment and

---

[5] The idea that the real exchange rate cannot be managed in the long run is true only if the time interval implicit in this "long run" is very large – more than twenty years – but then the restriction becomes irrelevant. What is important is managing the exchange rate over a reasonable amount of time, which would be under the relative control of the economic policy maker.

consumption, and exports minus imports; gross income is the sum of workers' wages, salaries of the professional middle class, and profits; and the national income is the gross income minus the returns on capital sent abroad. Investment is equal to savings, with investment determining savings on the demand side, and savings financing investment ex post. The income level is determined by the expenditures in consumption, investment, and exports. Foreign savings, that is, savings that a country receives from abroad, are equal to the current account deficit, which, in turn, corresponds to the trade balance plus net returns sent abroad, which depend on the real exchange rate. The more appreciated it is, the smaller the export total and the bigger the import total, and therefore the bigger the current account deficit or foreign savings. Domestic savings are equal to returns on labor and on capital minus consumption.

As a strategic macroeconomic price, the exchange rate does not fully determine foreign savings or the current account deficit only because this deficit depends also on the level of the country's economic activity. Assuming that the country does not face the Dutch disease, we understand that the equilibrium exchange rate is the one that, intertemporally, ensures the equilibrium of the current account.[6] It oscillates around this point because of capital inflows and outflows. If we assume the country's international reserves to be constant, the exchange rate depends on the balance or deficit of the current account, determining it at the same time. From this fact results a crucial consequence for developing economies and for the critique we are developing here: when a country adopts the policy of growth with foreign savings, that is, growth with current account deficits, and finances them, whether with loans or with direct investments, the exchange rate will be appreciated (or overvalued)

---

[6] If the country does suffer the Dutch disease, we already saw that this definition is faulty because at this exchange rate, industries using state-of-the-art technology will not be economically viable.

as compared with the one that would prevail should the country keep the current account balance around zero.[7]

But the exchange rate has another, less discussed consequence. The greater the value of the exchange rate, the greater real wages (of workers) and salaries (of the professional middle class) will be, as long as the price of internationally tradable consumer goods (commodities) decreases with the appreciation of the local currency. As a trade-off, capitalists' profits will fall, whether because, on the income side, wages and salaries grew, or because, on the demand side, national capitalists would be exporting and investing less. Each economy will have a variation in wages and salaries in connection with the exchange rate, which will be greater for each household the greater the consumption of tradable goods and the greater the sensitivity of exports and imports to the exchange rate. In any case, it will be a relatively stable variation, which will be altered only in the long run. Therefore, profits, wages, and salaries, besides substantially depending on the economy's productivity level and on its income distribution pattern, depend on the exchange rate.

How does this relation occur? The profit rate is the opposite of the wage rate. On the assumption that workers receive a nominal wage, and acquire tradable goods and nontradable goods, workers' cost of living will depend on the nominal exchange rate and on the portion of tradable goods in their consumer basket. On the assumption also that prices are formed in the economy according to the known Kaleckian rule that relates price level to nominal wage, to the level of productivity, and to the markup, the real wage will be a function of productivity, of the real exchange rate, and of the markup or pattern of distribution of

---

[7] The existence of a current account deficit is associated with the relative exchange rate appreciation and therefore could involve market pressure to depreciate the exchange rate and to close the deficit. However, because we are talking here of a strategy, this means that the economic authorities are satisfied with the deficit and, especially through a high interest rate policy, try to keep the exchange rate at a relatively appreciated level, consistent with the deficit.

income (Bhaduri and Marglin 1990; Simonsen and Cysne 1995: 452). A devaluation of the real exchange rate with an increase in the price of tradable goods in relation to the nominal wage will mean a decrease in the real wage because the workers' consumer basket will become more expensive. The fundamental restriction to a real devaluation is that a possible rise in nominal wages resulting from nominal devaluation should not exceed the increase in the nominal exchange rate, given the price level. This will happen only if the prices of nontradable goods, especially nominal wages, remain constant or change less than proportionally to the exchange rate variation (Corden 1981: 31–2). Therefore, we are assuming here relative rigidity of nominal wages and flexibility of real wages, rather than flexibility of nominal wages and rigidity of real wages.

As for aggregate profits, we know that they depend on investments, which, in turn, besides depending on the expected profit rate, given the interest rate, depend on exports. Profits decline, therefore, when the exchange rate appreciates and exports drop – the decrease in capitalists' profits being complementary to the increase in wages and salaries of both workers and the professional middle class. Consumption, for its part, depends on real wages and salaries as well as on profits; that is, it depends on income and on the differential between the interest rate and the profit rate. Consumption varies in line with the variation of wages and salaries and the variation of profits and varies inversely to the differential between the expected profit rate and the interest rate. When the policy of growth with foreign savings prevails, the exchange rate will remain at a relatively appreciated level. This causes real wages and salaries to rise and the amount of wages and salaries to remain at an artificially high level (i.e., incompatible with their productivity or with the satisfactory profit rate that keeps the economy growing), whereas profits decline. On the assumption that the effect of the first movement on consumption is greater than the effect of the second one (because the propensity to consume of both workers and the middle class

189

is more than capitalists' propensity to consume), consumption will increase, and will remain high, with the relative currency appreciation reducing domestic savings. Domestic savings are therefore a function of the exchange rate.

It could be argued that the increase in workers' wages in medium-development economies in which a high concentration of income prevails is not something negative and that it will not necessarily reduce the profit rate in case of an insufficiency of demand. First, however, we must stress that wage increases resulting from a decrease in interests, rents, and speculative profits are always welcome; we do not believe, however, that an artificial increase in wages through the overvaluation of the exchange rate could be included among desirable wage increases. Second, we stress that we are reasoning, for the moment, in terms of supply, and therefore we are not presuming an insufficiency of demand. When examining overvaluation on the demand side, we notice that the insufficiency of demand resulting from the currency's excessive appreciation will cause an increase in unemployment. The artificial wage increase will provoke a decrease in employment and income because the production necessary to supply this demand will come from abroad as imports. On this side, the decrease in exports will cause a decrease in investment opportunities or in profit expectations; in investments themselves; and consequently, according to Keynes and Kalecki, in profits and domestic savings. At the same time, on the supply side, the increase in the amount of wages and salaries caused by the exchange rate appreciation will lead, by increasing consumption and decreasing the amount of profits, to a decline in the investment financed by domestic savings. The two movements therefore ratify one another and result in a reduction in investments. However, because there is an inflow of foreign capitals to finance the foreign savings or current account deficits, total investments and the rate of investment may increase, remain constant, or decrease, depending on the rate of substitution of foreign savings for domestic savings.

SUBSTITUTION OF FOREIGN SAVINGS FOR DOMESTIC SAVINGS

Whether foreign savings result in economic growth depends on the rate of substitution of foreign savings for domestic savings. If it is high – and we notice that it usually is – the portion of the current account deficit that becomes investment as opposed to consumption is small, disproportionate to the costs of interest and profit remittances made possible by the transfer of resources. We define this rate z as the variation of the domestic saving rate in relation to gross domestic product (GDP), S_i in relation to the variation of the rate of foreign savings in relation to GDP, S_x:

$$z = \partial S_i / \partial S_x.$$

Let us observe now the variables determining the rate of substitution of foreign savings for domestic savings. For the criticism developed here, although we work with variations in the exchange rate, we are more interested in its level. We are only secondarily interested in the moment of appreciation or depreciation of the exchange rate. What matters most is the level of the exchange rate and of the corresponding foreign savings. Let us assume two periods: t, when foreign savings are zero and the exchange rate is the reference exchange rate or the equilibrium exchange rate, and a period $t + 1$, in which a current account deficit (surplus) appears and the exchange rate is low (high) or appreciated (depreciated). Given this change, the new exchange rate will necessarily be more appreciated. What will be the consequence of this appreciation for investment? On the supply side, the key variable that will influence the amount of the increase in foreign savings that will go to consumption instead of investment, as a result of the exchange rate appreciation and the corresponding increase in wages, is the propensity to consume; the greater this propensity, the greater the portion that will go to consumption and the smaller the portion that will go to investment. It will also depend on the expected profit rate–interest rate differential: the greater this differential is, the smaller the portion of the additional foreign savings that will go to consumption. On the demand side, the key variable is the elasticity of exports to the variation of the exchange rate and, next, the elasticity of the investment rate in relation to exports, or more directly, of the variation of investment in relation to the exchange rate.

What will be the variation of domestic savings due to the appreciation of the currency of the country receiving foreign savings? In other words, on what will the rate of substitution of foreign for domestic savings depend? We have here a trade-off: an increase in the former tends to entail a decrease in the latter. An appreciation of the local currency may draw down domestic savings of the same amount, or even more, than the amount represented by the increase in foreign savings, thus causing a domestic savings displacement. If the decrease in domestic savings is greater than the increase in foreign savings, total savings drop, total investment drops, total consumption increases, and income remains stable. On what does this substitution depend? This rate depends on the variation of wages and salaries in relation to the exchange rate appreciation (the greater the variation, the greater the substitution will tend to be), on the variation of expected profits from export-oriented investments in relation to the exchange rate, on the propensity to consume, and on the interest rate–expected profit rate differential, that is, on investment opportunities. The most relevant of these variations is the variation of investment opportunities because, unlike the others, it varies strongly. If there are large profit opportunities, the capitalist class will use a larger portion of its expected and earned income to invest, increasing its marginal propensity to invest. In addition, the increases in working-class wages and (especially) middle-class salaries will also increase these classes' marginal propensity to invest, possibly offsetting the incentives to increased consumption arising from increases in real wages. On the demand side, the rate of substitution of foreign for domestic savings will be greater, the greater the elasticity of exports in relation to the variation of the exchange rate and the greater the elasticity of investments to exports, and therefore the greater the reaction of investments to the variation of the exchange rate. Demand and supply operate, therefore, in the same direction: on the demand side, the exchange rate appreciation successively triggers a decrease in exports, in investments destined for exports, and in savings as a residue of the investment; on the supply side, the decrease in investments is sanctioned by the direct decrease in domestic savings caused by the increase in real wages and by the increased consumption caused by the same exchange rate appreciation.

What is the meaning, in practice, of the rate of substitution of foreign savings for domestic savings? If we ignore the sign, if the rate is equal to 1 or 100 percent, it means that the increase in foreign savings corresponds to a similar decrease in domestic savings – in this case, there is total substitution. If the rate is zero, there is no substitution of savings. In the first case, the additional foreign savings do not cause any increase in the rate of investment; in the second, all of the additional foreign savings are transformed into an increase in investment and therefore in the rate of investment. In the intermediate cases, part of the foreign savings will be channeled into consumption and part into investment. The rate of substitution of foreign savings for domestic savings will be particularly greater the smaller the differential between the expected rate of profit and the interest rate is, that is, the fewer the investment opportunities. In this case, besides the fact that workers show a high propensity to consume, the middle class will also tend to consume nearly all the increase in its salaries, and not even the capitalists, who face falling profits, will significantly reduce their consumption. Therefore, if the differential between interest and profit is small, we will have normal investment opportunity, which will neither stimulate the middle class to transfer part of its salary increase to investment nor persuade capitalists to consume less. Consequently, the inflow of foreign savings will be strongly offset by decreased domestic savings resulting from increased consumption. In addition, profits themselves and their reinvestment will be modest. The outcome of both these facts is that there will be no new investment, in spite of the inflow of foreign savings. At the other end, if the profit rate–interest differential is great and the variation in consumption is small, a substantial part of the increase in wages and salaries will be directed not to consumption, but to investment.

In this chapter, our assumption is that under normal conditions, the rate of substitution of foreign savings for domestic savings tends to be high, above 50 percent; it will near 100 percent when current account deficits occur without any connection with investments and a particularly slow growth process prevails, as occurred in Latin America in the 1990s. However, historically or empirically, we know that under certain circumstances, countries have developed with foreign savings. What is the condition for this to occur, that is, for the substitution of foreign savings for domestic savings to remain close to zero? For the rate to remain closer to 0 than to 100 percent, it would be necessary that a favorable combination of externalities and increased demand gives rise to substantial investment opportunities, which are expressed in high expected profit rates, always combined with high GDP growth rates. It is important to remark that in much the same way as there is a substitution of foreign savings for domestic savings, when the current account deficit increases, the opposite may happen, that is, the substitution of domestic savings for foreign savings when the current account deficit or foreign savings are diminishing. In this case, on the supply side, wages and salaries will decrease; on the demand side, exports and investments will increase, causing the reverse substitution.

EMPIRICAL EVIDENCE

Many empirical studies have measured the relationship between the use of foreign savings and the level of domestic savings. Most of them show a substitution of foreign savings for domestic savings in what seems to be a near-consensus in the literature. Curiously enough, the exchange rate issue is set aside. Most studies in that field are not concerned with the role of the exchange rate in determining the level of domestic or foreign savings, nor do they offer an explanation of the rate of substitution of domestic savings for foreign savings. They simply present the results of their research – which are significant – without, however, offering any theories to explain them.

Before the classic research of Feldstein and Horioka (1980) regarding rich OECD countries,[8] Fry (1978) was one of the pioneers of econometric studies designed to measure the possible determinants of domestic savings. Although he is not primarily concerned with the relationship between domestic savings and foreign savings, in his empirical analyses, he provides indirect results on the degree of substitution between the two. He starts with a formulation that tries to explain the levels of domestic savings as a function of the growth rate and the level of GDP per capita, the real interest rate, and the level of foreign savings. The analyses are made with minimum chi-square regressions, with dummies standing in for different countries. Data are given for seven Asian countries for the period 1962–72: India (1962–72), South Korea (1962–72), Burma (1962–9), Malaysia (1963–72), the Philippines (1962–72), Singapore (1965–72), and Taiwan (1962–72), and the results point to a coefficient of roughly −0.5 connected to foreign savings. That is to say, 50 percent of the use of foreign savings would be neutralized by a decrease in domestic savings.

Sebastian Edwards (1995) carries out an extensive analysis on the determinants of private domestic savings. Besides discussing a few theoretical aspects involving several explanations for different levels of domestic savings, he presents an extensive empirical analysis of developed and developing countries. He makes estimations with a

---

[8] A large number of further studies have confirmed the findings of Feldstein and Horioka. Surprised economists, however, insisted on talking about the "Feldstein–Horioka puzzle." In recent years, however, econometric studies have shown that it was essentially a solvency constraint of those countries (Sinn 1992; Rocha 2004; Coakley et al. 1996).

panel of data from 1970 to 1992 for twenty-five developing countries and eleven developed countries. He uses an extensive list of independent variables and therefore of possible candidates for determinants of the private domestic savings rate: the demographic dependency rate (the population younger than fifteen years old plus the population older than sixty-five years old divided by the population between fifteen and sixty-five years old), urban population, government savings, growth rates, GDP per capita, money supply/GDP, credit to the private sector, public expenditure on social security and welfare, real interest rate, foreign savings, inflation, income distribution, and political stability. In the several estimated models, he finds once again a value of around -0.5 for the coefficient of foreign savings (minimum 0.38, maximum 0.625), showing a substantial substitution between private domestic savings and foreign savings.

Schmidt-Hebbel et al. (1992) study the behavior of domestic savings from a household perspective. Instead of focusing on aggregate savings, they base their empirical analysis on household savings as related to the available income. Among the independent variables used for estimation, they select, for instance, levels of household per capita income (rates and trend), real interest rates, rates of inflation, and foreign savings. Calculations are made for ten developing economies between 1970 and 1985 with panel data, using a model of fixed and random effects. The coefficients related to foreign savings point to values around -0.2, showing some degree of substitution between foreign savings and domestic savings. The authors call attention to this fact (Schmidt-Hebbel et al. 1992: 543): "foreign saving, which acts as an external liquidity constraint, boosts private consumption, as shown by its significantly negative influence on saving."

Still along these lines, Reinhart and Talvi (1998) make a comparison between Asia and Latin America concerning the relationships between foreign savings and domestic savings. They argue that the high levels of saving in Asia are related to historical trends rather than to the behavior of capital flows. They find empirical results that are in line with those of Schmidt-Hebbel et al. (1992) and Edwards (1995) in the sense that there is a reasonable degree of substitution between the two. The use of foreign savings correlates negatively with the level of domestic savings for both regions. Using a specification close to Fry's (1978), in which domestic savings are defined as a function of foreign savings and a vector of other determinants, Uthoff and Titelman (1998) equally find a negative relationship between levels of domestic savings and foreign savings, which stays around −0.5. They specify a model in which domestic savings rely on the trend, growth, and deviations of GDP per capita; on the inflation rate; on the demographic dependency rate, as in Edwards (1995); and on the trend and deviation of foreign savings and the real interest rate. The estimates cover fifteen Latin American and Caribbean countries between 1972 and 1993, totaling 330 observations, and the results regarding foreign savings indicate a highly significant negative coefficient of −0.47.

The authors also estimate the impact of foreign savings on domestic savings, from a separation between the foreign savings trend and the deviation from the trend. Again, the results point to a negative coefficient of around −0.48, with values between −0.31 and −0.46 for the impact of the trend increase, and between −0.48 and −0.49 for deviations from the trend. The Mexican case stands out. From 1983–90 to 1992–4, the use of foreign savings in Mexico increased by 7.4 percentage points of GDP, but the investment rate increased by only 4.4 percentage points of GDP. A large portion of the foreign resources was used to finance increased consumption, and domestic savings declined. For the average of Latin America, foreign savings increased by 2 percentage points between 1983–90 and 1992–4, whereas the investment rate increased by 0.3 percentage points of GDP, and domestic savings dropped by 1.7 percentage points (Uthoff and Titelman 1998: 36).

Although they do not use the exchange rate directly in the econometric measurements, these studies supply, however indirectly, empirical evidence supporting the theoretical arguments presented in this chapter. Assuming that situations of current account deficit are accompanied by some degree of exchange rate appreciation, we may conclude that the empirical studies presented in this chapter are in line with the argument that in general, the use of foreign savings is connected to a decrease in domestic savings and to an increase in the aggregate level of consumption. On the other hand, the observed substitution of foreign savings for domestic savings, depending on the country and the period for which data are collected, probably derives from the existence, or otherwise, at each given moment, of very high profit rate expectations, or in other words, of substantial investment opportunity transformed into high growth rates.

THE BRAZILIAN CASE IN THE 1990S

In the original studies by Bresser Pereira (2002b) and Bresser Pereira and Nakano (2002a), which criticized the policy of growth with foreign savings, there were already other empirical confirmations of the failure of foreign savings to promote growth. Using the methodology developed in this chapter, I estimated the rate of substitution of foreign savings for domestic savings in Brazil between 1994 and 1999, when the country's current account deficit increased strongly, and found a substitution rate of 131.9 percent; on the other hand, I estimated the rate of substitution of domestic savings for foreign savings between 1999 and 2006, when the reverse movement in the current account deficit took place, and found a rate of substitution of domestic savings for foreign savings of 68.4 percent.[9] As a consequence, the investment rate did not increase

---

[9] The variations were calculated on the basis of the average of the variables in the three years before each of the two periods. These data already take into consideration the change in the GDP calculation method announced by the Brazilian Institute of Geography and Statistics in March 2007.

Table 6.1: *Rate of substitution of foreign savings for domestic savings (1994–9) and of domestic savings for foreign savings (1999–2006)*

	Foreign savings, S_x (% GDP)	Domestic savings, S_i (% GDP)	Investment rate (% GDP)	Period	ΔS_x	ΔS_i	$\Delta S_i / \Delta S_x$ (%)
1994	0.44	19.83	21.27				–
1999	4.73	14.17	19.20	1994–9	4.29	−5.66	131.9
2006	−2.86	19.36	16.50	1999–2006	−7.59	5.19	68.4

Note: GDP, gross domestic product.

during the first period, when foreign savings increased, and practically did not decrease in the second period, when foreign savings received by the country declined and turned negative.[10]

As we can see from Table 6.1, the current account deficit, or the inflow of foreign savings, strongly increased in Brazil between 1994 and 1999: 4.29 percent of GDP. Nevertheless, as the theory that supports the criticism of the policy of growth with foreign savings would predict, the rate of investment did not increase; rather, it declined to 18.9 percent of GDP. On the other hand, the current account deficits in the period 1994–9 were met by two kinds of financing: loans and, principally, direct investment. Direct investment grew extraordinarily. Even so, the economy's total investment rate did not increase during the period, but rather it fell, as we can see in Table 6.1; instead, it was the net income sent abroad that increased.

From the devaluation of the real in 1999, the reverse process begins: a structural shock takes place and the current account deficit of 4.73 percent of GDP in 1999 becomes, in 2006, a surplus of 2.9 percent. We have,

---

[10] The positive structural shock suffered by the Brazilian economy transformed the current account deficit of 4.33% of GDP in 1999 into a surplus of 1.49% in 2005, corresponding to an external adjustment of 5.81% of GDP.

therefore, an external adjustment[11] of 7.6 percent of GDP between 1999 and 2006. These data are in Table 6.1, where we can also see that in much the same way as the rate of investment did not increase in the former period, when foreign savings were increasing, it did not increase when foreign savings declined but rather decreased to 16.50 percent of GDP – a decline of 2.7 percent of GDP against a decline of foreign savings of 7.6 percent of GDP.

In this second period, therefore, there is a substitution of domestic savings for foreign savings of 68.4 percent. This happens because, as I argued previously, wages decline as well as consumption, thus increasing domestic savings on the supply side, whereas on the demand side, exports increase (they almost doubled between 2002 and 2005), leading to increased investment in tradable goods and therefore to an increase in domestic savings. In the Brazilian case, this reverse process of substitution was fueled during that period by the fiscal adjustment beginning in 1999 and by the reduction in real wages caused by the sharp depreciation of the real in 1999 and late 2002. If the arguments presented here are correct, Brazil should have had, during the first period, a high rate of substitution of foreign savings for domestic savings and, in the second period, an equally high or even higher rate of substitution of domestic savings for foreign savings.

As we saw in the previous section, other researchers, although without a theory to explain the phenomenon, have measured the displacement of domestic savings caused by foreign savings in several countries and periods, and most of the results are around 50 percent. So in the 1990s, in Brazil, the rate was substantially higher than this already very high average rate. In turn, the reverse process of substitution of domestic savings for foreign savings, which began in 2000, could seem surprising but is equally foreseen by the model that we have presented. The increase of domestic savings was a result not only of the decline in real wages, but

---

[11] The difference between the 1999 and 2006 current account deficits.

also of the government's fiscal adjustment beginning in 1999[12] and of the increase in exports from 2002 on. This increase in exports is explained not only by a more favorable exchange rate but also, and mostly, by the improvement in the price of goods exported by Brazil, which increased by 30 percent between 2002 and 2005.[13]

Briefly, this chapter shows the negative effects of a nation's acceptance of the policy of growth with foreign savings, which is widely propounded in the economics literature and particularly by those intellectuals who accept conventional orthodoxy. Choosing this path, a country will face the problem of insufficiency of demand resulting from the lack of appropriate incentives to invest in investments destined for exports because the currency will tend to become overvalued. This exchange rate appreciation takes place in relation to the reference exchange rate, which, intertemporally, balances the country's current account. As discussed previously, the exchange rate determines not only exports and imports, and therefore foreign savings but also real wages and salaries as well as profits, and therefore consumption and domestic savings. Given the assumption of a stable relation between the exchange rate and wages, salaries, and profits, the fundamental variable in this case is the propensity to consume, which will vary depending on the existence of normal or large investment opportunities. On the demand side, investment, and therefore savings, depends on the elasticity of exports to the exchange rate and on the elasticity of investments to exports, or more directly, on the elasticity of investments to the exchange rate. Therefore, the exchange rate level also determines investment.

The inflow of capital or foreign savings tends to produce an exchange rate appreciation as well as an increase in real wages and imports because the variation or elasticity of consumption with regard to the

---

[12] Whereas between 1995 and 1998, the primary surplus was around 0%, in the period 1999–2002, it hovered around 3.5% and, in the following four-year period, around 4.5% of GDP.

[13] Funcex (Fundação Centro de Estudos do Comércio Exterior).

remuneration of workers and the middle class is generally near 1. On the demand side, it also tends to reduce exports and investments oriented to exports. As a consequence, we have a significant substitution of foreign savings for domestic savings, which research findings suggest hovers around 50 percent in normal circumstances but which may be more or less, depending on the economic situation. When, however, an economy experiences a period of high growth rates, in which there is a large differential between the expected profit rate and the long-term interest rate, the increase in consumption may be small because the middle class, in particular, may direct its real increase in salaries to investment, which is now much more attractive. This is the reason why, in certain periods, such as in the United States in the second half of the nineteenth century and in South Korea and Brazil in the first half of the 1970s, we had growth with foreign savings.

In most cases, however, our assumption is that, as happened during the 1990s, this exceptional condition is not present, and foreign savings will merely turn into increased consumption and increases in either the financial or the patrimonial (originated from direct investments) indebtedness of the country, both implying a heavy burden of remittances of income abroad, without an increase in investment or the growth rate. This also explains why Asian countries have so strongly defended their exchange rates, keeping them competitive, throughout the policy of growth with negative foreign savings, that is, with current account surpluses and an increase in reserves or investments abroad. This criticism contradicts the assumption of conventional economics that capital-rich countries transfer (and should transfer) their resources to capital-poor countries. We know, however, that the development of science, in any domain, lies in challenging several forms of conventional wisdom – a wisdom that, being often merely hypothetical-deductive, is readily refuted by countries' historical experience, which was always that capital is made at home. With this chapter, we hope to contribute to a theory that may explain this experience and the slow growth rates of countries that resort to foreign savings. We also hope to contribute to strengthening an emerging macroeconomics perspective that emphasizes the importance of aggregate demand and the need for a competitive exchange rate that ensures the sustainability of that demand.

7

Foreign Savings and Financial Crises*

In the previous chapter, we saw how the policy of growing with foreign savings, instead of causing growth by increasing investment, principally increases domestic consumption and causes the substitution of foreign for domestic savings. This substitution happens always – and only in particular situations, when the country is already growing fast and the propensity to consume has fallen – if this rate not high. In this chapter, we see the second perverse effect of the growth with foreign savings policy. As one of the factors that contribute to magnifying the tendency of the exchange rate toward overvaluation, the recourse to foreign capital to finance growth brings about recurrent balance-of-payment crises. As we saw in Chapter 4, the others factors are the capital deepening policy; the use of the exchange rate as a nominal anchor against inflation; exchange rate populism; and the policy of foreign indebtedness to overcome the insufficiency of foreign currencies, or the "two gaps," that would characterize developing economies. In this last chapter, we examine the financial crises of the 1990s, which began with the 1994 Mexican crisis and ended with the 2001 Argentinean crisis.

* This chapter was written with Lauro Gonzalez and Cláudio Lucinda.

We have chosen to examine the period 1994–2001 not only because balance-of-payment crises were frequent in this period but also because in the early 1990s, the U.S. Treasury, the IMF, and the World Bank defined growth with foreign savings as the official Washington Consensus policy to promote economic growth. This policy was also adopted in the 1970s, although more informally, and ended in the great foreign debt crisis of the 1980s. In this decade, capital inflows into developing countries were relatively retarded, but after the solution represented by the Brady Plan of 1989, capital outflows from rich to developing countries resumed, providing a destiny for the relative abundance of capital or excess of liquidity existing in the global economy.

Current account deficits (foreign savings), whether financed by loans, by portfolio investments, or by direct investment, cause, in a first stage, substitution of foreign for domestic savings; in a second stage, they cause increased financial fragility for the indebted country, constraining it to practice the *confidence-building policy*; finally, they result in a balance-of-payment crisis. The theoretical explanation of this sequence has already been developed in the two preceding chapters, but it becomes clearer and is based on additional evidence with the discussion, in this chapter, of the financial turbulence that characterized developing countries in the 1990s. Instead of relating these balance-of-payments crises to economic populism or loose fiscal policies, as conventional analysis does, we show that they derive from the growth with foreign savings policy. Instead of just calling them "financial crises," we call them "balance-of-payment crises" – the specific form of financial crisis that characterizes developing countries, whereas banking crises characterize rich countries.

Balance-of-payment crises are usually the consequence of current account deficits, which lead foreign creditors to suspend, suddenly, the rolling over of the debts of a given country. *Sudden stops* essentially have this nature. Current account deficits are accompanied by high and increasing foreign debt, but the sudden stop may also happen when the foreign debt is not too much, but the current account deficit is increasing fast and, in the understanding of the creditors, dangerously. This was the case with the 1997 Asian crisis. When current account deficits affect a country's capacity to attend to solvency and liquidity criteria, the crisis breaks. The solvency constraint simply says that the present value of future payments must be enough to liquidate the present debt stock. In its turn, the liquidity constraint is related to the country's short-term capacity to honor its ongoing obligations. From these two definitions, we see that solvency is a structural problem, whereas liquidity refers to the conjuncture. Yet the failure to observe both or either one of these constraints leads to financial crisis.

This approach applies to the financial opening policy that was recommended to the new, emerging countries, whose expected role was to absorb the high global liquidity that manifested itself in the early 1990s. The adoption of the growth with foreign savings policy seemed ideal in a moment of capital plenty.

A financial crisis may have different origins and dimensions, usually interrelated. It can originate in the banks, in the state, or in the corporations, or it can be a balance-of-payment crisis, depending on which sector of the economy has suddenly lost credit – or the whole country can lose credit. Usually, the kind of financial crisis that hits developing countries involves the whole country, which suddenly cannot meet its debt obligations, and so arise balance-of-payment crises. In the 1990s and early 2000s, the crises that developing countries faced were balance-of-payment or exchange rate crises. As we see, in all countries, the presence of large and recurrent current account deficits before the crisis is striking. On the other hand, the data of each country after the crisis and the sharp depreciation of the local currency that they imply show that these countries present large current account surpluses and a more effective control of the exchange rate.

Foreign Savings and Financial Crises

CONVENTIONAL EXPLANATIONS

The recent conventional explanations or models on balance-of-payment crises may be divided into three different generations, beginning with Krugman's (1979) model, which explained the crisis by reference to the inconsistency between the variables determining the exchange rate and the value fixed by the country's monetary authorities. Among these variables, a high public deficit was highlighted: fiscal policy would be inconsistent with exchange rate parity. Among the numerous works testing this model are Flood and Garber (1984), Ötker and Pazarbasioglu (1995), and, for Brazil, Miranda (2006). The second-generation models, like those by Obstfeld (1986, 1994), aimed to demonstrate that exchange rate crises cannot be identified or predicted only with macroeconomic indicators. Self-fulfilling prophecies, for instance, could be part of the explanation. In the framework of the accelerating inflation caused by expansive fiscal policies, creditors might prophesy the abandonment of exchange rate parity to keep the country growing, and in so doing, they help to fulfill the prophecy. Finally, the third-generation models (Krugman 1998) resort to the financial excess argument to explain financial crises. In this case, the crisis would be, principally, a banking crisis. The process begins with large capital inflows increasing the loan capacity of the domestic banks, which, for their part, adopt nonrecommended risk management practices.

The common and central assumption in these models is a moral hazard on the part of local banks: they have no incentive to adopt more prudent loan policies because they also assume that even high-risk loans will be warranted against default by the local authorities, who will not hesitate to bail out the banks if they are in danger. For that reason, these models are part of a framework of financial bubbles, moral hazard, and lax fiscal policies that implicates both irresponsible local authorities and irresponsible local banks. Speculative bubbles and financial crises are

207

caused by the poor quality of the loans; the consequence is a run on the local currency. There is, in this view, a clear disdain for the banking practices and government policies existing in developing countries, whereas the banks in rich countries that finance the current account deficits are forgotten. Additionally, the crises are viewed as banking crises (the typical crises in rich countries), not as the balance-of-payment crises that they in fact are.

Besides, all these models presuppose the twin deficits hypothesis (Gonzalez 2007). The current account deficit is understood as the net outcome of private and public savings and investment, presupposing, against empirical evidence, that both the exchange rate and the finances of the private sector are balanced. Intertemporal optimal decisions on savings and investment taken in a decentralized form will, according to these models, produce an equally optimal current account balance consistent with an intertemporally balanced exchange rate. If the current account shows a deficit, this deficit will also be optimal because it is the outcome of economic agents' maximizing decisions.

All this is fully inconsistent with the relative autonomy of the exchange rate and of the current account in relation to public deficits; more broadly, it is inconsistent with my claim in Chapter 4, that there is, in developing countries, a tendency toward overvaluation of the exchange rate – a tendency that is resolved only through a balance-of-payment crisis.[1] According to the neoclassical form of reasoning, there is no reason to assume that the state has better information on how much private agents should save and invest than the agents themselves. This would simply not be true in relation to the state and the public deficit.

---

[1] Besides, the assumptions of rational and optimal economic decisions imply the adoption of the hypothetical-deductive method as the main method of economic analysis – a form of reasoning that I criticized elsewhere because this method, applied to the substantive sciences, essentially builds castles in the air (Bresser Pereira 2009b). The hypothetical-deductive method is the main, if not the only, method in such methodological sciences as mathematics or decision theory.

Whereas the private sector would be able to become indebted without risk to the national economy, the same would not be true in relation to the public sector because one cannot assume public agents' rationality. Corden (1994: 78) sums up this view in the following manner:

> It follows that an increase in a current account deficit that results from a shift in private sector behavior should not be a matter of concern at all. On the other hand, the public budget deficit is a matter of public policy concern and the focus should be on this.

Thus, according to this conventional approach, my claim that the adoption of the growth with foreign savings policy or of intended current account deficits is the main cause of financial crises in developing countries makes no sense. Instead, at the root of poor-quality current account deficits, we would find fiscal imbalance and the determination of local governments to be engaged in the moral hazard of rescuing banks and business enterprises, whatever the cost. From these models follow macroeconomic policies. In 1981, when the current account deficit in Chile reached 14 percent of GDP, one IMF high official argued that there was no reason for worry once public accounts were under control and domestic savings were rising (Robischek 1981). A few months later, Chile experienced a major balance-of-payment crisis and sharply devalued its currency. A few years later, the *Lawson doctrine*, named after British finance minister Nigel Lawson (1987–99), became part of neoclassical macroeconomic reasoning. According to this doctrine, there would be no cause for concern in relation to private deficits because they would be automatically balanced by the market; financial crises would always originate in public sector fiscal unbalance. Reisen (1998: 11) quotes the following statement from a 1988 speech by Lawson:

> We are prisoners of the past, when UK current account deficits were almost invariably associated with large budget deficits, poor economic performance, low reserves and exiguous net overseas assets. The present position could not be more different.

Although the Lawson doctrine is not a theory, it brings together the various theoretical arguments that merge the twin deficits concept with the intertemporal approach to the current account. Thus, it is not surprising that in 1988, it opened the way for the early 1990s definition by the U.S. Treasury and the IMF of the growth with foreign savings policy and for the complementary financial opening recommendation to developing countries.

Mexico is a good example of the application of the Lawson doctrine. In the period 1992–4, the average Mexican current account deficit was almost 7 percent of GDP. Yet, in 1993, the Central Bank of Mexico asserted the following (quoted in Edwards 2000: 16):

> The current account deficit has been determined exclusively by the private sectors decisions. . . . Because of the above and the solid positions of public finances the current account should clearly not be a cause for undue concern.

To sum up, the conventional explanation uses, essentially, the twin deficits concept and the intertemporal approach to the current account, according to which the current account will be permanently reasonably balanced, provided that the exchange rate regime is the floating regime. Yet, when we examine the period that followed the Lawson doctrine and the U.S. Treasury's proposal of growth with foreign savings, we observe that many countries faced major balance-of-payment crises, despite showing reasonable fiscal equilibrium. Therefore, we must conclude that the conventional explanations are insufficient. In the next section, we propose an alternative explanation.

FOREIGN SAVINGS AND FINANCIAL CRISES

A balance-of-payment crisis begins when foreign creditors lose confidence and decide to stop financing the rollover of public and private debt in a given country. This decision is conditioned by the expected return on the credit operations. When the return turns negative, we have a breakdown in the flow of finance. What the creditor does is estimate the probability that he or she will receive back the value of his or her loans. Let us call P this success probability, R the expected return, K the valued loaned, and i the interest rate, which we can write in a simplified way[2]:

$$E[R] = P.[K(1 + i)] - K(1 + i^*),$$

where i^* is the international interest rate and represents the creditor's opportunity cost. Given a positive interest differential $(i - i^* > 0)$, the probability P will determine the signal of the creditor's expected return. Probability P depends on the liquidity and solvency conditions of the country. Such conditions – or their perception – may deteriorate fast to generate a negative expected return. The crisis breaks when two restrictions cease to be satisfied, namely, the solvency constraint and the liquidity constraint. When a country adopts the growth with foreign savings policy, it starts incurring large and continuous current account deficits that will have negative effects on both constraints. From the start, we will have substitution of foreign for domestic savings, foreign financial fragility will soon materialize, and finally, the country will face financial crisis.

Thus, this explanation for balance-of-payment crises brings to the floor its direct cause – the current account deficit or the growth with foreign savings policy – rather than a domestic cause, namely, the government's fiscal accounts. In each country, the budget deficit may contribute to the current account deficit, but not necessarily. The exchange rate may appreciate and the current account may turn negative, while the fiscal accounts are under control.

The intertemporal solvency constraint on a country is similar to the one faced by business firms when they borrow capital. Creditors

---

[2] The recovery tax, that is, the portion of the loan that is recovered after default is ignored.

will evaluate the intertemporal solvency of the country in the same way as they proceed with loans to business enterprises. They will evaluate the country's capacity to pay back loans. They will check the potential present value of the cash flow generated by the financed investments (defined as operation assets). A business enterprise is insolvent when this present value is not sufficient to meet liabilities, including loans.

In transferring this reasoning to the evaluation of the foreign solvency of a country, the more adequate measure of its capacity to pay back is the present value of resource transfers calculated in light of the surplus originating from exports minus imports and nonfactor services. It may be expressed in the following way:

$$(1 + i)D_{s-1} = \sum_{s=t}^{\infty} \left[\frac{1}{1+i} \right]^{s-t} \text{TLR}_s.$$

Thus, this surplus in a country corresponds to the operational cash flow generated by a business enterprise. The insolvency condition is the limit situation in which the present value of the transferences (TLR) is insufficient to liquidate the stock of debt (D) existing at that moment.

Yet the *stricto sensu* intertemporal solvency concept is not much use to creditors because there are infinite trajectories ensuring a country intertemporal solvency. Thus, we must consider the possible trajectories that creditors conventionally demand from debtors to keep rolling over the debt. Conventionally, creditors use the foreign debt to exports ratio (D/X) to control solvency. A country will be in a comfortable position if this ratio is less than 2, in a dubious position if it is between 2 and 4, and in a critical situation if the ratio is more than 4. These are rules of thumb, but they are widely accepted. Thus, the question is how the growth with foreign savings policy affects this ratio. It affects the D/X ratio negatively because a current account deficit is consistent with a more appreciated exchange rate than the rate that balances the current account so that if the current account deficit rises and the debt grows faster than exports, this ratio will increase.

The second financial constraint – liquidity – may be defined as the mismatch between the demand for foreign money and the central bank's stock of international reserves. The accumulation of current account deficits ends up causing this inconsistency between the potential dollars estimated to be on the patrimonial balance sheet of local financial institutions (FIs) and the international reserves. According to this approach, the local banks and the central bank are fundamental FIs that may change the country from a hedge to a speculative condition as a consequence of the growth with foreign savings policy.[3] The following assumptions are behind the claim that the liquidity constraint may cause (1) an exchange rate relatively fixed or floating but not responding quickly to market variations[4] and (2) balance-of-payment crises. Besides, we have to consider the well-known arbitrage equation, where the expected return (r) is equal to the international interest rate (r_f), which is the funding cost plus the expected depreciation of the local currency (e) plus the risk premium (p):

$$r = r_f + e + p.$$

Given these assumptions, we can evaluate the impact of the growth with foreign savings policy on liquidity – the latter measured by the mismatch between the potential demand for foreign money and the reserves. Following Neftci (2002), the indebtedness process, together with the appreciation of the exchange rate, coincides with the initial moments of the liquidity cycle. Beginning with the local FIs,[5] financial opening increases

---

[3] The concepts hedge, speculative, and Ponzi used here are from Hyman Minsky (1986). An FI is viewed as a hedge if its liabilities are small relative to sales or exports, and it is viewed as speculative if the institution becomes dependent on the goodwill of creditors. The Ponzi condition is one of insolvency.

[4] In supposing this condition, I am rejecting the conventional "fix or float" alternative because it does not really exist empirically. Countries always manage their exchange rates, although to varying degrees (Bresser Pereira 2004b). Besides, experience shows that a floating regime does not prevent balance-of-payment crises.

[5] We use the expressions *local FIs* and *local banks* interchangeably.

the rate of introduction of financial innovations and of the supply of differentiated products to capitalist rentiers. The elimination of barriers to capital flows allows local FIs to borrow resources in foreign hard currencies, which are sold to the central bank, the counterpart being invested in bonds and/or generating assets against the private sector.

From the systemic standpoint, increasing debt does not substantially affect the initial values borrowed and the consolidated patrimonial structure of the local FIs and of the central bank. Yet, as the returns incentivize the entry of new institutions into the market, the patrimonial balance sheets of the local FIs show typical speculative traits. To understand why this happens, it is necessary to consider the evolution of the balance sheet of the central bank as capital inflows greater than the growing current account deficits allow for the accumulation of international reserves and for the false perception of less foreign vulnerability. The buildup of reserves may be accompanied by an increase in the money supply, depending on the degree of sterilization implemented by the monetary authority. When there is an increase in the money supply, the conventional argument is that the fall in the interest rate will reduce the incentive for foreign borrowing, and the capital inflow process will lose momentum. This is a typical assumption of the efficient market hypothesis. What really happens is that the increase in systemic risk, the risk premium as defined previously, tends to grow, incentivizing the continuation of the borrowing process. Yet foreign creditors follow the increase in the debt ratio and, at a given moment, wave the red flag. From this moment on, loans just finance repayments of debt, that is, net capital inflows cease and the cycle's euphoric phase ends. As there is a current account to be financed, a mismatch exists between the FIs' contracted foreign obligations and reserves. In other words, the FIs' patrimonial balance sheets now show typical speculative characteristics.

It would be reasonable to assume that the central bank would intervene in the market in some fashion. Yet the financial fragility of the local banks, now consisting mostly of speculative units, will impose constraints on the central bank's actions. The classic "too big to fail" syndrome is now present. On the other hand, the national economy is booming. Thus, although foreign creditors know the central bank's incentives and constraints, they are also influenced by the euphoric mood. In consequence, the more likely scenario is that the local currency will remain overvalued for a long time and lead the economy into crisis.

Once the net inflow of foreign resources ceases to be sufficient to finance the current account deficit, the fluctuation of foreign reserves turns negative. For the central bank, a negative variation of reserves means a speculative patrimonial balance sheet because, previously, the dominant perception was that the possible liquidations of foreign loans counted with the guarantee of a growing stock of international reserves. Now, given the reversion to the previous condition, the money flow potentially required to finance the growing liabilities present on the balance sheets of local banks has become greater than the one present in the form of reserves in the assets of the central bank. The decision of just one creditor to liquidate his or her position totally or partially is sufficient to set off a herd effect that will soon trigger the crisis – a crisis whose causes are directly related to the growth with foreign savings policy or, in other words, to the foreign liquidity and solvency constraints.

EMPIRICAL ANALYSIS[6]

This chapter focuses on the balance-of-payment crises that broke in the 1990s and early 2000s after the early 1990s decision to include financial opening and the growth with foreign savings policy in the Washington Consensus.[7] By using a multivariable market exchange rate pressure

---

[6] In this section, we present only a brief summary of the econometric study. For a full report of the tests, see Gonzalez (2007).

[7] In the 1980s, the Washington Consensus, as originally set out by Williamson (1990), did not include financial opening. The decision to include financial opening was made by the U.S. Treasury in 1993, in the first year of the Clinton administration.

index (MEPI), we have been able to detect fourteen balance-of-payment crises in middle-income countries. Yet the identification of a financial crisis is not simple; thus, the conclusions or results of the several econometric studies are conditional on the adopted definitions.[8]

Because our theoretical approach is based on the idea that the recent financial crises are related to the deterioration of the external sector of the economy, the starting point of our empirical analysis was an extension of the first-generation models that explain financial crises by reference to macroeconomic fundamentals in the local banking sector. However, our main task was to select the variables that could test the hypothesis that the financial crisis is explained mainly by the deterioration of the external sector's fundamentals, which in turn stems from the buildup of current account deficits.

In this fashion, we have included two proxies that could potentially capture solvency and liquidity, whose deterioration causes the crises. As a proxy for solvency, we used the variation of the current account position lagged by one period. As for liquidity, we used the variation of the ratio of short-term external debt to international reserves. In addition, our first estimations included the following explanatory variables for MEPI: (1) fiscal deficit as a percentage of GDP, (2) credit (from the monetary authorities) extended to the banking sector as a percentage of GDP, (3) short-term liabilities of the central bank as a share of international reserves, (4) a proxy variable that captures the contagion effect, and (5) a measure of political risk (International Country Risk Guide, a wholly owned subsidiary of Political Risk Services).

We used quarterly data, and our sample of countries took into account the 2006 Financial Times Country Classification to obtain the emerging markets. Data availability allowed us to study fourteen countries: Argentina, Brazil, Korea, Ecuador, the Philippines, Indonesia,

---

[8] For a discussion of the definition of a crisis and the respective empirical results, see Gonzalez (2007).

Israel, Mexico, Peru, the Czech Republic, Russia, Thailand, Turkey, and Venezuela.

The first results that we obtained were in line with our theoretical hypothesis; that is, solvency and liquidity were significant in explaining the observed movements of the dependent variable – MEPI – and the fiscal deficit was not a significant variable. It is important to point out that the evidence for the nonsignificance of the fiscal variable is in line with other available empirical analyses such as that of Pereira and Seabra (2004). Moreover, following Eichengreen et al. (1994) and Radelet and Sachs (2000), we included macroeconomic fundamentals that could affect MEPI: (1) the banking credit extended to the private sector as a percentage of GDP; (2) the variation in the consumer price index, and (3) the unemployment rate. The new results presented similar evidence, mainly pointing to the importance of liquidity and solvency.

The next step in our empirical analysis was the creation of a formal definition of crisis. In this fashion, we have defined a binary variable (CRISE) based on the deviation (2.33 standard deviations) of MEPI from its average. In addition, based on Rodrik and Velasco (1999), for any quarter that CRISE equals 1, it was assumed that CRISE would be zero in the next three quarters. By such an assumption, we were able to avoid the double counting of crises.

This was even more important in view of the quarterly base of the data. For technical reasons, we had to exclude all those countries that did not show at least one crisis event, which meant removing Israel and Peru from the sample. Assuming 2.33 standard deviations, we identified nineteen crisis episodes. We chose to use a LOGIT – Log Odds Units – model for our new estimations. Once again, the results were in line with our theoretical hypothesis; that is, solvency and liquidity were significant in explaining the binary variable.

In short, the empirical analysis that was conducted and briefly discussed in this chapter supports the theoretical reasoning previously developed. By using different methods and model specifications, we were able to conclude that there is evidence that solvency and liquidity are eroded over time by the buildup of current account deficits, which increases the probability of financial crisis episodes.

CONCLUSION

To sum up, contrary to the claims of conventional economic analysis, the balance-of-payment crises in the 1990s and early 2000s were not principally caused by fiscal deficits but rather by recurrent current account deficits. Public deficits may cause crises, but only when the twin deficits hypothesis is confirmed – an outcome that often fails to materialize because the exchange rate is seldom in equilibrium in developing countries. Given the tendency of the exchange rate toward overvaluation, this rate may remain overvalued for relatively long periods, followed by a sudden stop or a sharp devaluation, which indicates a financial crisis. Attracted by greater returns, foreign creditors underestimate the liquidity and solvency constraints to which these countries are subject. The growth with foreign savings policy and the capital deepening policy on the part of conventional orthodoxy, and exchange rate populism on the part of local politicians, merely aggravate the overvaluation. The consequent capital inflows that, according to conventional wisdom, benefit developing countries actually follow a three-stage process: first, they cause the substitution of foreign for domestic savings, a small increase in the investment rate, and a substantial increase in the country's foreign indebtedness; second, they cause international financial fragility that entails a confidence-building policy; and third, they eventually cause a balance-of-payment crisis. As foreign indebtedness increases and pushes against the liquidity and solvency constraints, the probability of a financial crisis increases.

In econometric tests, the variables relating to liquidity and solvency were significant, while in the same tests, the fiscal variable was not significant. Thus, the data support the hypothesis that the growth with foreign savings policy, not fiscal laxity, was the main cause of the balance-of-payment crises. They confirm the thesis that there is, in developing countries, a tendency of the exchange rate toward overvaluation. The exchange rate does not vary around an equilibrium rate, as it would if markets were efficient in controlling it. Besides the well-known high volatility that characterizes the exchange rate in developing countries, including the middle-income ones, there is the tendency toward over-valuation, which, if not neutralized, ends in financial crisis.

Conclusion

In this book, I have focused on the middle-income countries developing in the framework of commercial globalization and financial globalization. The former is viewed as an opportunity, the latter as a danger or a curse: commercial globalization is an opportunity because middle-income countries dispose of some advantages in international competition, principally low-cost labor; financial globalization is a curse because the country that engages in it loses control of its exchange rate, the rate becomes overvalued, foreign indebtedness grows, foreign savings substitute for domestic savings, and the country is subjected to balance-of-payment crises. My objective has been to develop a theoretical framework able to explain why some emerging countries are successful in catching up but others are not.

Behind the analysis that I developed in this book is today's division of the world's countries into four types: the rich countries; the fast-growing middle-income countries, existing principally in Asia; the slow-growing middle-income countries, existing principally in Latin America; and the poor countries. Middle-income countries are those that have already completed their capitalist revolutions and have a modern state, a market able to allocate resources, and hard-working entrepreneurial and

Conclusion

professional social classes. Given that they dispose of cheap labor and are able to copy or buy technology, economic theory predicts that they will catch up. Yet, after the major foreign debt crisis that these countries confronted in the 1980s, they became vulnerable to the pressures and recommendations coming from the North. This has been particularly true in relation to the three larger Latin American countries: Brazil, Mexico, and Argentina. Their vulnerability originated not only in foreign debt but also in the fact that their successful growth strategies, based on import substitution and state intervention, were outdated. Meanwhile, the North, under the leadership of the United States, regained strength from the new weakness of the middle-income countries and also from two positive facts: the collapse of the Soviet Union and the dominance of neoliberalism – the ideology identified with U.S. elites and their hegemony. This market fundamentalist ideology aimed, domestically, at the minimum state and at the weakening of labor unions and state bureaucracies. In relation to middle-income countries, this pseudo-orthodoxy, based on high interest rates and overvalued currencies, was the practical way for rich countries to neutralize their cheap-labor competitors. To this was added globalism – the affirmation that nation-states had lost autonomy and relevance – from which it was concluded that the only way open to developing countries was to engage in institutional reform and adopt the globalists' macroeconomic policy recommendations. Yet some middle-income countries were able to resist the new times and the new truths. China, India, and Taiwan fully resisted them. Others, such as Korea, Indonesia, Malaysia, and Thailand, submitted to the North for some time and experienced a financial crisis in 1997, but learned the relevant lessons and returned to new developmentalism and to subsequent growth.

Countries that adopt new developmentalism grow with domestic savings, and their macroeconomic policy is based on a simple tripod: tight fiscal policy, moderate interest rates, and competitive exchange rates. In this book, after discussing globalization, national development strategies, and catching up, I focused on the hypothesis of the tendency of the exchange rate toward overvaluation. I emphasized two points: countries must reject the policy of growth with foreign savings, and they need to neutralize the Dutch disease to have a competitive exchange rate – a condition for industrial exports and an export-led growth strategy. It seems natural that capital-rich countries should transfer their capital to capital-poor countries, but I hope to have demonstrated that this is not the case. All countries that develop rely, essentially, on domestic savings. When a country resorts to foreign savings, that is, to current account deficits financed by borrowing or by foreign direct investment, it becomes prone to financial fragility and a balance-of-payments crisis. So long as the crisis does not materialize, the developing country will experience a high rate of substitution of foreign savings for domestic savings, or in other words, an increase in consumption rather than in investment. This is not the case only in special situations, when, because the country is already growing very fast, the marginal propensity to consume falls. The fact that countries like China receive substantial direct investment should not be confused with foreign savings. Given its persistent current account surplus, China grows with domestic savings. Direct investment brings technology to China and opens new markets, but the corresponding capital inflows are more than compensated for by China's investments and loans abroad.

The neutralization of the Dutch disease by developing countries has many domestic and international consequences. This disease consists in the fact that the Ricardian rents that benefit the country lead it to have two exchange rate equilibria, of which the industrial equilibrium (which makes industries utilizing state-of-the-art technology viable) is more appreciated than the current equilibrium exchange rate (which intertemporally balances the current account). The basic form of neutralizing the disease to reap the benefits of the rents, without incurring their negative effect, is to impose a tax on exports to shift the supply curve of the goods upward to the point where the two equilibria coincide. This policy is simple to explain but difficult to implement because it will temporarily increase inflation and reduce real wages. On the other hand, to the extent that countries are able to neutralize their Dutch disease, the depreciation of the exchange rate that has already equilibrated the current account will necessarily mean substantial current account surpluses. This is already happening with the oil-exporting countries, which are experiencing huge current account surpluses and establishing sovereign wealth funds. The counterpart is the current account deficit of the United States. Yet, insofar as this process gathers momentum, and more developing countries neutralize more fully their respective Dutch diseases, all non–Dutch disease countries will experience current account deficits. Rich countries will continue to grow, but their foreign accounts will be balanced through the transfer of substantial assets to developing countries.

I divided the argument of this book into two parts. In Part I, I developed six political economy propositions: (1) global capitalism is characterized by strong economic competition not only among business enterprises but also among countries or nation-states; (2) such competition made countries or nation-states more interdependent and relatively less autonomous but also made their governments more strategic because interdependence derived from increased economic competition; (3) the countries that are successful in global competition are those that strengthen their nations and adopt a national development strategy; (4) after World War II, many developing countries adopted a national developmentalist strategy, based on a combination of state intervention and private entrepreneurship, that was successful in promoting their industrial and capitalist revolutions, thus transforming them into middle-income countries; (5) in the 1980s, a major foreign debt crisis and the exhaustion of the state-led national strategy, coupled with the hegemony of neoliberal ideology at the world level, led most middle-income countries (except some Asian countries) to adopt conventional orthodoxy, or the Washington Consensus, which caused balance-of-payment crises and increased inequality, instead of growth; and (6) after the financial crises of the 1990s, and given the successful economic strategies of several Asian countries, a new national strategy is emerging – new developmentalism – which I compare with old national developmentalism and conventional orthodoxy.

In Part II, I presented seven development macroeconomics propositions that are part of the new developmentalist approach; they refer to the foreign economic relations of the middle-income country and are centered on the exchange rate. This choice does not mean that the domestic aspect and other macroeconomic prices (interest, inflation, profit, and wage rates) are not important, but that, given space constraints, I chose the price that is most strategic and on which I could possibly make an original contribution. The propositions are as follows: (1) new developmentalism is a development macroeconomics strategy that, although recognizing development obstacles on the supply side, assumes that the major obstacles are on the demand side; (2) at the domestic level, the major obstacle is the tendency of wages to grow less than productivity because of the unlimited supply of labor, while at the external level, the main obstacle is the tendency of the exchange rate toward overvaluation; (3) a competitive exchange rate is here understood to be the rate that makes viable economically tradable industries using state-of-the-art world technology – the industrial equilibrium exchange rate, which differs from the current equilibrium exchange rate, in the countries facing the Dutch disease; (4) the two structural causes behind the tendency of the exchange rate toward overvaluation (the Dutch disease and higher profit and interest rates attracting foreign capital) are magnified by frequent and mistaken economic policies, namely, the growth with foreign savings policy (current account deficits), capital deepening, exchange rate anchors, coping with the two-gap assumption, and the practice of exchange rate populism; to catch up, the developing country must neutralize this tendency; (5) the Dutch disease is a major market failure that makes the current equilibrium exchange rate more appreciated than

Conclusion

the industrial equilibrium exchange rate (which makes viable tradable industries using state-of-the-art technology); it is a fundamental obstacle to diversification and economic development, except in its initial phase; (6) contrary to widespread belief, the growth with foreign savings policy, coupled with financial opening, does not promote growth; rather, it causes financial crises and, always, an artificial increase of wages and consumption, or in other words, a high rate of substitution of foreign for domestic savings; (7) financial crises in developing countries are usually balance-of-payment crises deriving from a suspension of the rolling over of the foreign debt by foreign creditors. The financial crises of the 1990s and early 2000s were not a consequence of fiscal deficits, as conventional economics assumes, but rather of the growth with foreign savings policy that was an essential ingredient of the Washington Consensus.

These thirteen propositions imply bringing back the state. In the times of industrial capitalism and development economics around the 1950s, the challenge that developing countries faced was to industrialize, and for that the state was supposed to create forced savings. In global capitalism, at the beginning of the twenty-first century, the emerging countries have undergone their capitalist revolutions, are already industrialized, and dispose of large working, professional middle, and capitalist classes and a substantial domestic market. They have an advantage in catching up – low-cost labor – but face structural effective demand problems insofar as, to the extent that wages do not grow with productivity and there is a tendency of the exchange rate toward overvaluation, business enterprises lack investment opportunities. Contrary to the claims of its critics, globalization demonstrably offers a great opportunity for these countries to catch up insofar as it creates major export and investment possibilities. Yet, contrary to neoliberal ideologues (whom I call "globalists"), who argue that in globalization, nation-states have lost policy relevance, many middle-income countries profited from that opportunity insofar as they rejected conventional orthodoxy or the Washington

225

Consensus. By doing so, they were able to define a national development strategy; they rejected financial globalization or financial opening and neutralized the tendency of the exchange rate toward overvaluation. If, additionally, they also worked to neutralize the tendency of wages to grow more slowly than productivity, they were able to develop large domestic markets, thus combining an export-led with a domestically oriented strategy. I called this strategy *new developmentalism*, distinguishing it from old developmentalism and conventional orthodoxy. To define its main characteristics, I did not use the hypothetical-deductive method that conventional economics adopts but rather looked to the experience of the fast-growing Asian countries that moved the center of gravity of the world economy to the East.

In October 2008, the financial crisis that had broken a year before in the United States deepened, became global, and turned into the worst economic crisis capitalism had faced since the depression of the 1930s. Among middle-income countries, the ones that were more penalized were those that did not learn the lessons of the 1990s and incurred high current account deficits; that is, they insisted on adopting the growth with foreign savings policy. The Eastern European countries fall principally in this category. Contradictorily, the immediate consequence of the crisis in developing countries was a sharp devaluation of their currencies in relation to the dollar. The depreciation was sharpest in Brazil and Mexico, among other countries that had allowed their exchange rates to become strongly overvalued in the preceding years.

Yet the financial crises of the 1990s had made most middle-income developing countries more prudent in financial terms than rich countries. Thus, the consequences of the global financial crisis will not be as severe as they will be in the rich countries, and particularly in the United States and the United Kingdom – the countries in which the neoliberal ideology was dominant and the deregulation of financial markets was pronounced. These countries did not adopt the mistaken macroeconomic policies that they recommend to developing countries

Conclusion

(and which I have discussed in this book), but they adopted the micro-economic ones, namely, market deregulation. The result is that when the crisis broke, their institutions proved weaker than those in many middle-income countries. The regulation of the Brazilian stock market by the Comissão de Valores Imobiliários, for instance, proved to be considerably more effective than the regulation of the U.S. stock market by the U.S. Securities and Exchange Commission. The U.S. government was eager to recommend and impose institutional reforms on other countries, but eventually, its institutions for regulating markets proved to be poor. Today, it is clear that developing countries will also suffer in the crisis. The decoupling thesis that was popular in financial markets before October 2008 lost any credibility as developing countries saw their exchange rates sharply devalue, their commodity prices fall, their local stock market bubbles burst, and the first signs of cancellation of investment plans and of actual reduction in consumption.

The challenges confronting middle-income countries are great. Despite the major crisis they are facing, rich countries will continue to exert an ideological hegemony that neutralizes the competitive capacity of many middle-income countries. Yet I am supposing that the example of the countries that succeed in catching up will lead an increasing number of them to adopt national development strategies. This, however, will not represent a loss for rich countries. The game between the competing countries will be substantially positive-sum, rather than zero-sum. Developing countries will catch up, but rich countries will continue to grow, and probably at a faster rate than today. The huge growth of China since the 1970s has reduced the relative weight of the U.S. economy in the world, but if China's annual growth had been 2 percent, instead of 10 percent, the United States today would probably be less prosperous than it is – its rate of growth would have been less than it effectively was in this period.

Will Latin American middle-income countries turn to new developmentalism, or are they condemned to dependent and insufficient development? There is no simple answer to this question, but one thing is clear: the conditions that created the U.S. ideological hegemony in the 1990s no longer exist. The disaster represented by the Iraq War is one factor leading to that result and the major 2008 global economic crisis is another, but the central cause is the failure of neoliberal institutional reforms and of the corresponding macroeconomic policies to promote growth. The more a country surrendered to conventional orthodoxy, the less it grew. Countries like Argentina and Russia, which fully surrendered, experienced major crises. Subsequently, they adopted national strategies and resumed growth. In contrast, countries that remained attached to advice emanating from Washington, D.C., such as Brazil and Mexico, grew slowly. Mexico is a limiting case; a proud nation, it was caught in the trap of the North American Free Trade Agreement – an agreement between unequal countries that favors neither the Mexican people nor the American people, but only an elite class, principally in the United States. Mexico seems condemned to have an overvalued currency insofar as it remains associated with the United States. Mexico's entire manufacturing industry is being gradually transformed into a great maquiladora. In Brazil, under the second Lula administration, there are signs of change in the right direction, but the macroeconomic policy based on soft fiscal adjustment, high interest rates, and an overvalued currency remains in place. Among the four BRIC countries (Brazil, Russia, India, and China), Brazil grows the most slowly. Despite the high prices of the commodities exported by Brazil, the overvaluation of the real has brought back the current account deficit, and there is no guarantee that the modest present growth rates will be sustained. Since 2004, Brazil's growth rate has improved as a result of the high prices of the commodities it exports. Yet macroeconomic policy remains subordinated to conventional orthodoxy, insofar as a political coalition of interest rentiers, the financial sector, and foreign interests uses the widespread fear of inflation to justify incredibly high interest rates and an overvalued exchange rate. A return to power of a developmentalist political coalition consisting of manufacturing entrepreneurs, the public bureaucracy, and the working class cannot be ruled out. Lula's Workers' Party is nearer to this alternative political coalition than to the rentier and finance one. Yet the present administration probably lacks the requisite courage to change policy. A new balance-of-payment crisis will probably be needed to persuade the elites that conventional orthodoxy is a pseudo-orthodoxy that is in the interests only of rich countries. Among Latin American countries, only Argentina has adopted a strategy that approaches new developmentalism. Argentina probably learned from its debt default crisis in 2001 and is able to keep its fiscal budget balanced, its interest rate moderate, and its exchange rate competitive. The neutralization of the Dutch disease through export taxes (*retenciones*) is correct but faces strong domestic opposition. On the other hand, the North is pressing Argentina to control inflation by appreciating the peso. It is too early to predict if Argentina will be able to sustain its present fast growth rates.

Chile is a special case. During the 1990s, it was the only Latin American country to impose controls on capital inflows, and so it kept its exchange rate competitive, neutralizing the Dutch disease. Yet, in the early 2000s, Chile signed a bilateral agreement with the United States that reduced its policy space. Several other Latin American countries have elected left-wing and nationalist political leaders, but their chances of success are limited because these are poor countries characterized by weak nations and correspondingly weak states.

The crisis capitalism has faced since 2007 is financial and economic, but its causes are political and moral as well. The immediate cause of the crisis was the failure of U.S. banks as a result of households defaulting on mortgages that, in an increasingly deregulated financial market, were able to grow unchecked because banks relied on financial innovations that allowed them to repackage the relevant securities in such a manner that the new bundles looked safer than the original loans to their acquirers. When the fraud came to light and the banks failed, the confidence of consumers and businesses, which was already deeply shaken, finally collapsed, and they sought protection by avoiding consumption and investment. Besides, as banks also lost confidence, a credit crunch materialized. In consequence, aggregate demand plunged vertically everywhere, and the turmoil, which was at first limited to the banking industry, became an economic crisis.

This is a reasonable explanation, but given that the issue of confidence lies at its core, I ask, was confidence lost as a result merely of economic reasons – of the dynamics of the economic cycle or of the intrinsically unstable nature of capitalism – or does a political and moral issue lurk at the root of the crisis? True, the capitalist economic system is, in fact, inherently unstable, but over the course of the twentieth century, we developed a series of institutions that should, by all expectations, substantially mitigate the severity of crises. The thirty golden years of capitalism after the end of World War II (1945–75) – the times of the new welfare state and of Keynesian macroeconomics – confirmed this prediction: crises did, in fact, lose frequency and intensity, economic growth rates increased, and economic inequality went down.

In the past three decades, however – the years of neoliberal hegemony and the creation of fictitious wealth – growth rates slowed, income again concentrated in the hands of the wealthiest 2 percent of the population, and financial instability increased everywhere, culminating in the global crisis of 2008 – a crisis infinitely more severe than the modest economic deceleration combined with inflation that marked the end of the thirty golden years. Despite the confusion between neoliberalism and liberalism (a great and necessary ideology) and between neoliberalism and conservatism (a political stance worthy of respect), this ideology is neither liberal nor conservative but rather is characterized by fierce, immoral individualism. Whereas liberalism was originally the ideology of a bourgeois middle class against an oligarchy of landlords and the military and against an autocratic state, neoliberalism, which became prevalent in the last quarter of the twentieth century, is an ideology of the wealthy against the poor and the workers and against a democratic and social state. Although authentic liberals and conservatives are also republicans (as are socialists and environmentalists), that is, they harbor a belief in public interest or the common good and uphold the need for civic virtues so that the former can be ensured, neoliberals deny the notion of public interest, embrace an all-justifying individualism, make the invisible hand into a caricature, and encourage each one to fight for his or her individual interests, as collective interests will be ensured by the market and the law. The law, in its turn, must liberalize everything. In what new role is the state cast? Instead of identifying with the law itself, it is reduced to the bureaucratic organization that should enforce it, and even that is said to be performed poorly. And the state's purpose? According to neoliberal views, the state's purpose is to be a mere regulator, while in a show of Orwellian doublespeak, this prevalent ideology advocates general deregulation. In this perverse cultural process, neoclassical economics adopting a hypothetical-deductive method turned into a meta-ideology – into a scientific and mathematical bundle of ideas legitimizing hard-line individualism or neoliberalism.

Confidence, therefore, was not lost just for economic reasons. In addition to deregulating the markets, the neoliberal hegemony eroded society's moral standards. Virtue and civics were forgotten, or even ridiculed, in the name of an overarching market economy rationale. Performance bonuses became the only legitimate performance incentive. Corporate scandals multiplied. Bribery of civil servants and politicians became a generalized practice. They, in turn, adapted to the new times, thereby confirming the public choice claim that they ignore the public interest and make trade-offs between rent seeking and being elected (politicians) or promoted (public bureaucrats). Instead of regarding the state as the principal instrument for collective social action, as the expression of the institutional rationality each society attains at its respective stage of development, and as the legal steward of morality, society came to see it as an organization of corrupt functionaries and politicians. On the basis of this political reductionism, the state and the law were demoralized, the role of values was reduced, and new latitude was given for easy gains. It is no accident that John Kenneth Galbraith's (2004) book is titled *The Economics of Innocent Fraud*. Compared to the same author's *American Capitalism: The Concept of Countervailing Power* (Galbraith 1952), this final book by the great economist, who died a while later at the age of ninety-seven, gives a sense of the decline of ethical standards over the past thirty years. While I was writing this book, I was concentrating on criticizing the evils of neoliberalism and of its meta-ideology – conventional economics ensuring scientific legitimacy to that ideology – in relation to middle-income countries. The present major crisis, however, fell back on the rich countries. This boomerang effect is regrettable not only because it hits the poor in the rich countries but also because it eventually harms everybody, everywhere. Yet this crisis also represents an opportunity for economists to review their science and to build a more historical economic theory (instead of a hypothetical-deductive one), and, more important, for citizens and politicians to gather together in the democratic state aiming to reform capitalism, with the goal of organizing society toward economic, political, social, and sustained development.

References

Acosta, Pablo A., Emmanuel K. Lartey, and Frederico S. Mandelman (2007) "Remittances and Dutch disease." Working paper, Federal Reserve Bank of Atlanta, Atlanta, GA.

Aglietta, Michel, and Laurent Berrebi (2007) *Désordres dans le Capitalisme Mondial.* Paris: Odile, Jacob.

Albert, Michel (1991) *Capitalisme Contre Capitalisme.* Paris: Seuil.

Alves, Antonio J., Jr., Fernando Ferrari Filho, and Luiz Fernando de Paula (2004) "Crise cambial, instabilidade financeira e reforma do sistema monetário." In Fernando Ferrari Filho and Luiz Fernando de Paula, eds., *Globalização Financeira: Ensaios de Macroeconomia Aberta.* Petrópolis, Brazil: Vozes; 369–461.

Bacha, Edmar L. (1973) "Sobre a dinâmica de crescimento da economia industrial subdesenvolvida." *Pesquisa e Planejamento Econômico* **3**: 937–952.

Baland, Jean-Marie, and Patrick François (2000) "Rent-seeking and resource booms." *Journal of Development Economics* **61**: 527–42.

Baldwin, Richard (2006) "The great unbundling(s)." Economic Council of Finland. Available at http://www.tinyurl.com/2ol2n8.

Barbosa Lima Sobrinho, Alexandre (1973) *Japão: O Capital se Faz em Casa.* Rio de Janeiro: Paz e Terra.

Beck, Ulrich (2000) *What Is Globalization?* Cambridge: Polity Press.

Benaroya, François, and Didier Janci (1999) "Measuring exchange rates misalignment with purchasing power parity estimates." In Stefan Collignon, Jean

233

References

Pisani-Ferry, and Yung Chul Park, eds., *Exchange Rate Policies in Emerging Asian Countries*. New York: Routledge; 199–217.

Berger, Suzanne, and Richard Robert (2003) *Nôtre Première Mondialisation*. Paris: Seuil.

Bhaduri, Amit, and Stephen Marglin (1990) "Unemployment and the real wages: The economic basis for contesting political ideologies." *Cambridge Journal of Economics* **14**: 375–93.

Blinder, Alan S. (2006) "Offshoring: The next industrial revolution?" *Foreign Affairs* **85**: 113–28.

Boyer, Robert (2001) "Comprendre un changement d'époque." In Robert Boyer and Pierre-François Souyri, eds., *Mondialisation et Régulations*. Paris: La Découverte; 7–22.

Boyer, Robert, and Pierre-François Souyri, eds. (2001) *Mondialisation et Régulations*. Paris: La Découverte.

Braudel, Fernand (1979) *Les Jeux de l'Echange*. Volume 2 of *Civilisation Matérielle, Économie et Capitalisme XVᵉ–XVIIIᵉ Siècle*. Paris: Armand, Colin.

Bresser Pereira, Luiz Carlos (1977) *Estado e Subdesenvolvimento Industrializado* [State and Industrialized Underdevelopment]. São Paulo: Brasiliense.

Bresser Pereira, Luiz Carlos ([1970] 1984) "Concentration of income and the economy's recuperation." In *Development and Crisis in Brazil*. Boulder, CO: Westview Press; 143–8.

Bresser Pereira, Luiz Carlos (1986) *Lucro, Acumulação and Crise* [Profit, Accumulation, and Crisis]. São Paulo: Brasiliense. Available in English at http://www.bresserpereira.org.br.

Bresser Pereira, Luiz Carlos (1991a) "A crise da América Latina: Consenso de Washington ou crise fiscal?" [Latin American crisis: Washington Consensus or fiscal crisis?]. *Pesquisa e Planejamento Econômico* **21**: 3–23. Available in English at http://www.bresserpereira.org.br.

Bresser Pereira, Luiz Carlos, ed. (1991b) *Populismo Econômico* [Economic Populism]. São Paulo: Nobel.

Bresser Pereira, Luiz Carlos (1995) "Development economics and World Bank's identity crisis." *Review of International Political Economy* **2**: 211–47.

Bresser Pereira, Luiz Carlos ([1999] 2002a) "Latin America's quasi-stagnation." In Paul Davidson, ed., *A Post Keynesian Perspective on Twenty-First Century Economic Problems*. Cheltenham, UK: Edward Elgar; 1–28.

Bresser Pereira, Luiz Carlos (2002b) "Financiamento para o subdesenvolvimento: o Brasil e o Segundo Consenso de Washington" [Finance for underdevelopment: Brazil and the second Washington Consensus]. In Ana Célia

References

Castro, ed., *Desenvolvimento em Debate: Painéis do Desenvolvimento Brasileiro*. Volume. **2**. Rio de Janeiro: Mauad/BNDES; 359–98.

Bresser Pereira, Luiz Carlos (2004a) "Exchange rate: Fix, float, or manage it?" Preface to Mathias Vernengo, ed., *Monetary Integration and Dollarization: No Panacea*. Cheltenham, UK: Edward Elgar; xiii–xix.

Bresser Pereira, Luiz Carlos (2004b) *Democracy and Public Management Reform: Building the Republican State*. Oxford: Oxford University Press.

Bresser Pereira, Luiz Carlos (2006) "New developmentalism and conventional orthodoxy." *Economie Appliquée* **59**: 61–94.

Bresser Pereira, Luiz Carlos (2008) "Dutch disease and its neutralization: A Ricardian approach." *Brazilian Journal of Political Economy* **28**: 47–71.

Bresser Pereira, Luiz Carlos (2009a) *Developing Brazil: Overcoming the Failure of the Washington Consensus*. Boulder, CO: Lynne Rienner.

Bresser Pereira, Luiz Carlos (2009b) "The two methods and the hard core of economics." *Journal of Post Keynesian Economics* **31**: 133–63.

Bresser Pereira, Luiz Carlos, and Paulo Gala (2008) "Foreign savings, insufficiency of demand, and low growth." *Journal of Post Keynesian Economics* **30**: 315–34.

Bresser Pereira, Luiz Carlos, Lauro Gonzales, and Claudio Lucinda (2008) "Crises financeiras nos anos 1990 e poupança externa" [Financial crisis in the 1990s and foreign savings]. *Nova Economia* **18**: 327–57.

Bresser Pereira, Luiz Carlos, and Yoshiaki Nakano (1987) *The Theory of Inertial Inflation*. Boulder, CO: Lynne Rienner.

Bresser Pereira, Luiz Carlos, and Yoshiaki Nakano (2002a) "Uma estratégia de desenvolvimento com estabilidade" [A strategy of development with stability]. *Brazilian Journal of Political Economy* **21**: 146–77.

Bresser Pereira, Luiz Carlos, and Yoshiaki Nakano (2002b) "Economic growth with foreign savings?" (in Portuguese). *Brazilian Journal of Political Economy* **22**: 3–27. Available in English at http://www.bresserpereira.ed.br.

Bruno, Miguel (2006) "Lucro, acumulação de capital e crescimento econômico sob finanças liberalizadas: o caso brasileiro" [Profit, capital accumulation, and economic growth under liberalized finances: The Brazilian case]. In Luiz Fernando de Paula, Léo da Rocha Ferreira, and Milton de Assis, eds., *Perspectivas para a Economia Brasileira: inserção internacional e políticas públicas* [Perspectives for the Brazilian Economy: International Insertion and Public Policies]. Rio de Janeiro: UERJ – Universidade Estadual do Rio de Janeiro; 91–116.

Calvo, Guillermo, Leonard Leiderman, and Carmen Reinhart (1995) "Capital inflows to Latin America with reference to the Asian experience." In Sebastian

References

Edwards, ed., *Capital Controls, Exchange Rates, and Monetary Policy in the World Economy.* Cambridge: Cambridge University Press; 339–80.

Canitrot, Adolfo (1975) "La experiencia populista de distribución de renta" [The populist experience of income distribution]. *Desarrollo Económico* **15**: 331–51.

Chang, Ha-Joon (2002a) *Kicking Away the Ladder.* London: Anthem Press.

Chang, Ha-Joon (2002b) "The East Asian model of economic policy." In Evelyne Huber, ed., *Models of Capitalism: Lessons for Latin America.* University Park: Pennsylvania State University Press; 197–236.

Chang, Ha-Joon (2006) "Policy space in historical perspective, with a special reference to trade and industrial policies." *Economic and Political Weekly* **41**: 32–48.

Chatterji, Monojit, and Simon Price (1988) "Unions, Dutch disease and unemployment." *Oxford Economic Papers* **40**: 302–21.

Chesnais, François (1994) *La Mondialisation du Capital.* Paris: Syros.

Coakley, Jerry, Farida Kulasi, and Ronald Smith (1996) "Current account solvency and the Feldstein-Horioka puzzle." *Economic Journal* **106**: 620–27.

Collier, Paul (2007) *The Bottom Billion.* Oxford: Oxford University Press.

Collier, Paul, and Anke Hoeffler (2004) "Greed and grievance in civil war." *Oxford Economic Papers* **54**: 563–95.

Comparato, Fábio Konder (2005) "Brasil, um país em busca de futuro." *Folha de S. Paulo* **270**.

Corden, W. Max (1981) *Inflation, Exchange Rates and the World Economy.* 2nd ed. Oxford: Clarendon Press.

Corden, W. Max (1984) "Booming sector and Dutch disease economics: Survey and consolidation." *Oxford Economic Papers* **36**: 359–80.

Corden, W. Max (1994) *Economic Policy, Exchange Rates, and the International System.* Chicago: University of Chicago Press.

Corden, W. Max, and Peter J. Neary (1982) "Booming sector and de-industrialization in a small open economy." *Economic Journal* **92**: 825–48.

Correa de Moraes, Reginaldo C. (2006) *Estado, Desenvolvimento e Globalização* [State, Development, and Globalization]. São Paulo: UNESP – Universidade Estadual Paulista.

Diaz-Alejandro, Carlos (1981) "Southern Cone stabilization plans." In William R. Cline and Sidney Weintraub, eds., *Economic Stabilization in Developing Countries.* Washington, DC: Brookings Institution; 119–48.

Dollar, David (1992) "Outward-oriented developing economies really do grow more rapidly: Evidence from 95 LDCs, 1976–1985." *Economic Development and Cultural Change* **40**: 523–44.

References

Dornbusch, Rudy, and Sebastian Edwards, eds. (1991) *The Macroeconomics of Populism in Latin America*. Chicago: University of Chicago Press.

Dupas, Gilberto (2006) *O Mito do Progresso* [The Myth of Progress]. São Paulo: UNESP – Universidade Estadual Paulista.

Easterly, William (2001) "The lost decades: Developing countries' stagnation in spite of policy reform 1980–1998." *Journal of Economic Growth* 6: 135–57.

Edwards, Sebastian (1995) "Why are saving rates so different across countries? An international comparative analysis." Working paper 5097, NBER – National Bureau of Economic Research, Cambridge, MA.

Edwards, Sebastian (2000) "Does current account matter?" Working Paper 8275, NBER – National Bureau of Economic Research, Cambridge, MA.

Eichengreen, Barry (2003) *Capital Flows and Crises*. Cambridge, MA: MIT Press.

Eichengreen, Barry, and David Leblang (2002) "Capital account liberalization and growth: Was Mr. Mahathir right?" Working paper 9427, NBER – National Bureau of Economic Research, Cambridge, MA.

Eichengreen, Barry, Andrew K. Rose, and Charles Wyplosz (1994) "Speculative attacks on pegged exchange rates: An empirical exploration with special reference to the European monetary system." Working paper 4898, NBER – National Bureau of Economic Research, Cambridge, MA.

Esping-Andersen, Gøsta (1990) *The Three Worlds of Welfare Capitalism*. Princeton, NJ: Princeton University Press.

Evans, Peter (1995) *Embedded Autonomy*. Princeton, NJ: Princeton University Press.

Fajnzylber, P., N. Loyaza, and C. Calderón (2004) "Economic growth in Latin America and Caribbean." Working paper 265, World Bank, Washington, DC.

Feldstein, Martin, and Charles Horioka (1980) "Domestic savings and international capital flows." *Economic Journal* 90: 314–29.

Ferreira, João Marcelo Grossi, Jolanda E. Ygosse Baptista, and Samuel Abreu Pessôa (2006) "Why did the Brazilian investment ratio not recover after inflation stabilization? An econometric study on the culprits." Report EESP/FGV, EPGR/FGV, Banco Itaú, São, Paulo.

Ffrench-Davis, Ricardo (2003) *Entre el Neoliberalismo y el Crescimiento com Equidad* [Between Neoliberalism and Growth with Equity]. 3rd ed. Santiago de Chile: J. C. Sáes.

Fine, Ben (2004) "Examining the ideas of globalisation and development critically: What role for political economy?" *New Political Economy* 9: 213–32.

Fiori, José Luís (2002) *60 Lições dos 90* [Sixty Lessons of the 1990s]. Rio de Janeiro: Record.

References

Flood, Robert P., and Peter M. Garber (1984) "Collapsing exchange-rate regimes: Some linear examples." *Journal of International Economics* **17**: 1–13.

Frenkel, Roberto (2003) "Globalización y crisis financieras en América Latina" [Globalization and financial crisis in Latin America]. *Brazilian Journal of Political Economy* **23**: 94–111.

Friedman, Thomas L. (1999) *The Lexus and the Olive Tree*. New York: Farrar, Straus, Girous.

Fry, Maxwell (1978) "Money and capital or financial deepening in economic development?" *Journal of Money, Credit and Banking* **10**: 464–75.

Fukuyama, Francis (2004) *Construção de Estados: governo e organização no século XXI* [Construction of States: Government and Organization in the Twenty-first Century]. Rio de Janeiro: Rocco.

Furtado, Celso (1963) *Plano Trienal de Desenvolvimento Econômico e Social (1963–1965)*. Rio de Janeiro: Síntese.

Furtado, Celso (1965) *Development and Stagnation in Latin America: A Structuralist Approach*. St. Louis, MO: Social Science Institute, Washington University.

Gala, Paulo (2006) "Política Cambial e Macroeconomia do Desenvolvimento" [Exchange policies and macroeconomics of development]. PhD dissertation, São Paulo School of Economics of Getulio Vargas Foundation.

Galbraith, John Kenneth (1952) *American Capitalism: The Concept of Countervailing Power*. Boston: Houghton Mifflin.

Galbraith, John Kenneth (2004) *The Economics of Innocent Fraud*. Boston: Houghton Mifflin.

Gellner, Ernest (1983) *Nations and Nationalism*. Ithaca, NY: Cornell University Press.

Gerschenkron, Alexander (1962) *Economic Backwardness in Historical Perspective: A Book of Essays*. New York: Praeger.

Glatzer, Miguel, and Dietrich Rueschmeyer, eds. (2005) *Globalization and the Future of the Welfare State*. Pittsburgh, PA: University of Pittsburgh Press.

Godoi, Alexandra Strommer de Farias (2007) "O milagre irlandês como exemplo da adoção de uma estratégia nacional de desenvolvimento" [The Irish miracle as an example of the adoption of a national development strategy]. *Brazilian Journal of Political Economy* **27**: 546–66.

Gonzalez, Lauro (2007) "Crises Financeiras Recentes: Revisitando as Experiências da América Latina e da Ásia" [Recent financial crisis: Revisiting Latin American and Asian experiences]. PhD dissertation, São Paulo School of Economics of Getulio Vargas Foundation.

References

Goodin, Robert E., Bruce Headey, Ruud Muffels, and Henk-Jan Dirvin (1999) *The Real Worlds of Welfare Capitalism*. Cambridge: Cambridge University Press.

Grossmann, Gene, and Esteban Rossi-Hansberg (2006) "The rise of offshoring: It's not wine for cloth anymore." Available at http://www.princeton.edu/~grossman/TheRiseofOffshoring.pdf.

Grunberg, Gerard, and Zali Laïd (2007) *Sortir du Pessimisme Social*. Paris: Hachette and Science Po.

Haass, Richard (2008) "What follows American dominion?" *Financial Times*, April 26.

Habermas, Jurgen (2000) *Après l'État-nation* [After the Nation-State]. Paris: Fayard.

Hall, Peter A., and David Soskice, eds. (2001) Introduction to *Varieties of Capitalism: The Institutional Foundations of Comparative Advantage*. Oxford: Oxford University Press; 1–70.

Held, David, and Anthony McGrew, eds. (2002) Introduction to *Governing Globalization*. Cambridge: Polity Press; 1–25.

Hirst, Paul, and Grahame Thompson (1996) *Globalization in Question*. Cambridge: Polity Press.

Hoogvelt, Ankie (2001) *Globalization and the Postcolonial World: The New Political Economy of Development*. 2nd ed. Baltimore: Johns Hopkins University Press.

Huber, Evelyne, ed. (2002) *Models of Capitalism: Lessons for Latin America*. University Park: Pennsylvania State University Press.

Ianni, Octavio (1995) *Teorias da Globalização* [Theories of Globalization]. Rio de Janeiro: Civilização Brasileira.

Johnson, Chalmers (1982) *MITI and the Japanese Miracle*. Stanford, CA: Stanford University Press.

Johnson, Simon H., Jonathan Ostry, and Arvind Subramanian (2007) "The prospects for sustained growth in Africa; benchmarking the constraints." Working paper 07/52, International Monetary Fund, Washington, DC.

Kaldor, Nicholas (1978) "Causes of the low rate of growth of the United Kingdom." In *Further Essays in Economic Growth*. London: Duckworth; 100–38.

Karl, Terry Lynn (1997) *The Paradox of Plenty*. Berkeley: University of California Press.

Keohane, Robert O., and Joseph S. Nye (2001) *Power and Interdependence*. 3rd ed. New York: Longman.

Krugman, Paul (1979) "A model of balance of payments crises." *Journal of Money, Credit, and Banking* 11: 311–25.

References

Krugman, Paul (1995) "Growing world trade: Causes and consequences." *Brookings Papers on Economic Activity* **1**: 327–77.

Krugman, Paul (1998) "What happened to Asia?" Available at http://web .mit.edu/krugman/www/DISINTER.html.

Krugman, Paul (2008) "Trade and wages, reconsidered." Draft for the spring meeting of the Brookings Panel on Economic Activity. Available at http:// www.princeton.edu/~pkrugman/pk-bpea-draft.pdf.

Kuttner, Robert (2008) "The Copenhagen consensus." *Foreign Affairs*, **87**: 78–94.

Larsen, Erling R. (2004) "Escaping the resource curse and the Dutch disease: When and why Norway caught up with and forged ahead of its neighbors." Discussion Chapter 377, Statistics Norway, Oslo.

Lederman, Daniel, and William F. Maloney (2007) "Trade structure and growth." In Daniel Lederman and William F. Maloney, eds., *Natural Resources: Neither Curse nor Destiny*. Stanford, CA: Stanford University Press/World Bank; 15–40.

Levy-Yeyati, Eduardo, and Federico Sturzenegger (2007) "Fear of floating in reverse: Exchange rate policy in the 2000s." Universidad Torcuato di Tella. Available at http://www.bankofengland.co.uk/publications/events/ccbs _cornell2007/paper_5levy_yeyati.pdf.

Lewis, Arthur W. (1954) "Economic development with unlimited supply of labor." *Manchester School* **22**: 139–91.

List, Friedrich ([1846] 1999) *National System of Political Economy*. Roseville, CA: Dry Bones Press, 1999.

Mankiw, N. Gregory (2006) "The macroeconomist as scientist and engineer." *Journal of Economic Perspectives* **20**: 29–46.

McKinnon, Ronald (1973) *Money and Capital in Economic Development*. Washington, DC: Brookings Institution.

Minsky, Herman P. (1986) *Stabilizing an Unstable Economy*. New Haven, CT: Yale University Press.

Miranda, Mauro Costa (2006) "Crises Cambiais e Ataques Especulativos no Brasil." *Revista de Economia Aplicada* **10**: 287–301.

Mosley, Layna (2005) "Globalisation and the state." *New Political Economy* **10**: 355–62.

Neftci, Salih N. (2002) "FX short positions, balance sheets and financial turbulence: An interpretation of the Asian financial crisis." In John Eatwell and Lance Taylor, eds., *International Capital Markets*. Oxford: Oxford University Press; 277–93.

References

Nogueira Batista, Paulo, Jr. (1998) "Mitos da globalização" [Myths of globalization]. *Estudos Avançados* 12: 125–86.

North, Douglass C. (1990) *Institutions, Institutional Change, and Economic Performance.* Cambridge: Cambridge University Press.

Nurkse, Ragnar (1953) *Problems of Capital Formation in Underdeveloped Countries.* Oxford: Basil Blackwell.

Obstfeld, Maurice (1986) "Rational and self-fulfilling balance-of-payments crises." *American Economic Review* 76: 72–81.

Obstfeld, Maurice (1994) "The logic of currency crises." *Cahiers Economiques et Monetaires* 43: 189–213.

Ohmae, Kenich (1990) *The Borderless World.* New York: HarperCollins Publishers.

Oomes, Nienke, and Katerina Kalcheva (2007) "Diagnosing Dutch disease: Does Russia have the symptoms?" Working paper 07/102, International Monetary Fund, Washington, DC.

Oreiro, José Luís, Luciano Nakabashi, and Breno Pascualote Lemos (2007) "A economia do crescimento puxado pela demanda agregada: teoria e aplicações ao caso brasileiro" [The economy of growth pulled by the aggregate demand: Theory and applications to the Brazilian case]. Working paper, Universidade Federal do Paraná, Departamento de Economia, Centro de Pesquisas Econômicas, Curitiba, Brazil.

Ötker, Inci, and Ceyla Pazarbasioglu (1995) "Speculative attacks and currency crises: The Mexican Experience," IMF working paper 95/112, International Monetary Fund, Washington, DC.

Palma, Gabriel (2005) "Quatro fuentes de 'desindustrialización' en América Latina: Una trampa de bajo crecimiento" [Four sources of deindustrialization in Latin America: A trap of small growth]. In José Antonio Ocampo, ed., *Beyond Reforms: Structural Dynamics and Macroeconomic Vulnerability.* Stanford, CA: Stanford University Press / World Bank; 79–130.

Pastore, Afonso Celso, Maria Cristina Pinotti, and Leonardo Porto de Almeida (2008) "Câmbio e crescimento: o que podemos aprender?" [Exchange rate and growth: What can we learn?]. In Octavio de Barros and Fabio Giambiagi, eds., *Brasil Globalizado* [Globalized Brazil]. São Paulo: Campus; 268–98.

Pereira, Ana Paula M., and Fernando Seabra (2004) "Crises cambiais e bancárias na década de 1990: uma análise de painel aplicada a mercados emergentes" [Exchange rate and banking crises in the 1990s: A panel analysis applied to emergent markets]. Working paper, ANPEC Associação Nacional dos Centros de Pós-Graduação em Economia, João Pessoa, Brazil.

References

Polanyi, Karl (1957) *The Great Transformation.* 2nd ed. Boston: Beacon Press, 1957.

Prebisch, Raúl (1950) *The Economic Development of Latin America and Its Principal Problems.* New York: United Nations, Department of Economic Affairs.

Radelet, Steven, and Jeffrey Sachs (2000) "The onset of the East Asian financial crisis." In Paul Krugman, ed., *Currency Crises.* Chicago: University of Chicago Press; 105–62.

Razin, Ofair, and Suzan M. Collins (1997) "Real exchange rate misalignments and growth." Working paper 6147, National Bureau of Economic Research, Washington, DC.

Reinhart, Carmen M., and Ernesto Talvi (1998) "Capital flows and saving in Latin America and Asia: A reinterpretation." *Journal of Development Economics* **57**: 45–66.

Reisen, Helmut (1998) "Sustainable and excessive current account deficits." Working paper 132, Organisation for Economic Co-operation and Development – Development Centre, Paris.

Renan, Ernest ([1882] 1992) *Qu'est-ce qu'une Nation?* Paris: Pocket/Agora.

Robichek, E. Walter (1981) "Some reflections about external public debt management." Estudios Monetarios VII, Banco Central de Chile.

Rocha, Fabiana (2004) "Correlação Feldstein-Horioka: indicador de mobilidade de capitais ou de solvência?" [The Feldstein: Horioka correlation: Indicator of capital mobility or of solvency?] *Brazilian Journal of Political Economy* **23**: 3–11.

Rodrik, Dani (1998) "Who needs capital-account convertibility?" *Princeton Essays in International Finance* **207**: 55–65.

Rodrik, Dani (2007) "The real exchange rate and economic growth: Theory and evidence." Working paper, John F. Kennedy School of Government, Harvard University, Cambridge, MA.

Rodrik, Dani, and André Velasco (1999) "Short-term capital flows." Working paper 7364, NBER – National Bureau of Economic Research, Cambridge, MA.

Roemer, Michael (1994) "Asia and Africa: Towards a policy frontier." Development discussion paper 485, Harvard Institute of International Development, Cambridge, MA.

Rosenstein-Rodan, Paul (1943) "Problems of industrialization in eastern Europe and south-eastern Europe." *Economic Journal* **53**: 202–11.

Sachs, Jeffrey D. (1989) "Social conflict and populist policies in Latin America." In R. Brunetta and C. Dell-Arringa, eds., *Labor Relations and Economic Performance.* London: Macmillan Press; 137–69.

References

Sachs, Jeffrey D., and Andrew M. Warner (1999) "The big push, natural resource booms, and growth." *Journal of Development Economics* **59**: 43–76.

Sachs, Jeffrey D., and Andrew M. Warner (2001) "The curse of natural resources." *European Economic Review* **45**: 827–38.

Sassen, Saskia (2005) "When national territory is home to the global: Old borders to novel borderings." *New Political Economy* **10**: 523–42.

Schmidt-Hebbel, Klaus, Steven Webb, and Giancarlo Corsetti (1992) "Household saving in developing countries: First cross-country evidence." *World Bank Economic Review* **6**: 529–47.

Schmitter, Philippe C. (1974) "Still a century of corporatism?" *Review of Politics* **36**: 7–52.

Shaw, Edward (1973) *Financial Deepening in Economic Development*. Oxford: Oxford University Press.

Simon, Herbert A., and Peter A. Simon ([1962] 1979) "Trial and error search in solving difficult problems." In Herbert A. Simon, ed., *Models of Thought*. New Haven, CT: Yale University Press; 175–80.

Simonsen, Mário Henrique, and Rubens Penha Cysne (1995) *Macroeconomia* [Macroeconomics]. São Paulo: Atlas.

Sinn, Stefan (1992) "Saving-investment correlations and capital mobility: On the evidence from annual data." *Economic Journal* **102**: 1162–70.

Stephens, John D. (2002) "European welfare state regimes: Configurations, outcomes, transformations." In Evelyne Huber, ed., *Models of Capitalism: Lessons for Latin America*. University Park: Pennsylvania State University Press; 303–38.

Stephens, John D. (2005) "Economic internationalization and domestic compensation." In Miguel Glatzer and Dietrich Rueschmeyer, eds., *Globalization and the Future of the Welfare State*. Pittsburgh, PA: University of Pittsburgh Press; 49–74.

Tavares, Maria da Conceição, and José Serra (1972) "Beyond stagnation." In Maria da Conceição Tavares, ed., *From Import Substitution to Finance Capitalism*. Rio de Janeiro: Zahar; 153–59.

Torvik, Ragnar (2001) "Learning by doing and the Dutch disease." *European Economic Review* **45**: 285–306.

Usui, Norio (1998) "Dutch disease and policy adjustments to the oil boom: A comparative study of Indonesia and Mexico." *Resources Policy* **23**: 151–62.

Uthoff, Andras, and Daniel Titelman (1998) "The relationship between foreign and national savings under financial liberalization." In Ricardo Ffrench-Davis and Helmut Reisen, eds., *Capital Flows and Investment Performance: Lessons from Latin America*: Economic Commission for Latin America and the Caribbean / Organisation for Economic Co-operation and Development; 23–40.

Wade, Robert H. (1996) "Globalization and its limits: Reports of the death of the national economy are greatly exaggerated." In Suzanne Berger and Ronald Dore, eds., *National Diversity and Global Capitalism.* Ithaca, NY: Cornell University Press; 60–88.

Wade, Robert H. (2003) "What strategies are viable for developing countries today? The World Trade Organization and the shrinking of 'development space.'" *Review of International Political Economy* **10**: 621–44.

Wallerstein, Immanuel (1974) *The Modern World System.* New York: Academic Press.

Williamson, John (1990) "The progress of policy reform in Latin America." In John Williamson, ed., *Latin American Adjustment: How Much Has Happened?* Washington, DC: Institute for International Economics; 353–420.

Wolf, Martin (2004) *Why Globalization Works.* New Haven, CT: Yale University Press.

Woo-Cummings, Meredith, ed. (1999) *The Developmental State.* Ithaca, NY: Cornell University Press.

Woodall, Pam (2006) "The new titans." *The Economist,* September 14; 1–4.

World Bank (2002) *Globalization, Growth, and Poverty.* Oxford: Oxford University Press / World Bank.

Index

Index

Index

Index

Index

Index

Index

Index

Index

Index

Index

globalization as threat vs. opportunity to, 44–45, 48
immigration barriers, 47
income inequity in, 47–49, 173–174
relationship with other countries, characteristics
of competition and exploitation, 32–33, 38–39, 50–51, 52, 95, 130
international division of labor, 46, 168–169
Rodrik, Dani, 134–135, 217
Roemer, Michael, 109
Rosenstein-Rodan, Paul, 142–143
rule of law, 72–73
Russia, 49, 108

salaries, 56, 76, 92, 127, 133, 136, 174, 181, 187, 188, 189, 190, 192, 193, 194, 201, 202
Sachs, Jeffrey D., 127–128, 150–151, 153–154, 217
Saudi Arabia, 164, 165–166
savings
forced, 6, 12, 67, 68, 75, 98, 132, 225
substitution of foreign for domestic, 6, 8, 14, 21, 52, 127, 140, 184, 192, 204, 205, 211, 218, 225
Say's law, 182
Scandinavia, 47. *See also specific countries*
Schmidt-Hebbel, K. S., 196–197
Schumpeter, Joseph, 56
Schumpeterian entrepreneurs, 56
Seabra, F., 217
shareholders, 24, 28
Shaw, Edward, 142
Simon, Herbert, 61–62
Simon, Peter, 61–62
Singapore, 65, 195
slavery, 51
Smith, Adam, 41–42, 79, 102–103
Sobrinho, Barbosa Lima, 140
sovereign funds, 14, 171
sovereignty, defined, 40–41
Soviet Union, 30–31
Soviet Empire collapse, 37–38

state
intervention, 12, 63, 74, 75, 113, 114, 132, 221, 223
liberal 72
liberal democratic, 28
defined, 42–44
government vs., 37, 57
minimal, 101
size of the, 7, 74, 106
social, 28, 29, 34, 48, 69, 231
social democratic state, 28
democratic, 74, 232
welfare, 28, 34, 69, 95, 230
Stephens, John, 47
Sturzenegger, Federico, 134–135

Taiwan, 48, 64, 96, 128, 195, 221
technological
change, 22, 56
technology
best existing, 151
Thailand, 48, 65, 137, 217, 221
Talvi, E., 196–197
taxation to neutralize the Dutch disease, 159–165, 170–171, 179, 222–223
theory of associated dependence, 82
Thompson, Grahame, 23
Titleman, D., 198
trade globalization. *See also* commercial globalization; financial globalization
income inequity and, 47
moment defining, 31–32
as opportunity, 20–21, 118–119
positive-sum game, 41–42, 47–49
trade in tasks, 32
trade liberalization, 166
Treasury Department, U.S., 99–100, 205, 209–210
two-gap model, 142–143

unbundling, 32
United States. *See also* Washington Consensus
financial crisis (2007), 229–230

Index